WINNING THOUGHTS

For Any Season...Of Life

DR. GEORGE MATHISON

*Thoughts to inspire, encourage, motivate, comfort, challenge –
and to instill within a winning attitude towards life.*

All proceeds from the sales of this book will go to and benefit Habitat for Humanity.

George and Monteigne Mathison pictured with Auburn University President Dr. William Muse and his wife, Marlene, at Jordan-Hare Stadium.

Photography: Jeff Etheridge, AU Photographic Services.

Printing: Craftmaster Printers, Inc., Auburn, Ala.

ISBN 0-9649877-1-6

Printed in the United States of America
First Edition

Dedicated to
Monteigne and Mallory

TABLE OF CONTENTS

SECTION I
Helpful Hints On How To Live

SECTION II
Looking For Leaders

SECTION III
The Tunnels In Life

SECTION IV
The Importance of A Good Finish
To finish well, we need:

Winning Thoughts For Any Season...Of Life

(Thoughts to inspire, encourage, motivate, comfort, challenge – and to instill within a winning attitude towards life.)

A thrilling part of my ministry in the Auburn community is my association with the Auburn University football team. Several of the players faithfully attend our worship services, and many of the coaches are active members of our church. It is an inspiration to see them in worship each Sunday.

I love and appreciate our coaches so much. Over these past six years I have learned to respect their coaching ability, appreciate their leadership skills, admire their care for their players and to genuinely love them as dear brothers in Christ.

They are a blessing to my life and ministry.

I remember a tough loss in a Southeastern Conference game on a Saturday night right after I became closely associated with our football team. The plane ride back was long, we were late flying into Montgomery, and it was in the wee hours when we bused back to Auburn.

I was feeling a little sorry for myself because I thought of how I had three sermons to preach the next morning. I did not even feel like getting out of bed that day. Late that Sunday morning, I looked out upon the congregation and saw several of the coaches present. On the second row (as he does every Sunday during the football season) sat Coach Bowden, his wife, Shryl, and their three little girls. I found out that he had gotten in later than I had on Saturday night, gotten up earlier that Sunday morning, driven to Montgomery to tape his television program, driven back to Auburn, attended Sunday School and was in his place at worship.

Yes, our coaches are an inspiration to my life and ministry.

This is the second book I've written, and like the first it is a compilation of the Monday morning studies I shared with the coaching staff in the coaches conference room in the Auburn University Athletic Complex.

On a recent Sunday, a young lady shared with me that her boyfriend had given to her a copy of my first book, *Positive Thoughts From a Perfect Season...And Beyond.* As she was leaving church on that Sunday morning, she said to me, "I am enjoying your book, and I read from it every night before I go to bed. It reminds me so much of the sermons you preach here each Sunday. After I read a chapter or two, I just fall right off to sleep each night!"

Now I'm sure she did not mean that my sermons put her to sleep each Sunday, but if my sermonic endeavors can help her get a good night of restful peace – then for this I am thankful.

The title of this volume is *Winning Thoughts For Any Season...Of Life*, and as the subtitle suggests, these are thoughts to inspire, encourage, motivate, comfort, challenge and to instill within you a winning attitude towards life.

I have a personal conviction that we all want to be winners. We all want to be victorious in life because winning represents the crowning achievement for our best efforts. Winning represents the ultimate accolade for our noblest labors. I believe God has placed within us a desire to be our very best. When we look to God and believe in ourselves, we can develop a winning mentality. Just as losing can become a way of life, so with God's help, with a positive attitude and with a belief in ourselves, a winning attitude can become a way of life.

I remember reading these lines by the late Vince Lombardi, "Winning is not a sometime thing; it's an all-the-time thing. You don't win once in a while, you don't do things right once in a while, you do them right all the time. Winning is a habit. Unfortunately, so is losing."

Over the years I have observed that there is a distinctive difference between winners and losers. I remember hearing my Brother, John Ed, share in a sermon these revealing thoughts about winners and losers, and they provide excellent insight into the basic differences of these two ways of life.

A winner is always a part of the solution.
    A loser is always a part of the problem.
A winner always has a winning program.
    A loser always has a wonderful excuse.
A winner says, "I'll pitch-in and I'll do what it takes."
    A loser says, "It's not in my job description."
A winner sees an answer for every problem.
    A loser sees a problem for every answer.
A winner sees a green near every sand trap.
    A loser sees several sand traps near every green.
A winner sees a possibility in every difficulty.
    A loser sees a difficulty in every possibility.
A winner is always positive.
    A loser is always negative.
A winner is always optimistic.
    A loser is always pessimistic.
A winner works harder than a loser and has more time.
    A loser is always too busy to do what is necessary.
A winner goes through a problem.
    A loser goes around it, and he never gets past it.
A winner makes commitments.
    A loser makes promises.
A winner says, "I'm good, but not as good as I ought to be."

A loser says, "I'm not as bad as a lot of other people."
A winner listens.
A loser just waits until it's his turn to talk.
A winner respects those who are superior to him and always tries to learn from them.
A loser resents those who are superior to him and
tries to find flaws in their program.
A winner says, "There ought to be a better way to do it."
A loser says, "That's the way it's always been done."
When a winner makes a mistake, he says, "I was wrong."
When a loser makes a mistake, he says, "It was not my fault,"
and he blames somebody else.

I don't know where John Ed got these revealing thoughts, but I do know they speak volumes in helping us understand what it takes to form winning thoughts within our minds and a winning style for our lives.

Now in reality, all of God's children, and all of our brothers and sisters in Christ are winners, because someday when the working tools of life have slipped from our tired and weary hands, and we stand before a just God we will hear these words, "Well done, thou good and faithful servant. You have been faithful to that which I have entrusted to you, now enter in and receive that which I have prepared for you;" but I believe we all can be winners in this life NOW.

How can we be winners in this life? How can we develop our fullest potential? How can we truly be victorious in the big game of life? How can we inculcate winning thoughts into our minds, and then translate them into actions of success in every realm of life? The following chapters seek to answer these questions.

Now these are thoughts for any season of life: the courageous seasons, the happy seasons, the relational seasons, the family seasons, the victorious seasons, the lonely seasons, the hurting seasons, the aging seasons, the growing seasons, and the seasons of everyday living as we journey down the highway of life.

These thoughts can relate to any realm of your life: business, school, social or athletic. These are simple principles that I've seen work within different types of teams: academic, personal, football, basketball, church groups, businesses, communities, staffs – and they can work for you. These thoughts can be your vistas for victorious living.

These thoughts are compiled from studies that took place over several football seasons, and their content will reflect what we as coaches, players and friends were feeling and experiencing.

They are divided into four sections, and each section represents a series of studies that was presented over a certain time. They are arranged so they can be read and studied not only a section at a time, but also a chapter at a time. If you choose to read one chapter a night before retiring, you will go through this book in less than a month.

Hopefully, it will help you sleep better. It just might even put you to sleep.

Chapters 1-17 (Section I) were shared with the coaches in a series under the title, "Helpful Hints on How to Live." (With the exception of Chapters 10 and 11 which were preached in the Auburn United Methodist Church as a part of this particular series. I've included these two chapters on *How To Discover Your Vocational Call* for the benefit of the many University students who are seeking to find "their vocational call in life." The two Sundays these sermons were preached we had approximately 800-900 University students in attendance in each service, and it is my prayer that the messages were helpful to them – and thus by having them in printed form here, they can continue to provide help, inspiration and direction in determining their vocation in life.)

I might point out that these particular studies on "Helpful Hints..." among the coaches on Monday mornings were a part of some of the most helpful, inspiring and beneficial times we had together as friends and brothers in Christ.

Chapters 18-21 (Section II) make up a four-part series that was presented on the subject of leadership, "Looking For Leaders," for there are few vocations where leadership skills are as needed as in the field of coaching.

Chapters 22-24 (Section III) reflect a three-part study that was done on the subject, "The Tunnels In Life," for coaches (like people in all professions) today find that the roadway of life certainly has its dark and deep tunnels.

Chapters 25-29 (Section IV) contain a four-part study that was presented on "The Importance of a Good Finish," for if I've learned anything in my association with our coaches, it is the ultra importance of following through, working hard and staying with it right up to the very finish – for in the final analysis that is the true mark of victory.

Allow me to say just a word about how these thoughts in this book were put together. Ministers have different ways of studying, researching, compiling, preaching and writing. My approach is probably different from most others. I get up early every morning to read, study and pray. I then try to set aside a good part of Wednesday and Friday for in depth study and sermon preparation. Then, when I go into the Sanctuary on Sunday morning, I simply stand up before my people and preach without any notes and from the overflow of my study during the previous week.

Like the chapters in the first book, these thoughts were first shared with the coaches during our Monday morning Bible Studies. They were then preached to my people extemporaneously and without notes, and then they were dictated to my secretary, Carol Owen, and typed out in final form.

Auburn United Methodist Church is one of the great churches in Methodism. I do not know of a church anywhere that has as many University students in attendance as does Auburn United Methodist. During the fall and winter, it is a thrilling thing to see several hundred University students in worship every Sunday. Some of the greatest preachers in our denomination have served this church, and I am truly honored and humbled to be able to follow in their footsteps.

I sincerely believe God wants us to be our very best. I believe He wants us to be winners. As you read this book, you will find motivation to help you get started in the big business of every day living. You will find thoughts to help you gain courage, happiness, faith and positive relationships. You will find thoughts to help you overcome the daily problems of life. You will find thoughts that will help you grow and become stronger in your spiritual pilgrimage and faith walk. You will find thoughts to encourage you when you stumble and find yourself in the dark and deep tunnels of life; you will find thoughts to assist you in becoming a competent, caring and committed leader; and then you will find thoughts to help you attain the crowning goal for any winner in any sport – that of finishing well.

It is my prayer that these thoughts will help you go from "victory to victory." God bless you.

Dr. George Mathison
Senior Minister
Auburn United Methodist Church
Auburn, Alabama

I wish to say a special thank you to Mr. Mike Hubbard, President of *Auburn Network, Inc.* Mike is a dear friend, a member of the church I serve, and a man whom I greatly admire and respect. I appreciate his confidence in me and his assistance in helping put this project together. I also wish to thank my secretary, Carol Owen, for her patience in typing notes that I extemporaneously dictated, and then checking for accuracy, proper punctuation, correct spelling and organization. I deeply appreciate her kindness and patience.

SECTION I
Helpful Hints On How To Live

Helpful Hints On How To Live

HOW TO MAKE YOUR DREAMS COME TRUE
"Where there is no vision, the people perish..."
(Proverbs 19:18a)

With this section and chapter we begin a series of studies on the theme, "Helpful Hints on How to Live." My goal for these studies is to help make us better coaches, better students, better football players, better church members, better Christians, and better men and women. The chapters in this first section address and deal with practical problems and issues that we face everyday, for it is only in the mastering of the problems in life that we become true winners in the game of life.

Just like a plan for a big football game, these are winning thoughts and helpful hints that can make us victorious as we live life each day.

These chapters deal with the many complex issues of life such as goal setting, courage, family happiness, personal happiness, personal pain, loneliness, our jobs, getting along with people, growing older, and the place of prayer in our lives – for it is only when we, with God's help, master these areas of life that we become true winners in the big game of life. These winning thoughts and helpful hints in this series are directed to that end.

As I shared these thoughts with our football coaching staff on Monday mornings and then with our worshiping congregation in Auburn on Sunday mornings, I felt and appreciated their love, support and prayers so very much. As I shared with them, these studies are Biblical in their exegesis, very practical in their approach, and I trust they will be helpful to you during the living of these days.

The first study in this series is entitled, *How To Make Your Dreams Come True*. Our text for this message is a very familiar verse taken from Proverbs 29:18. It simply says, "Where there is no vision, the people perish..." And may God add His blessing to this, the reading of His Word.

Our Father, as individuals, I pray that you will give to us vision. I also pray that you will show each of us how to dream, and then through your grace help us make those dreams come true.

One of the great Bishops during the early part of this century was a man by the name of Bishop William Quayle. Once Bishop Quayle was on a train, and he was engaged in conversation with several businessmen. He did not have on his ecclesiastical garb, so they did not know that he was a minister, much less a Bishop. The businessmen were greatly impressed with his charisma, his confidence, his demeanor and his spirited exchanges. One of the businessmen then said to him, "Mister, you have got to be in sales. What product do you sell?" Bishop Quayle immediately replied, "I sell horizons! I sale horizons!"

Now, our Lord does not sell horizons. He does not sell vision, and He does not sell dreams. But He makes these things available to us through faith in Him, and it is through His grace that we claim them. The people who do claim them are the people who will make a difference in this world in which we live. They will also make a difference in the world tomorrow.

Scott Peck in his book, *A World Waiting to Be Born*, writes, "I have never known a genuinely talented person who achieved 'greatness' without a sense of destiny...who did not, years before such achievement, experience an almost burning sense that she or he was called to grand and glorious achievements."

Now those "grand and glorious achievements" which Peck refers to are made possible by our dreams.

Vision and horizons are vital. Dreams are very important because it is through our dreams that we set goals. It is through our dreams that we establish a plan of action and a sense of direction to attain those goals. And it is through our dreams that we are motivated to begin in the first place to attain those goals.

Now, if dreams are so important, how can we make them come true? May I share with you three simple steps* that can help you in this process? They are:

I.   **See the Invisible**
II. **Believe the Incredible**
III. **Attempt the Impossible**

I.   **See the Invisible**

When you look, what do you see? When you listen, what do you hear? Jesus spoke about people who have ears, but yet they do not hear. He spoke of people who have eyes, but they do not see.

Luke tells of when Jesus was in Jericho. There was a large group of people gathered. Jesus and the people looked up in a tree, and they saw something. The people looked up, and they saw a man by the name of Zacchaeus who was a greedy little tax collector. Jesus looked up, and He did not see <u>something</u>. He saw <u>somebody</u>. He saw a precious soul. He saw a person of sacred worth. He saw potential within a human being.

Luke tells of how Jesus invited Zacchaeus down, and He went home with him. Following that meeting in the home of Zacchaeus, Jesus said of Zacchaeus, "Behold, today salvation has come to this house."

Now the simple point I want to make is this: The people looked, and they saw a problem. Jesus looked, and He saw a possibility.

I think of little David in the field watching his father's sheep. Many people looked upon David, and they only saw a little shepherd boy. God looked upon David, and He saw a king.

Once Michelangelo and another artist were gazing upon a piece of marble. Michelangelo said to his companion, "What do you see?" The man said, "Why, I see a block of marble. What do you see?" Michelangelo, with a gleam in his eye as he placed his chisel to the marble and raised his hammer said, "Friend, I see an angel in that marble, and I am going to set that angel free!" Yes, when you look, what do you see? Can you see those intangibles that make for greatness. Can you see the invisible?

Yes, it is our horizons that stretch us. It is our dreams that enable us to grow. And it is vision that infuses life into our very being, for without vision we are not truly alive. Notice again the words of our text as it says, "Where there is no vision, the people perish."

II.   Believe the Incredible

To make our dreams come true we must believe the incredible, and the most incredible fact of history, the most the incredible fact of the universe is that God loves you.

For centuries theologians have tried to fathom and interpret the love of God. They have tried to fathom it spiritually, emotionally, mentally and intellectually. And they have tried to interpret it, but God's love is so incredible that it is difficult to interpret and explain.

One of my favorite vocalists is George Beverly Shea. I think Bev Shea was enthralled in the very throes of the incredibleness of God's love when he penned the lines to this beautiful hymn:

There's the wonder of sunrise at morning;
The wondrous sunset I see.
But the wonder of wonders that thrills my soul;
Is the wonder that God loves me.
Oh the wonder of it all;
The wonder of it all,
Just to think that God loves me.

And to help us understand His love for us is precisely why God revealed Himself through Jesus Christ.

I have a good friend who is a minister in this Annual Conference, and he shared a story with his people that was found, he said, in an old ***Colliers*** magazine.

Many years ago in an orphanage there was a young girl by the name of Susan. Susan was not attractive, and she was overweight. When the other children were not teasing her, they simply avoided her. When guests came to the orphanage, they shunned Susan. The orphanage had a strict rule that when the children were outside the walls, they were not allowed to talk or communicate with anybody. One day while outside the big walls of the orphanage, Susan took a piece of paper, and she scribbled some words upon it. She then took a pin and fastened the note to a tree. The Superintendent of the orphanage saw it, and he immediately snatched the note down and instructed Susan to report to his office.

The Superintendent went to his office first, he straightened out the paper and read the note. What he read literally broke his heart for it said, "Whoever finds this, please know that I love you. Susan."

Isn't that what God did on Calvary's Cross? God's Son was nailed to another tree. The inspired writer said, "He had no form or comeliness that we should look at Him and no beauty that we should desire Him. He was despised and rejected..."

Isn't that what God said upon Calvary's Cross: "Whoever sees this; whoever understands this; whoever believes this, I want you to know I love you."

How incredible is God's love? Like the theologians, we have difficulty fathoming it. It is almost too much to take in. We sang about it a moment ago;

> *And when I think that God, his Son not sparing;*
> *Sent Him to die, I scarce can take it in;*
> *That on the cross, my burden gladly bearing,*
> *He bled and died to take away my sin.*

Yes, to make your dreams come true, believe the incredible fact that God loves you. Saint Augustine of Hippo, the great church father of the Fourth Century said, "God loves everyone of us as though there was only one of us to love."

Tell me, can you fathom God's love? Can you accept God's love? Can you believe God's incredible love? I'll challenge you to believe the incredible.

III.   Attempt the Impossible

Now after we have seen the invisible, and after we have believed the incredible, we then need to attempt the impossible.

And the way we begin to attempt the impossible is by memorizing Luke 1:37. For that verse says, "With God, all things are possible." I don't know of a more meaningful verse of Scripture you can commit to memory than that verse. Now, when you read it in the original language, it is presented with several negatives, and it literally reads, "For with God, nothing shall be impossible." Are you willing to attempt the impossible?

Bruce Larson is on Schuller's staff in California. He told of receiving a telephone call from Millard Fuller in Americus, Georgia. Fuller shared with Larson that he was beginning a new organization. It was one of the goals of his organization to build over 100,000 homes for poverty stricken people. He then invited Larson to serve on his Board of Directors.

Larson declined as he thought to himself, "Why, that's impossible." He shared with Fuller that he was too busy to take on that responsibility. Later Bruce Larson was to say, "There are many regrets, and one is that I did not take that position to attempt the impossible."

Yes, there was a man who, with a saw in one hand and a hammer in the other hand, and with a heart that beat with compassion for impoverished people, and that man, Milliard Fuller, attempted the impossible, and Habitat for Humanity was born.

There was a physician who had a Bible in one hand and a stethoscope in the other. That physician stepped out of the comfort and security of old England, and he stepped in to the unexpected in the Lamberene jungle in French Equatorial Africa. And there Dr. Albert Schweitzer attempted the impossible.

Several years ago in Alabama there was a little girl who was either born deaf or she became deaf at a very early age. She worked through six years of physical therapy to learn how to even pronounce her last name.

That little girl had a mother who was positive about life. The word "impossible" was not even in her vocabulary. That mother taught her daughter that the last four letters in American spell "I Can."

She constantly shared with her that famous quote by Helen Keller when Ms. Keller said, "The most handicapped person in the world is a negative thinker."

As that little girl grew older she wanted so much to learn to dance. Because of her hearing impairment it was very difficult, but she gave it her best, and she learned to dance by memorizing the time in between beats.

On September 17, 1994, that young lady stepped upon a stage and did a contemporary ballet to Sandi Patti's "Via Dolorosa," and on that September night Heather Whitestone attempted the impossible, and she was crowned Miss America.

What is your vision today? How challenging are your horizons? How real are your dreams? It is my firm conviction that you can make your dreams come true if you will put your faith in God, and then "<u>see</u> the invisible, <u>believe</u> the incredible, and then with God's grace, <u>attempt</u> the impossible."

* *One of my closest friends in the ministry is Dr. Bob Baggott. I assist him as our Chaplains together, and he has so kindly and graciously taken me under his wing. I appreciate so very much his kindness to me. I love Bob like a brother, and we room together when we travel with the team. Other than his loud snoring, that*

sounds like a small freight train coming through the room about 2:00 a.m. each Saturday morning, I love everything about my dear friend and brother. Bob is a Baptist and I am a Methodist, but I tease him by telling him that he is the most "Methodist-Baptist" that I have ever met. I told him that I could get him a robe and teach him the Apostle's Creed, and he would make a good Methodist. I've preached for Bob, and he has preached for me. He and his Betty are a blessing and inspiration to Monteigne and me. Bob and I enjoy sharing sermon ideas and outlines with each other. Bob shared this outline for this study with me, and for this idea I am grateful to my friend.

HOW TO HAVE COURAGE

*"Wait on the Lord: be of good courage,
and He will strengthen your heart."*
(Psalm 27:14)

My brother, John Ed, told the story of a couple who lived in the country. They were people of the soil, and they did not enjoy any of the modern conveniences. They did not even have a television set. They had never even been to the city.

One day as they were sitting on the front porch swinging, the farmer said to his wife, "Wife, we have got to go to town!" So they made the long trek into town. For the first time they saw the busy traffic, the tall sky scrappers and the apartment buildings. Then for the first time they went into a department store. The farmer was dressed in his over-alls, and his wife was a rather homely looking woman.

For the first time they saw an elevator. They stood looking at the doors of the elevator. The doors opened, and the wife stepped inside the elevator. The doors closed, and the lights flashed. About 20 seconds later, the lights flashed again, and the elevator doors opened. Out walked a beautiful young lady. The old farmer looked at her, scratched his head, and said, "Wife, I don't know where you went, and I don't know what you did–but we have got to come to town more often!"

And I feel we ministers need to teach and preach more often on subjects that directly relate to people and the everyday problems they are facing. We need to supply answers to questions people are asking. We face many problems in life, and it is important for us to know the Bible has answers to these many questions. The Bible has solutions to the many problems of life. We encounter many obstacles as we journey through life.

Sister Theresa wrote in her journal, "Lord, when wilt thou cease to strew our path with obstacles?" The Lord answered,

"Murmur not, for it is thus that I treat my friends." Theresa replied, "Ah, dear Lord, and that is why thou hast so few friends."

As we travel through life we encounter many obstacles and problems. I believe the first step we must take in addressing these problems is to be courageous. We need to have courage. We even need courage to come before God for the Bible says, "Let us come boldly unto the throne of grace so we can find mercy and grace to help in our time of need." (Hebrews 4:16)

God wants us to have this boldness and courage. The text I've chosen for this study is Psalm 27:14. The Psalmist says, "Wait on the Lord: be of good courage, and He will strengthen your heart." This verse tells us when we wait upon the Lord, He will give us courage and strengthen our hearts.

We need this kind of courage. The world admires people who are courageous. It thrills us to read about a courageous fireman who rushes into a burning building and rescues a child.

It thrills us to read about a courageous policeman who lays his life upon the line. It thrills us to read of mighty acts of courage and valor that have taken place upon the battle field.

Sometime ago my wife and I made a trip to the state of Virginia to visit several Civil War Battle fields. One of the most fascinating battle fields is in Petersburg, Virginia. The guides tell of how there in Petersburg occurred one of the most unusual strategies in military history.

In mid 1864, General U. S. Grant was the commander of the Army of the Potomac. He had commenced his "War of Attrition." It was a type of warfare that was to gradually grind down the Confederacy.

Things were moving rather slowly so Grant ordered his engineers to dig a tunnel 510 feet deep beneath the Confederate lines. There they deposited 300 kegs of dynamic. A fuse was prepared, and it was set to go off at 3:00 AM on the morning of July 30, 1864. The assault troops were ready to rush in following the explosion. They lit the fuse and they waited for the 3:00 hour. At 3:00 AM nothing happened. It became apparent to the Union high command that the fuse had gone out.

Grant asked for volunteers for what would possibly be a suicide mission as he sought men to go into the tunnel and find the detached fuse. Two men from the 48th Pennsylvania Regiment volunteered. There names were Daugherty and Reese. They were from the Anthracite coal mining region of Pennsylvania. They had worked in the mines there, and they were familiar with the underground.

Crawling on their hands and knees in the bosom of the earth, through a narrow corridor, they came to where the fuse had gone out. They reattached it, and then made their way back to safety. The fuse was ignited, and in a short time there was a devastating explosion.

What is known in Civil War history as "The Battle of the Crater" took place. You can visit Petersburg, Virginia, today, and you can see the massive crater made by the huge explosion. As I stood there and looked at that wide crater, I thought of the courage of those two men. The bravery of those two men from Pennsylvania has gone down as one of the most courageous acts in Civil War history because what they did was not on the outside in the sunshine, in full view of everybody, but it was underground in the dark, out of the view of everyone.

An act of courage like this moves and thrills us beyond words, but we need to realize courage is not something marked strictly for emergency use. God wants us to be courageous everyday of our lives. As we face the problems of life each day we need this courage in our lives on a daily basis. We need courage to brace our convictions, to boost our confidence, and to bolster our commitment. I believe the type of courage described in our text is available to us on a daily basis. It is my conviction that we experience this courage when we embrace four beliefs. These four beliefs will make you a courageous person. You need to:

I.   Believe In the <u>Importance</u> of Yourself
II. Believe In the <u>Interest</u> Other People Have In You
III. Believe In the <u>Inspiration</u> of Those Who Have Gone On Before You
IV. Believe In the <u>Infinite</u> Greatness of Your God

I.   Believe In the Importance Of Yourself

Perhaps you are saying, "George, that does not sound too spiritual for me to believe in the importance of myself." My friend, not only is it spiritual for you to believe in yourself – it is also scriptural.

A person asked our Lord, "What is the great commandment?" Jesus said, "You are to love the Lord your God with all of your heart, your soul, your strength and your mind. And the second is like unto it as, you are to love your neighbor as yourself."

Think about that for a moment. If we don't love ourselves, how can we love our neighbors? And if the second commandment is like unto the first, how can we even love God if we do not love and believe in ourselves?

You are unique, different and important. As a child of God you need to celebrate your uniqueness and importance.

I heard the story of a third grade teacher who was instructing the boys and girls in her class about new developments in Science. She said to the class, "Boys and girls, tell me something important that is in the world today that was not here ten years ago." A little boy on the back row raised his hand. The teacher acknowledged him and said, "O.K., Johnny, tell me something important in the world today that was not here ten years ago." The little boy confidently asserted, "Me, Teacher, me!" And that little boy was right because he is important.

You are important, and you need to believe in the importance of yourself. It is amazing what we can accomplish when we truly believe in ourselves. It is also amazing what we fail to accomplish when we do not believe in ourselves.

During the Civil War, Rear Admiral DuPont was asked why he failed to take his ships into Charleston Harbor. Admiral Farragut listened to DuPont's reasons. Admiral Farragut then said, "Sir, that is a good explanation, but you and I both know the real reason you did not bring your ships into the harbor was because you did not believe you could do it!"

In Matthew 25, our Lord tells the parable of the Talents. One man was given five talents, another man was given two talents and another man was given one. The man with one talent became fearful and failed to believe in himself as he went out and buried his talent.

As you study the New Testament you will find one of the harshest rebukes leveled by our Lord was toward this man who became fearful and failed to believe in himself.

With a firm resolve we need to believe in the importance of ourselves.

When young Benjamin Disraeli was jeered down upon the occasion of his first speech in Parliament, he shook his fist in the face of his critics and said, "You will hear me again!" And the Parliament of Britain did hear him again. With a high level of self-esteem and a belief in the importance of himself, Disraeli rose up to become the beloved Prime Minister of England. Belief in one's self brings courage, and courage brings victory and success.

I was driving out of Atlanta the other day, and I saw a bumper sticker that especially touched me. The grammar is not all that good, but the theology is not all that bad. This bumper sticker simply said, "You are special! You are important because God don't make no junk!" Believe in the importance of yourself!

II. Believe In The Interest Other People Have In You

It is wonderful when a person stands against great odds as God's man or God's woman in a dark hour. But there are times when that man needs to know there is some-body who believes in him.

There are times when that woman needs to know somebody is interested in her.

There are times when they need to know there are those who truly care.

There are those times when we need to know we are a part of the brotherhood, the sisterhood and a part of the community and fellowship of faith. We need to know others believe in us and care.

I read about a kind priest who was entering St. Paul's Cathedral in London. He noticed to the side of the steps a beggar asking for alms. The caring priest put his hands in his pockets and produced nothing. He looked at the beggar and sadly said, "I am so sorry, my Brother, but I have nothing." The beggar replied, "Oh, you have given me more than money. You have called me brother."

The Bible says, "A friend loves at all times, and there is a friend who sticks closer than a brother." And we need to know our brothers and sisters care for us, are interested in us and truly believe in us.

It was Bishop Goodson who told this moving story of Dr. James Franklin. He said Dr. Franklin was traveling cross-country by train many years ago. He was approached by a porter who asked him if he was a minister. Dr. Franklin replied to him that he was a minister, and he asked the porter why he would ask such a question. The porter said, "I saw the Bible in the seat next to you, and I felt you must be a minister."

The porter then said, "At one time I wanted to become a minister more than anything in the world. Dr. Franklin asked the porter why he did not go into the ministry.

The porter replied, "I have an older brother. It was the great desire of his heart to go to college, seminary and become a minister himself. Our parents were very poor, and we prayed about it. It was my decision that he go to college, and I work on the railroad."

The porter then said to Dr. Franklin, "Since you are a minister, perhaps you know my brother. His name is Bishop Scott. Bishop Isaiah Benjamin Scott."

Dr. Franklin jumped to his feet and exclaimed, "You mean Bishop Scott is your brother? I am well aware of the great work he is doing in Africa as well as the United States here. He was the first African American elected to the high office of Bishop in the Methodist Episcopal Church."

Some time after that experience on the train Dr. Franklin was attending a General Conference. He heard Bishop Scott speak. After the Bishop's eloquent sermon, Dr. Franklin sought the Bishop out and asked to speak with him.

Dr. Franklin said, "Bishop Scott, do you have a relative who works as a porter on the railroad?" As soon as he asked the question, tears started to well up in the eyes of Bishop Scott. The Bishop stood there for a moment and said nothing. And then with tears rolling down his cheeks he said, "That is my only brother. He sacrificed so I could go to college, seminary and go into the ministry. It was his belief in me that gave me the courage to go on against seemingly insurmountable odds. His belief in me made the difference. All I am or ever hope to be I owe to my Lord and precious brother." Like Bishop Scott, we need to believe that others are interested and truly believe in us also.

III. Believe In the Inspiration Of Those Who Have Gone On Before

Just rest your mind upon those people who have meant so much to you over the years. Scan the panorama of your mind and reflect upon those who have touched your life in a significant way. Think of those whose shadow of influence has fallen across your life and made you what you are, who you are, and Whose you are today.

Dr. Harry Emerson Fosdick said, "We are tempted to see only the finger prints of evil men, but we need to balance that view with the footprints of goodness and greatness that have been made in the sands of time."

Think of those whom you have loved and lost for a while. There are many whose footsteps have graced the very aisles of our sanctuary in years past.

There are those who have taught Sunday School within the hallowed halls of this and other churches.

There are great ones who are known by reputation to many, and there are those who are known only to you and God. Believe in the inspiration of these who mean so much to you. In our Affirmation of Faith, I am so thankful we say, "I believe in the communion of saints." That is a beautiful statement that reminds us of the inspiration of those who have laid down their crosses, taken up their crowns and made heaven all the more lovelier with their presence. It is a beautiful creedal statement that reminds us we gain inspiration even in this hour from those who touched our lives earlier.

The writer of Hebrews sounds this same note when he says, "We are surrounded by a great cloud of witnesses." One scholar reminds us of the beauty of this verse as it calls to mind a mighty coliseum where we are surrounded by the saints of God who sit in the grand-stands and cheer us on. They encourage us, inspire us and challenge us to be courageous as we fight the good fight of faith.

Yes, we begin to find courage as we understand what the Biblical record means when it says, "Thou they be dead, yet they live", and we gain courage from the inspiration they provide us.

IV. Believe In The Infinite Greatness Of Your God

Maybe right now you are fighting an awful battle. Perhaps you are engaged in a conflict or a fight. Maybe you are in the midst of a terrible struggle.

You need to realize that as a child of God it is not your battle entirely. The fight is the Lord's, and you need to commit it to Him. This is what the Bible means when it says, "Cast all of your care upon Him because He surely cares for you."

During the 16th Century, the Pope sent a Cardinal to visit Martin Luther. His purpose was to get Luther to renounce his belief.

The Cardinal said, "Do you think the Pope cares about a German Boor? Do you expect the Princes to take up arms and defend a wretched worm like you? No, I can tell you they will not. And, Luther, where will you be then?"

Luther replied, "Where will I be then? I will be where I've always been, where I am now, and where I'll always be: in the hands of my infinite great God."

And it was this belief in the infinite greatness of his God that gave him the courage to say at the Diet of Worms, "Here I stand! I cannot do otherwise so help me God!"

Our Lord wants us to live courageous lives. He wants us to experience this courage on an everyday basis as we deal with the problems of life, and we become courageous persons only when we embrace these THOUGHTS. This book is about a winning attitude in life. It is about winning thoughts for any season of life. Genuine and lasting victory commences with a courageous spirit. As you commence to read and study these positive principles, it is my prayer that you will begin by committing yourself to these four vital beliefs that will bring courage to your life.

HOW TO BUILD A HAPPY HOME

"Except the Lord build the home,
they labor in vain who build it..."
(Psalm 127:1a)

I read about a minister in a large city who went into a used bookstore. As he was browsing through a dusty shelf, he found a volume entitled *How To Acquire A Home.*

Looking for possible sermon illustrations, he started to thumb through the index. He was disappointed because the titles of the chapters were: "How to acquire a loan," "How to borrow money," "Locating the right real estate agent," "Getting the right interior decorator," "Selecting the proper landscaper," etc.

Now that book was mistitled, it should have been entitled *How To Acquire A House*, for you do not buy a home. You buy a house, and then you build it into a home.

You see, there is a distinctive difference between a house and a home.

A house is an institution. A home is an ideal.

A house can be cold and empty, but a home is where one comes at the end of a long hard day to find love, understanding and courage to keep fighting the good fight of faith until the final sunset.

A house stands alone, but a home has within it people who genuinely care for one another.

A house is built with money, but a home is built with human love, divine grace and the sympathizing tear.

You construct a house with brick, cement, wood and glass, but you build a home with the precious materials of human sacrifices, human personalities and human desires.

Home is in your heart. You may have to house it under a modest roof, but it can be a castle of dreams if love is there.

A little shack on the outskirts of town can be a home if the lights of love are burning brightly, while a palatial mansion in the most exclusive section of the city can be a little corner of hell if the lamps of love have started to flicker and the ashes are cold and dead upon the hearth.

Now, home is a subject in which all people are interested. I do not know of any word that strikes a more responsive cord than the word home.

Home is a part of the American dream. America gave to the world those haunting and wistful lines, "Be it ever so humble, there is no place like home."

Those words have caused lonely and homesick people around the world to listen and weep. When the author of those lines died on a far away strand, his body was brought back to America on a battleship with highest honors. He was no powerful, popular, political leader. He was no great athlete. He was no outstanding military leader who had won battles on land, sea or the in the air. All he did was give to the world those tender lines, "Home, sweet home."

Now the question is, how can we build a home? Our text very plainly tells us, "Except the Lord build the home, they labor in vain who build it."

It is interesting to note that the Hebrew word for home is *bayith*, and to the Jewish mindset it was a very dear and important place, and it was possible to build a home only through the work of God.

Now while our text tells us that only God can build a home, we can help Him by providing three elements. These three elements are:

I.   **Human Love**
II.   **Honest Appreciation**
III.   **Heartfelt Understanding**

I.   **Human Love**

I am almost reluctant to use the word love because we use this word to cover so many different subjects. Perhaps we even over use the word, and in many ways, we have just about worn it out.

Dr. Clovis Chappel once said that the word love is like that poor fellow in the parable of the Good Samaritan. It has been "robbed, stripped of its raiment, and left by the roadside wounded."

We use the word love to describe all types of things. We say that we love everything.

While I was in seminary I served the Perote Charge. It was made up of five churches, and the strongest church on the charge was the little Pleasant Hill Church. We had preaching every first Sunday of the month, and on that Sunday quite often I would, as they say in the country, "take dinner" with some of the members of that church.

In that church were two sisters and a brother who lived together. Their names were Sally, Jewel and Will. They felt their special calling by God was to take the young ministers under their wings and care for them, and they did a great job. At the time they were in their mid-eighties, and they were three of the sweetest people that I've ever known in my life.

The first Sunday that I preached there they invited me to have Sunday dinner with them. Miss Sally (that is what she wanted me to call her) said that she would ride from the church with me to give directions to the house. I remember how she got in the car and braced herself. She became very rigid, and I said, "Miss Sally, I'm a pretty good driver. You can relax." I'm not sure she had ridden in a car that many times.

We drove to their house which was way out in the country.

I remember when we got out of the car, I went around to her side of the car to open the door. As I opened the door she looked up and said, "Brother George, I just loved your sermon."

Well, as I was admiring her judgement and helping her out of the car we both nearly stepped on one of her chickens. Her eyes immediately glanced at her chicken, and she said, "Brother George, I love these chickens."

When we got into the front yard we saw some goats, and she pointed to them and said, "Brother George, I just love my goats so much." And I'm not real sure that we didn't have something that was like goat milk for lunch that day.

She then pointed to some pigs over by the side of the house, and she said, "Brother George, I just love my pigs."

Now, I don't think she realized it, but she took my sermon and just mixed it in with those chickens, pigs and goats. She put them all in the same package together, and she tied that package together with the string of love.

She put all of those different nouns into the same verbal context and underscored it with the verb, love, making it descriptive of each one of them.

But like Miss Sally, often we say that we love everything. I'm not real sure we can adequately define the word love. If I were to ask you, how would you define love, what would you say?

If you ask a romanticist to define love, he will write you a poem.

If you ask a young girl who is engaged to be married, she will write an essay.

If you ask some ole country boy to define love, he'll probably kick the dirt with his shoe, hang his hand, grin and say, "I can't explain it or define it, but I shore can feel it deep within my heart."

It's interesting that in the beautiful Greek language there are several words that describe the powerful emotion of love. In our English language we have only one word, but in the Greek language there are several.

There is the word agape, which is love in a spiritual dimension.

There is the word eros, which is love with a sexual connotation.

There is philia, which is love in a brotherly sense, hence Philadelphia is called "The City of Brotherly Love."

There is the word storge, and this particular usage refers to love in a familial context.

But the type of love I am referring to is a special kind of love that is vitally important in building a home. It is a love that commences with the affection of two people. It grows, and it is consummated through marriage. It then is nurtured and matures with the blessing of God upon it and it lasts forever. Yes, it lasts eternally.

While I was working on my doctorate in the Sewanee-Vanderbilt Joint Doctorate Program, I spent several summers taking course work at Vanderbilt in Nashville.

One of the real joys of being in that program was having the opportunity to worship in various churches in the Nashville area.

One particular church I especially enjoyed was the McKendree United Methodist Church in Downtown Nashville. It is an old historical church named after the venerable Bishop McKendree.

While I was studying there at Vanderbilt, the pastor at McKendree was Dr. Wallace Chappell.

He told the story of a young girl in his church he was planning to marry. She had recently graduated from Vanderbilt. It was at a time when the Vietnam War had just escalated, and it was at its height.

This young lady came to Wallace and said to him, "Could I please change one part of the service? We're getting married on Sunday, and on Tuesday, Jonathan is shipping out for Vietnam. His orders will send him into the very thick of the fighting. You know that part in the service where I take his hand, look into his eyes and say, 'to have and to hold, to love and to cherish, till death us do part,' I do not like the way that ends, 'till death us do part.' Could we please change that so I could simply put my arms around him, hold him and say, 'to love and to cherish <u>forever</u>, and <u>ever</u> and <u>ever</u>?'"

That is the kind of love that I am speaking of when I speak of the love that is needed within the home. It is a love that is eternal, and it lasts forever.

When Abraham Lincoln married Mary Todd, she had inscribed inside his wedding ring, "Love is eternal." And that is a good definition for love, for love is truly everlasting.

When I married my wife, she knew of my great admiration for Abraham Lincoln, and she had inscribed on the inside of my ring those same three words, "Love is Eternal."

So, this type of love – a love that lasts forever, a love that is nurtured daily with the blessing of God upon it, and a love that is born and commences with the affection of two people – this human love is absolutely essential in building a home.

II.   Honest Appreciation

Honest appreciation is so important in building a home. The need to be appreciated is one of the basic drives in human nature, and it is needed in the home as much as anywhere.

When William James was sick, some friends brought some flowers to him along with a note of personal appreciation. This great scholar replied to them by saying that he was reminded of the fact that in writing his text book on psychology he had omitted the deepest quality of human nature, the desire to be appreciated.

Yes, honest appreciation is so very important in the home.

Wives need to appreciate their husbands. A woman wrote a letter to Dorothy Dix asking how she could keep the love of her husband. Dorothy Dix wrote back telling her to learn a hundred ways of saying, "I think you're wonderful."

Husbands need to appreciate their wives. Wives need to appreciate their husbands. Children need to honestly appreciate their parents, and parents need to appreciate their children. Yes, we especially need to appreciate our children because children have a way of growing up, and getting away before we realize it and before we're ready.

This past week in my study I came across the words of a song that were sung by Mike Douglas. Having a daughter who is a senior in high school, these words brought tears to my eyes, and they tugged at the strings of my heart. The words go like this:

The men in my little girl's life,
The men in my little girl's life.
It seems like only yesterday,
I could hear my little girl saying –
"Daddy, there's a boy outside,
His name is Rob-
He wants to play in our backyard-
Can he, Daddy? Can he, Daddy-
Oh, please, Daddy."

Was it really so long ago,
She had come to me and she wanted to know-
"Dad, there's a boy outside,
His name is Lee-
He wants to carry my books for me-
Can he, Daddy?
Is it alright, Dad?
He's got a bicycle, Dad."

The men in my little girl's life,
The men in my little girl's life.

Then came ponytails and jeans,
And my little girl was in her teens.
"Pop, there's a boy outside,
His name is Tom –
He wants to take me to the prom –
O.K., Pop? He's cute, Pop –
We'll be home early, Pop?"

17

Before I knew it, time had flown,
And how my little girl had grown-
Now "Father, there's a boy outside,
His name is Eddie-
He wants to know if we can go steady-
Can we, Father? Yes, Father?
Oh can we borrow the car, Pop?

Yes, it seems like only yesterday,
I heard my lovely daughter say,
"Daddy, there's a boy outside-
His name is Jim-
He asked me if I'd marry him.
I said, 'yes,' Dad.
You've got something in your eye, Dad?
I love him, Dad."

The men in my little girl's life,
The men in my little girl's life.

A child, an adolescent, a young lady, a wife-
And-oh, yes-
There's another man in my little girl's life.
"Hi, Dad, there's a boy outside-
His name is Tim-
I told him Grandpa was going to babysit with him.
Thanks, Dad. Bless you, Dad.
Good night, Dad."

The men in my little girl's life,
The men in my little girl's life.

Yes, time has a way of passing by quickly and leaving us with a bunch of empty yesterdays filled with anticipated words of appreciation.

We need to express our appreciation to our wives and parents – and especially our children.

As I previously stated, my daughter is a senior in high school. In addition to expressing my appreciation to her, I also wrote her this personal letter as she prepared to graduate, and I hope and trust the words will be helpful to you:

My Dear Mallory...

It seems like April 1, 1979, was only yesterday. Early that Sunday morning I took your Mother to Providence Hospital in Mobile and later that day God blessed us with the creation of a little life called Mallory Spear Mathison. That was one of the two happiest days of my life. As you graduate from high school, there are some thoughts I wish to share with you.

First, I want to thank you for the happiness you've brought to your Mother and me – and scores of other people. Watching you grow up has been so exciting. Some of my most precious memories are associated with you and your formative years:

.... Like hearing you cry in the Saraland Church on Sunday night when you thought I had preached long enough.

.... Like watching your Daddy Si hold you in his arms and baptize you "In the name of the Father, and the Son and the Holy Spirit."

.... Like the night your mother was attending a Junior League meeting in Mobile, and I was home keeping you; and I had an emergency phone call, and you, a little 2 year old baby girl, got into all of your mother's watercolors, paints, canvasses and everything else that had to do with her artwork – and you painted and water colored the sofa, the T.V., the walls, a picture of John Wesley, my Bible and yourself (the picture of you and your artistic work that evening occupies a special place in my office at the church.)

.... Like the Sunday afternoon you rode your bike into the curb, you flipped over the top, and you landed on your stomach. We took you to the doctor, and in his office your little hands gripped my leg and you said, "Daddy, please don't leave me."

.... Like watching you as a little 7 year old girl sing, "God Bless America" during the evening worship service at Kingswood.

.... Like watching you cry when I tried to explain to you that the Bishop was moving us from Kingswood to a new church.

.... Like watching you change from a little girl into a beautiful young lady here in Auburn – going from a robed acolyte to a robed graduating senior.

.... Like hearing your compassionate voice on the other end of the line on that August night tell me, "Daddy, Mother Mary just died."

.... Like seeing how "excited and thrilled" you were when you found out that your Mother and I were going to be chaperons for the Junior/Senior prom.

.... Like the comfort you gave me when your Mother changed the name of our little dog, "Princess," to "No! No! My name is Bad Doggie! What is yours?"

Secondly, I want to share some thoughts that I hope will be helpful to you as you begin a new chapter in the book of your life.

The first two thoughts I've borrowed from a man whom I deeply admire, love and respect. He is the President of Auburn University, a member of our church and a dear friend. Dr. Muse said that his mother taught him two valuable lessons. They are worth repeating, and they are worth emulating.

One, "Do your homework." Always be prepared, and always remember the words of Abraham Lincoln, "I will prepare, and some day my time will come." Take your studies seriously, and always go to class. Woody Allen said, "Ninety percent of success is showing up." Now I'm not sure every professor will agree with that, but that is a pretty good quote anyway. Work hard, and give extra effort with the courses you take. Do more than what is expected of you. Jesus called it "going the second mile."

Two, "Be nice to people." God has blessed you with a warmth and kindness and sensitivity to the needs of people – especially to those who are less fortunate. Continue to be nice. As your Pastor-Father, one thing I've observed about people is – they don't care how much I know nearly as much as they want to know how much I care. Like you've always been, Dear, continue to be nice to people – and always have a positive hello and a big smile for everybody you meet, regardless of what they say or do to you.

Also...

.... Remember to "roll with the punches." Life is not all sunshine. Some days are dark. Learn to get through those days realizing the bright days will come. At times the road will be rocky, but remember it is the bumps upon the mountain that we climb on, and the important thing is to go a little bit higher everyday. Every life has sadness mixed in with gladness, and the key to a happy life is to make the smiles outweigh the tears.

.... Remember to laugh with life. A sense of humor will be one of your best friends, and you will find laughter to be the emotional lubricant that helps make the complex machinery of life run smoothly. And remember the words of Proverbs: "A merry heart does good like a medicine."

.... Remember to always look to God in everything you do, ever remembering again the words of Proverbs: "In all thy ways acknowledge Him, and He will direct your path."

.... Remember to take time each day to nurture those deep spiritual recesses of your soul. Set aside time each day to pray, read from the Bible, and study the lives of the Saints, For as you develop physically, and mentally, and socially, it is so important that you grow spiritually each day in your faith.

.... Remember that life is good, and fun, and exciting, and fall in love everyday with God, people, sports, the arts, mountains, dogs, cats, the ocean, the Bible, God's "special people," little country churches, majestic cathedrals,

*flowers, the beach, music, God's "interesting people," fields and clover –
with everything, except money.*

*Your Mother and I had been married for nine years, and upon our knees we
prayed that God would bless us with a little child. When we received word that
you were coming, we wept with joy. You were His answer to our prayers – and
you are everything we could have ever hoped for. You've brought us so much happiness. Again, as you close one chapter in the book of your life and prepare to
open another one, I want you to know how much we love you and how precious
you are to our hearts. God bless.*

Love,
Dad

III. Heartfelt Understanding

Like <u>human</u> <u>love</u> and <u>honest</u> <u>appreciation</u>, <u>heartfelt understanding</u> is so important in
building a home.

It is needed in the community, the church, and it is especially needed in the home.

Most problems in the home are precipitated by two factors: <u>one</u>, an inability to communicate and <u>two</u>, a failure to understand, and we solve many problems in the home
when we begin to communicate more effectively and to understand more empatheti-
cally.

Let me ask you a question: Do you have an educated heart? Now, with this being a
university community, we all are well familiar with an educated mind. But I'm talking
about something different here. I am speaking of an educated heart. What is an educated heart?

An educated heart is characteristic of a well adjusted person. An educated heart is
absolutely essential for a happy home.

An educated heart means you know how to bring happiness into the life of another
person.

An educated heart means you know how to make somebody feel comfortable in an
uneasy situation.

An educated heart means you know something kind and wonderful to say about
somebody, and you say it.

An educated heart means you know something ugly and vicious to say about somebody, and you do <u>not</u> say it.

An educated heart means you are able to see the other person's point of view.

An educated heart means you are able to do something that many people in this
world are incapable of doing, and that is to understand people.

21

People everywhere are crying out to be understood, and these cries are especially heard within the home, and sometimes the most important thing we can do is simply listen and seek to understand other people.

There was a minister who served a church in a certain community. In that church was a poor man who lived on the other side of the tracks. He was poor in the material things of the world, but he was rich spiritually. He was highly respected by everybody, and he was a leader in his church. He was also a very close friend of the pastor.

This man had one son who was constantly in and out of trouble. The minister had two sons.

One Sunday morning, the man's son committed a terrible crime in that little community, and he was arrested. He was put in the city jail. It devastated the boy's father.

On that Saturday night, the minister went to the jail to visit the incarcerated boy. He found the boy's father there, and after visiting, the two of them walked out of the jail together. The minister walked with the boy's father all the way to the man's home.

The minister then came home, and his two boys were on the front porch waiting for him. They immediately began to ask him questions.

They asked, "Dad, was Mr. Smith (that was not his name) angry? Was he mad? Was he upset because his son had been arrested? What did he say to you at the jail? What did he say to you while you walked home with him?"

The minister-father said, "Boys, he did not say anything to me. We just sat in the cell block and not hardly a word was spoken. He just sat over next to his son on the side of the bed, and he kept his arm around him."

"We then walked out of the jail together. He still did not say anything to me. We started walking towards his home, and about halfway there I simply lifted my hand, put it upon his shoulder and squeezed it."

"We then crossed over the railroad tracks to the other side of town where he lives. We walked down Railroad Street to the front steps of the little white framed house. A train came rumbling by, and it shook the steps, the front porch and the entire house as it had done many, many times before. We just stood and listened to the train."

"We then walked up on the front porch together. All the time he did not say anything. He was very quiet. Then, just as I started to leave, he did say something to me."

"He took my hand in both of his hands, looked into my eyes, and with a quivering voice said, 'Thank you for three things: one, thank you for being my friend; not just my minister, but also my friend. Two, thank you for being here with me. But most importantly, three, thank you for understanding. Thank you for understanding.'"

This day, the world around us is crying for someone to put a tender and loving hand upon its shoulder and say, "I understand." There are people in your very home today who are crying out for your heartfelt understanding. I'll challenge you to respond and seek to truly understand the people with whom you live.

Now, let's go back and pick up our text and take it home with us. It says, "Unless

God builds our homes, then we are laboring in vain." While He does the building, it is my prayer that we can help Him by providing these three important elements of human love, honest appreciation and heartfelt understanding, and when we truly look to Him and provide these elements, then we will build a home that will bring happiness to us and honor to Him.

HOW TO BE HAPPY
(John 15:7-11)
"...that your joy may be full."
(John 15:11b)

The next study in this series is <u>How To Be Happy</u>. It is one thing to harbor winning thoughts in your mind, but it is quite another thing to have those thoughts rooted in the furtile soil of a happy heart. So, I want us to think about this subject, <u>How To Be Happy</u>. Now I don't pretend to know everything there is to know about happiness. I do not have all the answers to this question. I do not know everything there is to know about happiness.

I heard about a dear lady who was married to a man who talked all the time. The lady put this classified ad in the newspaper: "For Sale: Complete 25 volume set of <u>Encyclopedia Britannica</u>; latest edition-never used- – <u>husband knows everything</u>!"

I don't know everything about happiness, but I do want to share with you some Biblical insights into this subject, and I trust that as a result we all will understand it better and seek to find an answer to the question that is the title of our message.

Our text tells us that our Lord wants us to experience joy that is full and happiness that is complete, and this is a subject that ought to be of interest to every person here.

We all want to be happy. I have never met a person who wanted to be unhappy. I have never met a person who wanted to be bitter. I've never met a person who wanted to have a negative attitude about life. I have never met a person who wanted to be sad. I have never met a person who wanted to be sour on life, but the fact is there are many unhappy people in this world today.

Now, I want you to notice the title of the sermon. It is not "How to Find Happiness." I am not so sure that we find happiness. If anything, happiness finds us.

The title of the message is not "The Goal of Happiness." Happiness is not a goal we attain nearly as much as it is a process of achieving.

Happiness is not a station we arrive at in life, but rather it is a means of traveling.

In his book, <u>Freedom of Simplicity</u>, Richard Foster says, "Never put happiness at center stage. It is the by-product of a life of service, never the chief end of life. Happiness is not a right to be grasped, but a serendipity to be enjoyed."

Now how can we set our feet upon this highway of happiness? How can we tap into and get in on this quest of whole-hearted happiness? How can we experience the "full joy" of which our text speaks?

I believe there are three simple steps we need to take beginning today. We need to:

I.   **Count our blessings**
II.   **Commit ourselves to serve others**
III.   **Consecrate ourselves anew to God each day**

I.   Count Our Blessings

First of all, we need to count our blessings. The reason many people today are not happy is, they cannot enjoy what they have because they worry about what other people have.

You can make yourself miserable by envying your neighbor's luxury automobile instead of enjoying your own car.

You can make yourself absolutely wretched by coveting your neighbor's palatial mansion instead of appreciating your own humble abode.

I read an interesting article about the escalating salaries in professional sports. One agent said, "Annual salaries of $5-$7 million a year now are not uncommon, and my client is always content with the salary I negotiate for him until he finds out that one of his teammates or someone on another team playing a similar position makes more. Then he becomes very unhappy!"

Yes, many people are unhappy because they do not appreciate what they have. They worry about others, and they try to stay up with them.

Someone has said that we in America are a peculiar people. We buy things we don't need with money we don't have to impress people we don't like.

And then many people are unhappy and do not enjoy what they have because they think only of what they lack.

G.K. Chesterton said, "There are two ways to get enough: one, is to continue to accumulate more and more. The other is to desire less."

George MacDonald said, "To have what we want is riches, but to be able to do without is power."

We experience happiness when we cease to worry about what other people have and what we lack and begin to thank God for His many blessings in our lives.

I have a dear friend who lives in Brewton. His name is Hosea Rodgers, and I greatly love and admire Brother Hosea. He collects articles, essays and poems that are inspirational, and all along he sends some of them to me. He recently sent one that especially warmed my heart. It also made me appreciate the many blessings of God in my own life. I do not know the author. It is simply entitled "The World is Mine." Perhaps you are familiar with it. It goes like this:

Today, upon a bus, I saw a maid.
  with golden hair,

I envied her – she seemed so happy, and I
*   wished I was so fair.*
When suddenly she rose to leave, I saw
*   her hobble down the aisle.*
She had one foot and wore a crutch
*   but as she passed she smiled.*

Oh, God, forgive me when I whine;
*   I have two feet, the world is mine!*

And then I stopped to buy some sweets,
*   the lad who sold them had such charm.*
I talked with him – he said to me,
"It's nice to talk with folks like you.
*   For you see," he said, "I'm blind."*

Oh, God, forgive me when I whine;
*   I have two eyes, the world is mine!*

Then walking down the street I saw a
*   child with eyes of blue.*
He stood and watched the others play;
*   It seemed he knew not what to do.*
I stopped for a moment, then said:
*   "Why don't you join the others, Dear?"*
He looked ahead without a word, and then
*   I knew he could not hear.*

Oh, God, forgive me when I whine,
*   I have two ears – the world is mine!*

With feet to take me where I go,
With eyes to see the sunsets glow,
With ears to hear what I would know,
Oh, God, forgive me when I whine;
*   I'm blessed indeed! The world is mine.*

When I read that little poem, it made me realize how blessed I am, and I began to thank God for the many ways He has blessed my life, and a by-product of the realization of those many blessings is the happiness that God gives to us. Yes, we need to sing and believe the words to the old Gospel Hymn,

Count your many blessings;
Name them one by one,
and it will surprise you
what the Lord has done.

I read in a bulletin that crossed my desk the moving story of an experience of Jack Hinton. Jack Hinton is an outstanding minister who lives in North Carolina. Sometime ago he was a part of a preaching mission in the West Indies. As a part of that mission, they were leading a worship service at a leper colony on the Island of Tobago.

Jack stood up to preach, and before he delivered his sermon he asked the congregation if they would like to sing one more song.

A few feet in front of him was a woman who had been facing the other direction. He could only see her back. She then turned around and looked at him. Jack said, "It was the most hideous face I had ever seen." The woman's nose and ears were entirely gone. The disease had destroyed her lips as well. She lifted a fingerless hand in the air and asked, "Can we sing, 'Count Your Many Blessings?'"

For one of the first times in his ministry, Jack did not know what to do or what to say. He simply stood there as tears welled up in his eyes and was completely overcome with emotion. Unable to say anything, he simply turned and left the service. He was followed by another member of the team who said, "Brother Jack, I guess you will never be able to sing that song again."

He replied, "Yes, I will. Yes, I will. But I will never sing it the same way."

And it is my prayer that after this sermon we will never be able to sing that song the same way.

And so, the first step to happiness is to realize God's goodness and grace in your life and count your many blessings.

II.   Commit Yourself to Serve Other People

I recently read an interesting account of the life of John D. Rockefeller. At the age of 53, Rockefeller was a broken and dejected old man. Although he was worth millions, his diet consisted of saltine crackers and milk. Those were the only things he could keep on his stomach.

Then Rockefeller made a change. Instead of serving his money, he decided to let his money start serving him. He began to think of others and how he could help them as he began to engage in philanthropic causes like the University of Chicago, Tuskegee Institute, and the Rockefeller Foundation.

He got his mind off himself, and he began to think of others and how he could help and serve them; and then an amazing thing happened. He became a happy person.

This biographer described him like this: "He was dying at 53; but he lived to 98!," and he ascribed his prolonged years and happiness to his decision to dedicate himself and his money to helping others.

Yes, a second step to happiness is to commit yourself in service to others.

Hans Christian Andersen said, "To be of use in the world is the only way to happiness."

May I share with you again a part of the quote from Richard Foster? Foster says, "Never put happiness at center stage. It is the by-product of a life of service."

You see, happiness is not necessarily something you do for yourself, but it is a bonus that life slips into your pocket when you do something for somebody else.

I am thinking of a dear lady right now. Her name is Lois Roberts, and the people in our church know and love her. She is a very busy person, but she takes time every week to visit the hospitals, nursing homes and elderly shut-ins. She carries sunshine and good will every where she goes. She writes letters of encouragement, and nearly everyday she calls people just to let them know that she is thinking about them, praying for them, and she tells them how much she genuinely loves them, and she means it.

I asked her this question: "Lois, as busy as you are, how are you able to do so much?" She looked at me with a twinkle in her eye, and she said, "Brother George, we have time to do what we want to do. I have time to do what I want to do, and you have time to do what you want to do. Most people do." And then she gave insight into the basic dynamic of happiness when she said, "Besides, I am just not happy unless I am doing something for somebody else."

Yes, happiness is committing ourselves in service to other people.

III.   Consecrate Ourselves Anew to God Each Day

Each morning when we awaken we need to consecrate ourselves anew and afresh to our Lord, and we need to repeat the words of the Psalmist, "This is the day the Lord has made, I will rejoice and be glad in it."

The Gospel writers record Jesus as saying, "If any person will come after me, let him deny himself, take up his cross and follow me." It is interesting that Luke inserts the word "daily" as he records, "If any person will come after me, let him deny himself daily..." The Psalmist writes, "Thanks be unto God who daily loads us with His benefits."

You see, it is important that we consecrate our lives anew to God each day.

We need to begin the day by blocking out the faults and failures of yesterday, and we need to shut off the fears and frustrations of tomorrow and consecrate ourselves to our

Lord this day. Just for today, we need to put our trust in Him, and in so doing we need to remember the words of the wise writer in Proverbs when he says, "Happy is he who trusts in the Lord."

Yes, happiness is to consecrate ourselves to God this day, and to live this day trusting Him in the center of His Will.

Dr. Albert Schweitzer said, "To know God is the greatest knowledge. To suffer the will of God is the greatest heroism. To do the will of God is the greatest achievement. To have the approval of God on your work is the greatest happiness."

Just for today, we can know Him. We can suffer His Will. We can do His Will, and we can have His approval on our work as we consecrate ourselves to Him and trust Him each step of the way.

How can you be happy? I'm not sure that I have the complete answer, but there are two things I know.

One, God wants you to be happy. Our text tells us that He wants the joy that is in Him to be within you. He wants you to experience His happiness.

Secondly, happiness is very much like a butterfly. It is like chasing a butterfly.

You chase it, you chase it, and you chase it; and it will always just elude you.

But then, you sit down and <u>count</u> your many blessings. You think of God's goodness and God's grace within your life.

Then you <u>commit</u> yourself to serve others as you take your thoughts off yourself, and you begin to think of other people. You don't focus upon your problems and your worries, but you think of how you can serve other people and make life better for them.

Then, in your own way you <u>consecrate</u> your life afresh and anew to your God this very day, not worrying about yesterday or fretting about tomorrow, but you put your trust in Him for today. Then an amazing thing happens. Then that little butterfly comes, and it softly, gently and tenderly lights upon your shoulder. That, my friend, is real happiness.

Chapter 5
<u>Helpful Hints On How To Live</u>

HOW TO OVERCOME YOUR FEARS

"God has not given us a spirit of fear,
but of power, love and a sound mind."
(II Timothy 1:7)

Like other ministers I am deeply appreciative of the loving support of the people in the church I serve. I am also appreciative of our coaching staff here at Auburn. They are a great source of help to me with their love and prayers. All ministers find immense help in their people.

I heard the story of a minister whose son enjoyed playing cards. He was very good at every type of card game. The minister was very concerned about his son because card playing was taking too much of the lad's time. He was also concerned because his son was learning some games that he did not think were appropriate.

One morning the son was in the closet playing solitaire. He heard his father coming, and he immediately gathered the cards up and put them in the first pocket he saw, which happened to be his father's baptismal robe. His father entered the closet, saw his son and said to him, "Johnny, I want you and your mother to go with me to a neighbor's house as I've been invited to baptize a man by immersion."

The minister's wife and son accompanied him to the neighbor's house. They went to the swimming pool where the baptism was to take place.

There was a big crowd of people present. The minister and the baptismal candidate waded into the shallow part of the pool. As the minister started to go down his robe flowed up, and the cards floated out. They floated out in full view of everybody in this order: an ace of spades, a king of spades, a queen of spades, jack of spades, and a ten of spades. They were right there in full view of everybody in that order.

The mother was very embarrassed, and she said to her son "Johnny, do something and help your Dad!" Little Johnny, with his eyes big said, "Mama, with a hand like that, Daddy don't need no help!"

But the truth of the matter is we all need help. And the people in the churches we serve and our coaching friends are a great source of help when we ministers stand to preach. And I am especially grateful for the prayers and support of my people when I deal with a subject like "FEAR".

The title of this chapter is <u>How To Face Our Fears.</u> The text is a very familiar passage from Paul's second letter to Timothy, chapter 1, verse 7. Paul writes to his young friend and says, "God has not given us the spirit of fear, but of power, love and a sound mind."

I read of a magazine that published a two page photograph of a busy street corner in a large city. It showed scores of people going about their various tasks. The caption over the picture simply said, "Of what are these people afraid?"

It was an interesting study of the psychological effect of fear upon the lives of people.

It showed a young mother with her arms filled with packages, her children by her side and anxiety and stress written all over her face.

It showed a man, immaculately attired in a business suit, going into a bank. He missed the first section of the revolving door, and his very demeanor displays his frustration.

It also shows a young man leaning against a wall with an aimless expression on his face. It appears he has no where to go, and his eyes manifest his great fear.

The photograph shows the strain and tension nearly every person is experiencing. The picture provides revealing insight into the problem of fear and the way it grips people. Fear is a terrible problem that so many people experience, both in the city and in the country.

Doctor Harold Roupp says, "Fear is private enemy number one; for out of fear comes a whole train of evils." Shakespeare said, "The minds of men are filled with dread, with fear."

Doctor Gaston Foote said, "You may write this down in indelible letters: what we fear we hate; what we hate we seek to kill; and when we seek to kill we destroy ourselves in the process."

There is a little verse in one of John's epistles that simply says, "Fear works torment." Fear does have a tormenting effect upon people. Fear can be deadly and destructive.

I heard the fable about a time that Death was entering a modern city. As Death was entering the city, it met a man who was coming out of the city. The man said to Death, "Who are you? Where are you going? What are you going to do?" Death said, "I am Death. I am going into the city. I am going to kill ten people." The man said, "That is terrible!" Death said, "I know that is terrible, but I am Death, and that is what I do." They both went their respective ways.

The next morning the man was entering the city, and he encountered Death coming out of the city. The man said to Death, "You said you were only going to kill ten people, but I read in the paper where one hundred people died in the modern city last night." Death said, "I did kill only ten people. The other ninety died of fear!" Fear is a deadly problem.

And it could be the biggest problem you as an individual face today, the problem of fear. It could be that every other problem in life stems from a basic fear.

Following the attack on Pearl Harbor on December 7, 1941, President Franklin D. Roosevelt spoke by radio to a frightened, attentive and united America. He addressed the real problem and properly assessed the situation when he said in that clear, resonant and authoritative voice, "The only thing we have to fear is fear itself!"

Now, as we discuss the problem of fear I think it is important that we realize that there are basically two types of fear.

There is a fear that builds up, and there is a fear that breaks down. There is a fear that brings life, and there is a fear that brings death. There is a fear that is constructive, and there is a fear that is destructive. There is a fear that is Godly, and there is a fear that is Godless. There is a fear that is positive, and there is a fear that is negative.

This positive fear is a holy awe with which we reverence God. This is what the Bible means when it says we are to fear God. This is what the writer of Proverbs means when he says, "Fear is the beginning of wisdom."

But the type of fear that is spoken of in our text is a negative type of fear. This fear is a debilitating spirit that cripples our minds, paralyzes our attitudes and renders us ineffective as we attempt to live life.

When we look at our text we immediately observe two important facts about fear. *One,* this negative and destructive fear is not of God. *Secondly,* as we face the fears of life, God has provided a triad of graces with which we can be triumphant. The three graces are power, purpose, and peace, and they are found in verse 17.

I.   The Grace of Power

Our text begins with Paul saying "God has not given us the spirit of fear, but of power...."

God wants to empower us to live above fear. The Greek word we translate as "power" is **dunamis**. It is the word from which we get our word "dynamite." It is interesting to note the same form of this particular word is used in Acts 1:8 when Jesus says to the early Church, "You will receive power when the Holy Spirit is come upon you." God wants to impart that power to us.

We need this power. Vance Havner said, "It concerns me that there are so many Christians who are content to live such fire-cracker lives when there is such dynamite power available. And God longs to confer this power upon us."

James Russell Lowell said, "There is dynamite enough in the Bible if illegitimately applied to blow all existing institutions to Atoms."

I think one of the greatest theologians to ever live was a man by the name of Dr. Walter Rauschenbusch. For many years he taught Church History at Colgate-Rochester Divinity School in New York. Interestingly enough, he is not remembered as a Church Historian but as an Ethicist. He was a Social Ethicist who wrote such books as A Theology Of The Social Gospel, Christianity and the Social Order and Christianity and the Social Crisis.

In one of his books, Dr. Rauschenbusch says, "Humanity is waiting for a revolutionary Christianity which will call the world evil and change it. We do not want to blow all our existing institutions to Atoms, but we do want to remold every one of them."

And then Dr. Rauschenbusch provides this excellent illustration which is so appropriate for this first point. He says, "A tank of gasoline can blow a car sky-high in a single explosion, or push it to the top of a hill in a perpetual succession of little explosions."

When I read that illustration I thought of how appropriate and applicable it is to the grace of power in our lives as we attempt to overcome fear. God dynamically and daily leads us to the top of the mountain so we can live above the fears of life. God wants us to reside on the mountain above the valley of the shadow of fear, and He enables us to do this through His Word and in His Spirit.

II.   The Grace of Purpose

God not only gives to us the grace of power, but He also gives to us the grace of purpose. Our text says, "God has not given us the spirit of fear, but of <u>power</u> and <u>love</u>...".

What is your purpose as an individual Christian? What is our purpose as a family of faith? What is our purpose as a community of believers? What is our purpose as the <u>ekklesia</u>, (called out ones of God)?

Our purpose is to love. That is it. Pure and simple -we are to love.

In Luke 10, our Lord summed up all the Old Testament laws and prophets in this credal statement of purpose when He said to a lawyer, "You are to love the Lord your God with all your heart, your soul, your strength, your mind and your neighbor as yourself." Again, Jesus said, "A new commandment I give to you that you love one another." And again Jesus said "By this shall all men know you are my disciples by the <u>love</u> that you have for one for the other."

And this love expresses itself in genuine caring. The Greek word we translate love here is from the root word *agape*. It is a special type of love that God has for us and a love with which we are to love other people. This *agape* love expresses itself through genuinely caring for people.

In one of his books, Dr. John Claypool tells the story about a man named Anthony DeMello. He tells of how this man looked upon a starving child. He then lifted his eyes to heaven and angrily said, "God, how could you allow such suffering? Why don't you do something?" And then, following a long silence DeMello heard the voice of God as He said, "I certainly have done something, I made you." And God has made us to share this *agape* love by caring for people.

And the Interesting thing is – when we become so absorbed with this purpose of loving, and we become so wrapped up in the task of caring, a by-product of this purposeful living is a life free from fear. When we direct all of our energies and efforts toward this

33

purpose, we do not have time to worry about our fears. And so a part of God's plan for us to face and overcome our fears is to fulfill His purpose for our lives.

What is our purpose as Christians? Our purpose as Christians is to love people and help them face and overcome their fears. And when we are totally committed to this purpose of caring and loving, we not only help other people face their fears, but we enable ourselves to overcome our own fears. God gives to us the grace of purpose to help us face and overcome our fears.

III.   The Grace of Peace

In addition to the graces of power and purpose, God gives to us the grace of peace.

Notice the last part of our text as it states, "God has not given the spirit of fear, but of power, love and a sound mind."

There are many translations of the statement we refer to as "a sound mind." Some translations render it as "self-discipline" or "self-control." It is the Greek word *sophronismos*, and Professor Barclay in his commentary on II Timothy describes it as "one of these great, Greek untranslatable words."

I personally like the rendering, "sound mind." A sound mind produces peace. An unsound mind produces instability and confusion. That is why James says, "A double minded person is unstable in all his ways."

It is interesting to study these three graces and observe how God gives them and where we find them.

The grace of power is given through God's Word. The writer of Hebrews says, "The Word of God is...powerful..." The grace of power is also given through God's Spirit. In Acts 1:8 Jesus said to His followers, "You shall receive power when the Holy Spirit is come upon you..."

The grace of purpose is given through God's *agape* love.

And the grace of peace is given through God's Son, Jesus Christ. That is why Jesus said in the 14th chapter of Saint John's Gospel, "My peace I leave with you, my peace I give unto you. It is a peace that the world does not give." And it is a peace this world knows nothing about. It is a peace this world can neither give nor take away. And this peace is given through God's Son, Jesus Christ.

In the Old Testament, when Isaiah prophesied the coming of Christ, he said in this Messianic prophecy, "His name shall be called Wonderful, Counsellor, the Mighty God, the Everlasting Father and the Prince of Peace."

The phrase "the Prince of Peace" is a beautiful phrase in the Old Testament. When Isaiah said His name shall be called "the Prince" he went to the very heart of the work of Jesus Christ. The word "prince" in the Hebrew means one who has absolute rule and dominion. It refers to one who is in control and one who is not only the source - but also the dispenser.

And how applicable this is to Jesus Christ, the one who is peace, and the One who gives peace.

The word "peace" is also a beautiful word in the Hebrew. We translate it as *shalom*. We do not have a word in English that means the exact same thing. For it refers to a type of peace that is more than the absence of war. It is the presence of inner resources to make us adequate for any task we face.

One scholar defines *shalom* as "totality, completeness, and wholeness. It means all the shattered and broken pieces have come together." And what a beautiful definition of the type of peace God gives to us to enable us to have sound minds when we face the fears of life. The Apostle Paul defined this peace as "a peace that keeps our hearts and minds in Christ Jesus."

The fears of life are real. But I want us to understand that God does not expect us to face these fears with our own strength.

For these fears, that are not of God, He provides this triad of graces: <u>power</u>, <u>purpose</u> and <u>peace</u>; and with them we cannot only face the fears of life, but in His grace, we can overcome them.

Chapter 6

HOW TO GET ALONG WITH PEOPLE

"...and be kind to one another, tenderhearted, forgiving
one another, as God in Christ forgave you."
(Ephesians 4:32)

It doesn't matter how gifted you are. It doesn't matter how graceful you are. It doesn't matter how talented you are. It doesn't matter how wealthy you are. And it doesn't matter how educated you are, for if you do not know how to get along with people then you are going to have a very difficult time in life.

Corporations spend millions of dollars every year helping their employees in this vital area because they know positive relations translate into productivity, and productivity translates into profit. Self-help books on this subject have flooded the market, but in this sermon I want to share with you a model that I believe is better than any corporate seminar or any book that you will find anywhere. This is a simple plan that is taken from God's Word, and I believe this is God's plan for us to get along with one another.

This plan is found in the last verse of Ephesians 4, as the Apostle Paul says, "And be kind to one another, tenderhearted, forgiving one another, as God in Christ forgave you."

In this verse there are three important rules we need to remember in our relationship with other people. They are:

**I.	Be Kind**
**II.	Be Tenderhearted**
**III.	Be Forgiving**

**I.	Be Kind**

Paul begins by telling us to "be kind to one another."
The Greek word we translate "kind" in the New Testament is *crestos*. The Greek word we translate as "Christ" in the New Testament is *cristos*. It is interesting that only one letter separates Christ from kind. And the kinder we become, the more Christ-like we become, and the more Christ-like we become the kinder we become.

Now I believe there are two directions in which we need to direct our kindness.

One, we need to be kind to our acquaintances, both old and new. We need to be kind to our friends and our family members. We need to be kind to those people whom we consider as just good folks.

There was a Methodist minister's little boy who was in elementary school. One night this little fellow said his prayers. As he got down upon his knees by his bed, this is what he prayed: "Dear Lord, please make all the bad people good. And Lord Jesus, please make all of those good folks in my Daddy's church kind to one another."

One of the greatest needs in the church today, if not the greatest need, is simply to learn to be kind to one another. It is also the greatest need within the home, the community, this nation, and even this world in which we live. We just need to learn to be kind to one another.

I saw a bumper sticker the other day that caught my attention. It simply said, "Commit random acts of kindness."

Now, when we direct our kindness to people like this, we are simply living out "the Golden Rule." This Scriptural rule simply tells us that we are to "do unto others as we would have them do unto us." We all want people to be kind to us, and in turn we should be kind to other people.

Any Chief Executive Officer of any successful company will tell you there is no substitute for implementing the Golden Rule and being kind to people. So if you want to get along with people, just flesh out this rule and be kind to others as you want them to extend kindness to you.

Now, for all pratical purposes, I could put the period to this sermon down right here for this is the key to good and positive relationships – just being kind to one another.

Secondly, we need to be kind to people who may not necessarily be kind to us.

One of our former Presidents spoke of a "kinder and gentler America." In many ways this great nation is kind and gentle, and yet there are some people in it who are not kind and gentle, and they need our kindness more than any others.

Dr. Pierce Harris, who served for many years as Senior Minister of the First United Methodist Church in Atlanta told the story about two ladies who did not particularly like each other. These two women were not kind to each other. He told of how one of the women, on a Saturday morning, went to the beauty parlor to get her hair ready for Sunday. This lady arrived at the beauty parlor, and she had to wait for two hours. After a two hour wait, the beautician finally saw her, and then she spent two hours working on her. When the lady left the beauty parlor, she was irate. She passed this other woman walking along the street coming from the other direction. This lady very angrily said to the other woman, "I am so mad I don't know what to do. I was in that beauty parlor for four hours!" The other woman simply replied, "My, my, four hours and you did not even get waited on." Now that is not the way to get along with other folks. That is not the way to win friends and influence people. We need to be kind to people who are not kind to us.

I want to challenge you to commit a verse of Scripture to memory. It is Proverbs 15:1. If you will memorize this verse, and then live it out, it will prevent many problems from ever occurring. It will save you much potential heartbreak before it ever comes, and it will stop many tears before they are ever shed. It will even help your blood pressure.

This verse simply says, "A soft answer turns away wrath, but grievous words stir up anger."

You see, it takes two people to have an argument, and Dale Carnegie in his famous book reminds us that in actuality we never really win an argument. We may get our point across, but we don't win the goodwill of people, and by being argumentative and abrasive we can lose many friends.

When I preached this sermon in my church at Auburn, one of my members, Carter Kyser, took me aside afterwards and said, "George, one of the greatest and wisest lessons in life was taught to me by my Dad, and it goes right along with point one of your sermon." He said, "Carter, son, don't ever argue with a fool. The people who are standing by may not be able to tell who is who."

And so, the next time somebody is ugly to you, you just be kind to them in return. The next time somebody comes upon you with the hot fire of meanness, you just respond with the cool water of sweetness and see what happens.

And so point number one is simply to be kind to one another.

II.   Be Tenderhearted

As we read on in our text, we find that Paul tells us secondly to be "tenderhearted." It is interesting to read how other versions translate this particular Greek phrase. The Amplified New Testament also uses the word, "understanding."

I personally like the word tenderhearted because there are many people who are understanding, but they are not understanding in a tenderhearted way. And there is a difference.

My good friend, Rev. Sandy Simmons who is a Methodist minister in Selma, tells in one of his sermons the story of four men who went hunting for deer together.

They left early one morning at 4:00 a.m., and they arrived in the woods at 5:00. Their names were Tom, Dick, Joe, and Fred.

They decided to divide into pairs and hunt through the day with a partner. Tom and Dick decided to go in one direction, and Joe and Fred then went in the other direction. Before they left they had an understanding that they all would meet back at that appointed place at 3:00 in the afternoon. So the men set out to hunt deer for the day.

At 3:00 p.m., Tom and Dick very punctually arrived back at the point where they started. Joe and Fred were no where to be found. Tom and Dick waited until 3:30, 4:00, 4:30 and then 5:00 p.m. They began to worry when they heard a rustle in the bushes. They looked up and saw Joe coming out of the woods dragging a big 10 point deer.

Joe was struggling to pull the deer out of the woods, but he made it and placed the deer before his friends, Tom and Dick.

Dick looked at the deer, and he was beside himself as he expressed to both Tom and Joe how beautiful the deer was. He admired the 10 points, and he said to Joe, "This is one of the most beautiful deer I have ever seen. It is such a prize and such a trophy."

Then he said to Joe, "By the way, where is Fred?" Joe then shared with him this story. He said, "Well, we had a little accident back in the woods. When I saw this deer, I took aim and Fred was standing right close to the deer. My first shot missed the deer, and I hit Fred in the leg. Fred reached over to grab his leg, and in so doing, he hit his head on a tree, and it knocked him out. I then shot the deer.

Then I left Fred there in the woods, I got the deer and brought the deer back to where we are now."

Dick was beside himself when he heard Joe share this story. He said, "You mean to tell me that you shot poor Fred in the leg. You then brought the deer back, but you left poor Fred in the woods. Why that is the most heartless and cruelest thing I've ever heard of in my life!" About that time, Tom, understanding Tom, interrupted Dick and said, "Dick, don't give Joe such a hard time. Man, ain't nobody gonna steal Fred!"

Now that is understanding, but I'm not real sure that is tenderhearted understanding. And I'm not real sure some of you understood that joke. But we need tenderhearted understanding if we are going to get along with other people.

Ian MacLaren was one of the most effective preachers in Great Britain. When he began preaching in his first church in the Highlands, he would attempt to preach without notes. The first time or two that he tried this, his mind went blank, and he completely lost his place. His train of thought became totally derailed.

He shared with his people that he was so sorry. He told them, "Friends, this is not very clear. It was clear in my study on Saturday, but I've lost my place, and now I will have to begin again."

He asked his people to simply bear with him, and then he struggled to get through his message.

After this happened the first time, one of his tenderhearted and understanding elders took him aside. This kind elder said to him, "When you don't remember your sermon, Lad, just call out a Psalm, and we will be singing while you are taking a rest. And if you are not ready, then we will sing the Psalm again."

Then this elder went on to tell him that while they were praising God with the Psalm, they would also be praying for him and pulling for him and loving him.

When I read that, I thought to myself, with tenderhearted elders like that, it is no wonder that Ian MacLaren became one of the great preachers of his day. It is no wonder that he moved the hearts of people in such a mighty way. And that same type of tenderhearted understanding is needed by all people everywhere.

Many of the people with whom you come in contact each day are having a rough time of it. Many of the people you meet simply want you to understand them in a tenderhearted way. Ralph Waldo Emerson said, "Enemies are just friends we have never taken the time to understand."

You see, the reason many relationships are strained and frayed is because we don't take the time to understand one another in a tenderhearted way. Instead of understanding, many times we have a tendency simply to assess people, issuses and situations, judge them with preconcieved ideas, and then jump to conclusions about them.

Jumping to conclusions can be a very dangerous thing. It can be dangerous to your relationship with other people. It can be dangerous to you.

I heard the story about a little dog by the name of August. As the story goes, August was always jumping at conclusions. One day August jumped at the conclusion of a mule. That was the last day of August.

And so, instead of jumping to conclusions, we need to try to understand people in a tenderhearted way for Paul tells us, "Be kind to one another, and be tenderhearted."

III. Be Forgiving

Now, in this model Paul goes on to tell us that we are to be forgiving. Paul even tells us how we are to forgive as he says, "forgiving one another as God in Christ forgave you."

Now this part of our text lifts up two important truths about forgiveness. One, it tells me that I can forgive for it simply says, "forgive one another." I can forgive, and you can forgive.

Secondly, it tells me that I have been forgiven, for it goes on to say, "as God in Christ forgave you," and really it is because I have been forgiven that I am able to forgive.

For several years Dr. John Killinger was the head of the Department of Homiletics and Literature at Vanderbilt Divinity School. Dr. Killinger is a former Professor, a dear friend and a mentor. In his book, The Teachings Of Jesus, Dr. Killinger has an excellent chapter on forgiveness.

He begins this chapter by writing about the Jivaro Indians in Ecuador. He tells of how the parents at night before their children go to sleep will continuously whisper in their ears the names of people they are suppose to hate.

They will continue to call these names over and over, and at the same time they will impress upon the little ones that they are to bitterly hate those people. It is their way of preserving and perpetuating enmities, feuds, and tribal hatreds.

Killinger correctly reminds us how we recoil at such a primitive practice. But he then goes on to discuss how there are many people who have been hurt and wounded by colleagues, former friends and even family members, and that pain of the past is very deep; they refuse to forgive, and by daily nurturing that resentment, that bitterness and those grudges they are in actuality doing the very same thing as those Jivaro Indians in Ecuador – only they are doing it on a more sophisticated level.

Tell me, has somebody hurt you in some way? My friend, don't you let your resentment of that person ruin and destroy your life.

You see, what happens is, if you fail to forgive somebody, that person can loom larger than life to you. That person will begin to affect and dominate your life without your even realizing it.

Perhaps this is what a wise person meant when he said, "He who has a thousand friends has not a friend to spare, but he who has one enemy will meet that enemy everywhere."

You see, an unforgiving spirit is very difficult to isolate. It has a way of spilling out and over and affecting your relationship with other people.

One of the wisest, most spiritual and most therapeutic things you can do is simply learn to forgive someone who has hurt you.

Now that can be very difficult to do in your own power, but when we look at our text again it tells us that we do not forgive in our own power, but we do it in the power of Christ because He has forgiven us.

Professor Dantzler points out that the word used most in the New Testament for forgiveness is the word *apheimi*. Professor Dantzler also points out that this particular word is used 142 times in the New Testament, but the interesting thing is that of those 142 times, it is used 129 times in the four Gospels. It is used only 13 times in the other chapters of the New Testament. He thus concludes that forgiveness is intrinsically woven into the very person of Jesus Christ as revealed in Matthew, Mark, Luke and John; and we can only truly forgive in His spirit and in His grace.

Dantzler also points out that in the Greek Old Testament, The Septuagint, this particular word was used to mean the release of a prisoner from jail or the release of one from a heavy debt. Then in the Greek New Testament this word was developed to also mean a casting away and releasing.

And there are those who need to be released from an unforgiving spirit. They need to cast that unforgiving spirit away. An unforgiving spirit is like a boat that is tied to a dock and firmly fastened. We need to cut the rope, and send the vessel of an unforgiving spirit into the sea of God's forgetfulness. We need to release it and cast it away; and just as God forgets it, so we need to forget it also.

You see, forgetting is an important part of forgiving. C.S. Lewis said, "Those who have not forgotten have not truly forgiven."

There are many excellent books that treat the subject of getting along with people. There are seminars on this subject held around the country every week. But I want to share again this simple plan with you that can help you get along with people in a more effective way than any seminar that is being held or any book that has been written. Our God, through the pen of Paul, tells us the way we get along with people is to "be kind to one another, tenderhearted, forgiving one another, as God in Christ forgave you."

My friend, if you will remember these three important rules in your relationships, and if you will implement and put them into practice this very day three things will happen in your life. *One*, you will be amazed at how smoothly and effectively you get along with people. *Two*, you will be a much happier person. And three, your Heavenly Father will look with greater approval upon you. May God help us to remember these rules and to put them in to practice.

HOW TO UNDERSTAND GOD'S LOVE
"...God is love."
(I John 4:8b)

The largest Sunday School Class in our church is the Nomad Class. These young couples keep out growing every classroom that is assigned to them, and they are constantly having to move from one room to a larger place to accommodate their growing number, thus the name, the Nomads. I recently met with about 80 members of this Sunday School class in our church, and we had a beautiful service of worship in Founders Chapel.

It was a service where we renewed our marriage vows, and it was one of the most meaningful worship experiences of which I have ever been a part. We renewed our marriage vows, and Tom Nunnally sang, "The Wedding Song" and "The Lord's Prayer." It was a moving service as we all felt such a closeness to our wives, our husbands, one another, and we especially felt a closeness to God.

I think it is good to renew our marriage vows because sometimes we have a tendency to forget. Even worse than forgetting, sometimes we get into a rut.

I heard the story about a farmer and his wife who were sitting on the front porch in a swing one Valentine's evening. They had been married for several years. The wife turned, looked into the face of her husband and said, "Herman, you have not told me in a long time that you love me." The farmer was chewing upon a straw. He very casually took the straw out of his mouth and said, "Wife, I told you I loved you on the day we got married, and if I change my mind, you will be the first one to know about it!"

Now, we need a better understanding of love than that, but it is very difficult to understand human love until we first understand something about divine love. It is very difficult to understand the natural love of people until we have some insight into the supernatural love of God.

Today I want us to think about the subject, "How To Understand God's Love," and our text is a part of I John 4:8 as John simply says, "God is love." That is one of the profoundest and most powerful statements in the New Testament, "God is love."

Now in this message I do not want to talk just about God's love, but I want to make a relevant application of this love to our lives and our relationship to other people within a contemporary context.

How do you understand God's love? I understand God's love in three ways. It is:

I.   A Revealing Love
II. A Redeeming Love

III.   A Reliable Love

I.   A Revealing Love

When God breathed His creation into existence, it was a revelation of His love, and as one song writer puts it, it is "a long line of love."

When I was working on my Doctorate, I spent several summers at Vanderbilt in Nashville. One of the things I enjoyed about Nashville was the cultural life of the city. As you may know, Nashville is the "Country Music Capital of the World." While I was there I learned to appreciate, to some degree, country music.

Now, my wife and I have different tastes in music. She loves classical music, and one of my favorite types of music is the folk music of the early 60's. The reason I like that particular music is because I love history, and many folk songs are in the form of ballads that simply recount historical events. I love to study and read history, and I also like having history sung to me.

I was interested to read that Supreme Court Justice William Douglas was a great fan of country music. It was also interesting to note that Supreme Court Justice Douglas actually liked many of the titles of the songs as much as he did the actual songs themselves.

I feel the same way. I find many of the titles to be much more interesting than the songs themselves. Some of the titles of country songs that Justice Douglas especially liked and that he enjoyed talking about were, "My Wife Ran Off With My Best Friend, and I Sure Do Miss Him." Another was, "When the Phone Don't Ring, You'll Know It's Me."

Now, you have to stop and think about that one for a moment. Another was, "Walk Out Backwards, So I'll Think You're Coming In." Now I must give credit to the source as this was found in a book entitled Supreme Folly by Rodney Jones and Gerald Uelmen, and these musical gems were taken from an album entitled, "Songs I Learned At My Mother's Knee, and at Other Joints."

I believe it was my good friend, Eddie Fox who raised the question in a sermon, "Do you know what you get when you play a country song backwards? Your wife comes back home. Your pick-up truck is returned, and your old dog named Blue does not die." Yes, there are many great and famous country songs.

But there is one particular country song that has really captured my heart. I had never heard this song until a minister friend mentioned it in a sermon. I immediately made a point to hear the record. I like the title of the song, but even more than the title, I like the words to the song. This country song is entitled, *A Long Line of Love.* The song is about a young man who is preparing to get married, and he speaks of the great love his grandparents had for one another and the love and affection of his parents. Fol-

44

lowing each stanza there is this poignant refrain, "Forever's in my heart and in my blood, I come from a long line of love."

Have you stopped to think – we who are a part of the community of faith emenate from a long line of love.

Yes, when God breathed this world into existence, it was a revelation of His love for His creation. As we study this long line of love of the Lord God Jehovah in the pages of the Old Testament, we see it as a love that is couched in legalism and characterized by justice.

It is when we get to the Book of Hosea that we see Yahweh, our God, as a God of love, mercy, forgiveness and divine affection.

Then through the eyes of the Prophets, especially Isaiah, we catch a glimpse of the prophesied Messiah.

And then God's love was ultimately and completely consummated in the gift of His Son, Christ Jesus our Lord, as John tells us, "For God so loved the world He gave His only son."

I remember several years ago hearing the story about a farmer who was plowing in his garden. He accidentally, with his plow, ran over a big ant hill. He immediately stopped and looked around at the ant hill. He then got down upon his knees and carefully scrutinized the hill as he saw many of the little ants were dead, many others were wounded and hurting, and still many of the others were going in all different directions.

The farmer felt so bad about what he had done. As he looked at the ants he thought to himself, "I wish there was some way I could let those little ants know how sorry I am. I wish there was some way I could reach out to them and care for them." Then the farmer realized that the only way he could express his care and help for them would be for him to become one of those little ants and go to where they were."

Isn't that exactly what God did with this world? He looked down and He saw a world that was misplaced and out of joint. He saw many of His children who were dead in their trespasses, many others who were wounded in their spirits, and even more who were wandering aimlessly and without any sense of direction. Then God said, "I wish that my children could know how much I love them and care for them, but the only way I could ever convey that would be to become as one of them."

And that is precisely what God did in Christ Jesus in the theology of the Incarnation.

This is what John means when he writes, "The word became flesh and dwelt among us, full of grace and truth." (John 1:14)

John Wesley captured this theological truth when he penned those lines, "Love divine all loves excelling, joy of heaven to earth come down."

Athanasius, the Church Father of the Fourth Century who defended Christian Orthodoxy against the Arian controversy at the Council of Nicea said, "He became what we are so that we may become what He is."

And just as God's love has been revealed to us in Christ Jesus, so we, in the spirit of this Christ, are to reveal our love to other people.

This is our most important task. Actually, this is our only task. John was the only Disciple to die of old age. All of the other Disciples met violent deaths of some type.

Tradition tells us that when John was an elderly man living in Ephesus that many of the young converts would come to see him. They would implore John to tell them about his time with Jesus, the Christ. They would ask about the day his Brother, James, and he met the Master. They would ask him to share with them the details of the many miracles Jesus performed. They would ask him about the parables and the Sermon on the Mount. They would ask him what it was like that day on Calvary's Mountain when Jesus bequeathed His precious mother to him. Tradition tells us that the only response John would make to them would be, "My little children, let us love one another. Little children, love one another."

Yes, our task is not to hate, hurt or even be indifferent to other people, but in the spirit of Christ we are to love all of God's children everywhere regardless of who they are or what they've done.

Because God's love has been revealed to us, we are to reveal our love to other people for Jesus said, "Greater love hath no man than he lay down his life for his friends."

Jesus also said, "By this, all men will know you are my Disciples...". By what? By the beautiful churches in which we worship? By the many programs we implement in ministry? No, Jesus said, "By this, all men will know you are my disciples; by the love you have one for the other." Yes, God's love is a revealing love, and in the spirit of Christ we are to reveal our love to others.

II. A Redeeming Love

Now, God revealed His love to us for a purpose, and that purpose was to redeem us.

And when we've experienced His redeeming grace, we will be able to sing with confidence the words to the old Camp Meeting hymn,

> *Redeemed how I love to proclaim it.*
> *Redeemed by the blood of the lamb,*
> *Redeemed and so happy in Jesus.*
> *His child and forever I am.*

But the real test of our redemption will be in the way we treat other people. It will be in the way we relate, influence and care for other people.

Because God, in His love, has redeemed us and has brought out the very best in us and made us better people; so our love will bring out the best in others and make them better people also.

Because we've experienced His redeeming love, so our love will be redemptive and sanctifying in the lives of other people. It will prompt other people to become their very best selves for this is what the writer of Proverbs means when he says, "As iron sharpens iron, so a person sharpens the countenance of his friends." (Proverbs 27:17)

III.   A Reliable Love

His love is a reliable love. I read about a farmer who placed a weather vane over his barn. Beneath the weather vane were three words, "God is love."

One of the neighbors was visiting with the farmer, and he noticed the weather vane with those three words beneath it. He said to the farmer, "Neighbor, does that mean God is love if the wind is blowing from a certain direction? Does that mean God is love only if the wind is blowing from the north, south, east or west?"

The farmer replied, "No, friend, that means God is love regardless of which direction the wind is blowing. That means God is love even if the wind is not blowing!" Such is the reliability of God's love.

If you ever visit Greenville, Tennessee, you can see the grave site of President Andrew Johnson. We remember that President Johnson was Vice President under Abraham Lincoln during the dark and trying days of the Civil War. He then was President during the turbulent time of Reconstruction in the deep South.

Over the resting remains of President Johnson is a marker that describes him. It simply says, "His faith in people never wavered."

You can take these words, "His faith in people never wavered," and you can multiply them a billion times, and you will have some insight into the reliability of God's love and God's faith in His people. It matters not where we go or what we do. It matters not how we treat Him, His faith in us never waivers, and His love never wanes.

He loves us when we are up, and He loves us when we are down. He loves us during the good times, and He especially loves us during the bad times. He loves us when things are going smoothly, and He especially loves us when we are passing through troubled waters. He loves us when our faces are covered with smiles, and He especially loves us when our eyes are blinded by tears. Such is the reliability of God's love.

Now, because we have experienced and know the reliability of His love, so our love for others will be reliable in all of our relationships.

Our love will be reliable in our relationship with God. Just as we can depend upon the reliability of His love, so He will be able to depend upon the reliability of our love.

Our love will be reliable in our relationship with all members of the human family, especially those who are the closest to us and those within our homes.

One of the most beautiful examples of this type of reliable love occurred in the lives of Ida and Isadore Straus. In 1914, the Straus Memorial was erected in New York City. Two years earlier, on April 15, 1912, when the Titanic went down, Mr. and Mrs.

Straus perished in that disaster.

The interesting thing is that Mrs. Straus could have been rescued because there was a life boat close by filled with women, and there was room for one other woman.

As she and her husband were on the sinking ship, the people in the life boat cried out to Mrs. Straus and pleaded with her to leave the Titanic and join them in the life boat.

It is said that Mrs. Straus looked at the women in the life boat, then she looked into the eyes of her husband, and with a smile upon her face and tears in her eyes, she said, "No, my husband and I have never been separated in life, and we will not be separated in death." They then put their arms around each other, held each other tightly, and they went down to a watery and icy grave there in the North Atlantic.

And this love will be reliable in your relationship with your church, and your church will be able to depend upon your faithfulness and your commitment in every way.

This love will also be reliable in your relationship with your friends. This love means you will always be there for them, and they will be able to count upon you and depend upon you. For this is what the writer of Proverbs means when he says, "A friend loves at all times, and a brother is born for adversity." (Proverbs 17:17)

How do you understand God's love? I understand it as a revealing love, a redeeming love, and a reliable love; and because we know and have experienced His love in these three capacities, so our love will also be revealing. It will be redemptive, and it will be reliable. May God help it so to be.

Chapter 8

HOW TO OVERCOME LONELINESS
"...and lo, I am with you always, even to the close of the age."
(Matthew 28:20b)

The title of this study is <u>How To Overcome Loneliness.</u>

Our text for this message is taken from Matthew 28:20. It is the very last part of Matthew's Gospel as Jesus says, "...and lo, I am with you always, even to the end of the age."

Each time I read this selection of Scripture, I am reminded of the man who approached his minister and shared with him his fear of flying. The Pastor in an effort to calm the man's anxiety said, "Why Brother, you should not fear flying. The Lord promises to be with you."

The man replied, "Reverend, the Lord says, '<u>lo</u>, I am with you always.' He doesn't say anything about being with us <u>high</u> up in the air."

But the truth of the matter is, God is with us all the time. He is with us when we are high, and He is with us when we are low. He is with us when we are upon the mountaintop of happiness, and He is with us when we are in the valley of sadness; and there is no time He is with us anymore than during our times of loneliness if we will only call upon Him.

He promises to be with us always, and He promises to never let us go. As I share this message, I hope we will keep this wonderful truth in the back of our minds.

What is loneliness?

It is David in the Old Testament crying out, "No man cares for my soul."

It is Paul in the New Testament languishing in a dark, damp and dingy prison cell writing to his young friend Timothy and asking him, "...to come before winter," and then adding these lonely lines, "Demas has forsaken me having loved this present world."

It is our blessed Lord hanging on Calvary's Cross and crying out, "My God, my God, why hast thou forsaken me?"

If I were to ask you to define or describe loneliness, what would you say:

Loneliness is an aged woman in a big house, sitting down for dinner, and looking across the table at an empty place, an empty plate and an empty chair, for the one with whom she has walked down the pathway of life some sixty years has recently been taken from her. Loneliness is the emptiness she feels deep within as she has to eat all by herself.

Loneliness is an elderly man in a nursing home sitting in a rocking chair in his room in front of his door. He is holding within his hands a picture of his son, his daughter-in-law, his grandchildren and his great grandchildren. As he sits there staring at the door, he hopes that someone in that picture will walk through and come over and hug his neck and gently kiss him upon the cheek. But it has been three months and no family member has come. He sits there all day clutching that picture with long, bony, arthritic fingers, and he holds it tightly to his breast, looks at the door and cries. That is loneliness.

It is the President of the United States sitting in the Oval Office faced with a big decision.

It is a minister with a pressing problem and no one with whom to talk.

It is a couple taking their only child, their daughter off to college for the first time and leaving her. As they pull out, they look in the rear-view mirror, and they see her standing there all by herself. For the first time they realize that she won't be there when they get home, and all of her many friends whom they have learned to love so much will no longer be coming over to the house. That is loneliness.

It is a little six year old boy whose parents drop him off for Sunday School. He stands there all by himself, and he's not real sure where to go or what to do, but he is sure that he wishes his parents were there with him. That is loneliness.

It is a little seven year old girl who has just found out that her parents are getting a divorce. She doesn't completely understand what a divorce is all about, but she is beginning to feel a thing called loneliness in a way that she has never felt before.

It is a University student who is engaged to a young lady. He loves her with all of her heart, and he worships the ground upon which she walks. On a cool fall night she shares with him that she no longer loves and cares for him in that way, and she thinks it would be best if they started dating other people. She very gently presses the engagement ring into the palm of his hand, kisses him on the cheek and says, "Good luck in the future." She then turns and walks away, and he is left there all by himself with a broken heart. That is loneliness.

It is a young couple standing in a cemetery on a cold winter morning looking down at a small casket in a little grave. It is their baby daughter.

The minister reads these words, "Suffer the little children to come unto me, and forbid them not, for of such is the kingdom of heaven."

He then reads those all too familiar words, "In my father's house are many mansions. If it were not so, I would have told you. I go to prepare a place for you, and if I go and prepare a place for you, I will come again and receive you unto myself so that where I am there you might be also."

The young husband and wife stand there, holding hands and then holding each other.

The cold winter wind bites their cheeks. Their eyes are filled with tears. Their minds are filled with many unanswered questions, and deep within their heart is an aching and throbbing loneliness that I do not have the words to describe. That is loneliness

It is the 1991 Super Bowl. Time is running out. The Buffalo Bills are trailing by one point.

They are within field goal range, and the kicker, Scott Norwood, has hit many field goals from that distance.

All the people in the stadium are watching, and the eyes of the nation are glued to their television sets for this last play.

If Norwood misses it, the Buffalo Bills will lose the Super Bowl. If he makes it, they will win the most important game in the sporting world.

The center snaps the ball. The holder puts it down, Scott Norwood kicks it, and then he watches it sail wide right.

Although there are over 100,000 people in that stadium, Scott Norwood is the loneliest guy in the universe.

When Dr. Charles Allen was Pastor of the Grace Church in Atlanta, he told of a lady who called a certain number in the Atlanta area that gave the time. She lived all by herself in an apartment.

Somebody asked the lady, "Don't you have a clock?" She responded, "Yes, I have a clock, but I just want to hear somebody speaking directly to me before I go to sleep at night."

Sometime ago, in one of Ann Landers' columns, there was a running debate about how a widowed woman should be addressed. There was no shortage of opinions.

In the midst of the discussion, one dear lady wrote these heart-rending lines. She told of losing her husband, and then she said, "About what I should be called, I do not care. It does not matter what people call me, just as long as they call me, come to see me and include me. My life is so lonely. Let people call me anything they wish, but please, let them call me."

Yes, loneliness is very real, and in this message there are three aspects of loneliness I want us to consider. I want us to think about:

I.   **The Causes Of It**
II.   **The Consequences In It**
III.   **The Cure For It**

I.   **The Causes Of It**

What are the causes of loneliness? I am sure there are many.

One, many people are lonely because they have been hurt. And in their hurt they retreat into a shell.

They say, and sometimes they say it consciously and sometimes they say it subconsciously, but they say, "I will never allow anybody to hurt me again!"

They become ingrown and withdrawn, and they completely cut themselves off from society. They do not make themselves vulnerable in anyway. They do not risk friendship, and they do not risk love; and because of their hurt they are lonely.

Some people are lonely because of the loss of a loved one and the inability to adjust.

Grief is a wonderful thing. Grief is natural, and grief is necessary. God has built into us the capacity to grieve, and there are certain stages through which we go. It is the culmination of these stages that brings fruition to the grief process, and when we lose a loved one it is natural to grieve.

But too much grief is not good. It can overwhelm you. It can emotionally devastate you. It can render you ineffective, and it can imprison you in a cell of loneliness.

Some people are lonely because their self-confidence has been destroyed. They feel inferior, and they feel inadequate. They fear failure, and their defense is to isolate themselves from any decisive issue and even from people; and in their isolation, they experience loneliness.

And then, some people are lonely just because they are hard to get along with and to know.

Have you ever met anybody like that? I'm not sure I have, but I understand there are people who are just hateful, abrasive and mean. They don't like people, and people don't like them. They don't like to be around folks. Folks don't like to be around them, and therefore they become very lonely.

My Brother, John Ed, told about a man who was like that. The old fellow did not like anybody, and nobody liked him. He was mean-spirited, and he would do cruel things.

You know, Will Rogers once said, "I never met a man I didn't like." Well, Will never met this fellow.

This old guy got sick and had to go into the hospital for a very serious operation. He was one of those patients that nurses hate to see coming.

After the operation, the man awakened, opened his eyes and realized that he was in his hospital room. It was pitch black. There were no lights on, and the curtains to the window had been pulled together.

The man was irate. He mashed the little button to summons the nurse, and he said, "If you don't get down here right away I will sue this hospital!" Those were not the exact words he used.

The nurse came, and the man then said to her, "I demand to know why the curtains to my window are pulled together!"

The nurse very politely said, "Well, sir, it is like this. There is a terrible fire raging across the street. You can see the flames from your room. Quite frankly, we were afraid you would wake up, look out the window, see those flames and think your operation had been a failure."

Yes, there are some people who are lonely simply because others do not want to be around them.

II.   The Consequences In It

Now, before I share with you the consequences, I need to make a clarification.

There is a distinctive difference between aloneness and loneliness. Aloneness is good. Loneliness is bad. Aloneness is positive. Loneliness is negative. Aloneness is productive. Loneliness is non-productive.

When you study the Scriptures, you find that Jesus spent much time alone. The Bible tells of how He alone went to the desert. He went to the mountains, and He went to the seashore.

And some of my most spiritually enriching times as your Pastor have been those occasions when I have come into this sanctuary all alone. Those are the times when I find strength, when I am alone here only with my Lord communing as friend to friend.

Another word for aloneness is solitude.

In his book, Celebration of Discipline, Richard Foster speaks of aloneness or solitude as one of the disciplines of the spirit.

Thomas Merton said, "Solitude cleanses the soul." Yes, solitude and aloneness are good.

I recently read again the old volume by Admiral Richard Byrd entitled Alone.

In this book, he tells about his excursion to the South Pole, and how he communicated by radio. When that radio connection was broken, he was all alone, but Byrd looked upon that time as one of the greatest experiences of his life. He described that aloneness as a time when he "gained a new set of values."

It was a time when he genuinely learned to appreciate beauty, and he became truly thankful for the sheer miracle of being alive. In his own words, Byrd said, "I felt that for the first time I was truly alive."

Yes, aloneness and solitude are very good, but loneliness can be very bad.

And there are certain consequences in loneliness.

Dr. James Lynch is a medical researcher at Johns Hopkins University, and in his book, The Broken Heart, he contends that loneliness is the number one killer in America today. His data and research support his contention in a very interesting and revealing way, and I appreciate his scholarship. While I do not completely agree with him, I do believe that loneliness has dire consequences.

For one thing, loneliness leads to bitterness. Many lonely people are very embittered people, and they can be very critical and negative about life.

Also, loneliness leads to self-pity. Quite often people in their loneliness begin to feel sorry for themselves, and they develop a martyr complex.

Loneliness leads to depression. One of the characteristics of a depressed person is a sense of loneliness and not wanting to be around other people. There is just a loss of interest in life and a separation from society.

Loneliness leads to moral breakdown. It is while people are lonely that they become sexually promiscuous. Many seek to escape out of their loneliness by having an illicit or extramarital affair.

Loneliness leads to alcoholism and drugs. Quite often, alcoholics want to drink only by themselves, and it is in their loneliness that they experience their alcoholism.

And there are those who seek to break out of the monotony and boredom of loneliness by turning to drugs.

Loneliness also leads to neurosis, and it can lead to psychosis.

By the way, do you know the definition of a neurotic and a psychotic? A neurotic is someone who, in his loneliness, builds dream castles in the air. A psychotic is the one who moves into those dream castles, and the psychiatrist is the fellow who collects the rent.

Yes, there are consequences in loneliness.

III.   The Cure For It

As we study the subject of loneliness, it is important that we know its causes and its consequences, but the most important thing we can know is the cure for it. In order for loneliness to be cured within our lives, I believe there are three essential steps we must follow.

One, we need to <u>think</u>. We need in our thought process to decide that we want to be cured of our loneliness. We need to pray and ask God to help us.

In his classic devotional writing, <u>The Dark Night of the Soul</u>, Saint John of the Cross says, "A willingness to be helped is the first step in overcoming sloth, despair and loneliness."

And we also need to think about verses of Scripture that can be helpful to us such as the words of Paul in Philippians when he says, "I can do all things through Christ who strengthens me." We need to think about that powerful verse from Isaiah when he says, "They that wait upon the Lord shall renew their strength, they shall mount up with wings like eagles."

Yes, we need to think.

Secondly, we need to <u>thank</u>. We need to thank God for our faith, for our family, and for our friends. But you say, "George, in my loneliness I do not have any friends." Then, thank God for the people who are the closest to you. Thank God for the people with whom you work.

Thanksgiving is so important because it gets our minds off ourselves. Thanksgiving is spiritually and psychologically therapeutic for when we begin to give thanks, it is then that the dark clouds of loneliness begin to disperse, and we start to see the bright sunshine of God's deep abiding presence.

We need to <u>take</u>. We need to take the initiative and do something about our loneliness. Are you lonely today? Take the initiative and get involved in activities.

Are you lonely today? Take the initiative to meet people and make friends. The writer of Proverbs says, "He that would have friends, must show himself friendly." Dale Carnegie said, "You can make more friends in one week by becoming interested in people than you can in one year by trying to get people interested in you." You assume the initiative and meet people. You make it happen.

A little girl was elected president of her class, and her Dad said to her, "Honey, how did that happen?" The little girl said, "Daddy, it did not just happen. I made it happen."

It was 1957 in the World Series. The Milwaukee Braves and the New York Yankees were playing. The Braves had a young right fielder from Mobile by the name of Henry Aaron. Henry came up to the plate to bat. The Yankee veteran catcher, Yogi Berra, noticed that Aaron was holding his bat the wrong way. Berra, in an effort to help Henry, said, "Henry, turn the bat so you can read the label."

Henry Aaron turned, looked at the catcher and said, "Yogi, I did not come up here to read, man, I came up here to hit."

It is important that we plan, pray and prepare. It is important that we think and thank, and it is important that we study and read; but there comes the time when we have to step up to the plate and hit. We have to take the initiative and make it happen, and you can do that with your life today.

Remember, you don't have to do it alone because our Lord promises, "I am with you always, even to the end of the age." And He promises to be with us everywhere we go and to never leave us. Praise HIS Name!

Chapter 9
Helpful Hints On How To Live

HOW TO HEAL A HURTING HEART
"He heals the broken hearted..."
(Psalm 147:3a)
"With His stripes we are healed."
(Isaiah 53:5)

The next study in this series is entitled <u>How to Heal a Hurting Heart.</u> I wish to lift up two verses of Scripture, and it is the margin between these two verses that I want us to occupy with our thinking. You will notice that the first verse tells us <u>what</u> God can do, and the second verse tells us <u>how</u> He does it.

The first verse from Psalm 147:3 says, "He heals the broken hearted."

Our second verse from Isaiah 53:5 says, "With His stripes we are healed." Let us pray:

Our Father, I know that in a gathering like this there are people whose hearts are hurting. Today may we experience your love, your tenderness, and your grace, And in experiencing these, your attributes, may we also know your healing and your wholeness within our lives. For I pray in the name of Christ our Savior and Lord. Amen.

How do you heal a hurting heart? I believe a starting point in answering this question is to know and understand three basic facts about a hurting heart. They are:

I.   The Meaning of It.
II.   The Mystery of It.
III. The Mastering of It.

I.   The Meaning of It

Now when I speak of the meaning of a hurting heart, I simply mean that it is very real, and there are reasons for it. To help us understand the meaning of a hurting heart, what are some of the causes and reasons for it? A hurting heart can be caused by:

One, the <u>disappointment</u> of a person. You see, people can hurt us, and people can disappoint us.

A man and woman have been married for 20 years. One evening he walks in, and he tells his wife that he no longer loves her. He is involved with somebody else, and he

56

asks for a divorce. As the husband then turns to walk out the door, the wife is left sitting there with tears in her eyes and a hurting heart.

A young man in the University is dating a girl. He loves her, and he literally worships the ground upon which she walks. One day she shares with him that she no longer cares for him, and she wants to date other guys. As she gently kisses him upon the cheek, and then turns to walk away, he is left standing there with a sickening sinking of the soul and a hurting heart.

A man hears that a friend has said some harsh and unkind things about him behind his back. He then discovers it is true, and the man is literally crushed. He is left with a hurting heart. Yes, people can disappoint us and break our hearts.

Secondly, the <u>death</u> of a loved one can cause the heart to hurt. I don't know of anything that can break a heart anymore quickly than a visit by the "pale horseman."

Dr. John Claypool in his book, <u>Tracks of A Fellow Struggler</u>, writes about the death of his little nine year old daughter. She died of Leukemia, and before her death she would look longingly into the eyes of her pastor father and ask, "Daddy have you talked to God about my leukemia?" She then would ask, "How long will the leukemia last? What did God say?"

One month after her death, Dr. Claypool climbed into the pulpit, and with a hurting heart, he preached the best he could.

In that powerful sermon, among other things, he shared three thoughts that especially ministered to me. One, he told his people that he needed them to help him during that crisis time. Secondly, he asked them to remind him that life is a gift, and perhaps for the first time he realized how precious and how important that gift is. Thirdly, with a heavy heart, he asked his people to help him as they joined hands together to walk "out of this darkness."

Thirdly, the <u>despondency</u> of a situation can break your heart.

A middle-aged man has worked with the same company for 20 some odd years. One day the boss comes in and says, "I've got word from the top that the company is beginning a process of (I believe the proper word in business circles is) 'down-sizing'." He tells how he is a casualty of that "down-sizing." The boss then goes on to thank him for his many years of faithfulness and loyalty to the company. He then swallows hard, bites his lip and turns and walks away.

The man is left sitting at his desk with his head in his hands realizing that effective soon he will no longer have a job. He is also thinking about payments on a big beautiful home, payments on two automobiles, and two kids in college. And he is left there with a hurting heart.

Also, despondent situations can break and hurt the hearts of athletes.

A tennis player in a third set tie-breaker double faults, loses the match, and he is left standing there on the tennis court with a hurting heart.

In a baseball game with the bases loaded in the bottom of the ninth, a relief pitcher comes in. He walks in the winning run, and he's left standing on the mound all alone with a hurting heart.

In a basketball game, a player is at the free-throw line to shoot a free-throw after time has expired. He is the only guy on the court. If he makes the free-throw, the game will go into overtime. He shoots, and he watches the ball hit the back of rim and bounce out, and he is left standing there on the court all alone with a hurting heart.

In a football game a field goal kicker can miss an important kick. One of my best pals is Matt Hawkins. He was the kicker for Auburn University during 1994-95. I remember the Auburn vs. Georgia game in 1994. The score was tied, and with time running out, he attempted a last second field goal. It could have won the game. The ball sailed wide left. I've got a feeling that Matt's heart was hurting on that November afternoon. (I might also point out that Matt Hawkins showed me and a multitude of other people how deep was his faith in Christ by the positive way he handled that situation. Through that I saw a young man with a deep faith and a genuine love for Christ that touched and witnessed to many people.)

Yes, a hurting heart is very real, and there are reasons for it.

II.   The Mystery of It

If you want to do an interesting word study in the New Testament sometimes, study the word "mystery." It is a word that we have transliterated almost bodily into the English language from the Greek. It is the word **mustarion**. Professor Strong points out that this word is used some 27 times in the New Testament.

And there are many mysteries in the Bible. Also, there are many mysteries in faith and life, but it is my opinion that the greatest mystery of all is the mystery of a hurting heart.

Why do some people experience pain, suffering, brokenness and hurt while others do not?

In the early days of World War II, Nazi Germany decided upon a blitz operation in England. They targeted two cities: Durham and Coventry. The two cities were similar in many ways. Both of them were industrial centers, and they manufactured armaments. Also, both of them had beautiful cathedrals.

I remember when we went to Durham, we visited the beautiful old Durham Cathedral. It's on a hilltop right next to the city. It was on a Sunday afternoon when we visited, and they were having a graduation ceremony. I remember how impressed I was with the beautiful Romanesque architecture that dates back to 1172. Durham Cathedral was also of interest to me because one of my heros of the faith, Venerable Bede, is buried in the cathedral. Brother Bede has been there a long time. He died in the Ninth Century.

But on the day Durham was to be bombed, the people began to fervently pray. They asked God to spare their city and their cathedral. Then an amazing thing happened. A misty-like cloud cover completely blanketed the city. Because the Germans were unable to see the city of Durham, they were unable to carry out the bombing operation. Durham was spared, and the people rejoiced and praised God. There in Durham, to this day, the people will point to the cathedral and explain how the providence of God spared their cathedral and city.

But on November 14, 1940, a day that will live in infamy for the people of Coventry, the planes came, the people prayed, but there was no misty-like cloud cover, and the bombs fell. The city was destroyed, and scores of women and children were killed.

It was the first time in modern warfare that an effort was made to completely wipe out a city from the air. Because of that raid by the Nazi Luftwaffe, a new word was coined not only in English, but in the word language lexicon. It was the word "coventrate" which literally means to obliterate a city with bombs, and the Nazis came very close to doing it. The city and the cathedral were destroyed.

Now, I remember when I read about Durham and Coventry, I asked myself the question, "Why was Durham spared, and why was Coventry not spared?" I believe the people in Coventry prayed just as hard as the people in Durham. And in answering that question, I have to say that it is one of the great mysteries of suffering in the history of warfare. It is a mystery that we do not understand.

It is the mystery of hurting hearts. To help us see it better, let me couch this mystery within the context of a Biblical illustration.

In Acts 12, two of God's servants were incarcerated: Peter and James. Both of them prayed to be delivered. You study the account. An angel of the Lord came, opened the door for Peter, and Brother Peter got out and went to a prayer meeting.

An angel did not come for James, but rather a guard came. He opened the door to the cell of James, and he led Brother James away to the executioner's block. As James stood there reflecting upon his unfulfilled ministry and preparing to seal his faith with his blood, I believe that deep within, James was trying to unravel the mystery of a hurting heart.

And I just have to say it is a mystery that we will not understand on this side of the River of Life. It will not be unveiled until we walk through the portals of glory and God, in His own good time and providential way, decides to explain it to us. Perhaps that is what Paul meant when he wrote to the Corinthians, "Now we see through a glass darkly, but someday we will see as we were meant to see." Yes, the hurting heart is a mystery.

Now, we can know something about the meaning of a hurting heart. But while we cannot completely understand the mystery of a hurting heart, I believe we can know and understand fully and unequivocally the mastering of a hurting heart.

III.   The Mastering Of It

In conclusion, let us think about how a hurting heart can be mastered and healed.

I mentioned earlier that we visited Durham. We also visited Coventry. That was one of the most unforgettable experiences of my life and ministry. I remember that July day as we walked through the remains of the old Coventry Cathedral. Only parts of the walls were standing.

Our guide shared with us how right after the air raid, the Dean of the Cathedral, Richard Howard, the caretaker and other members were walking through the bombed out remains of the cathedral. One of the members took some stones that had once been part of a wall and piled them together in what had once been the chancel area. The caretaker, one Jock Formes, then picked up two pieces of charred wood and fastened them together with three giant nails to make a cross. He situated the cross in the midst of the stones, and then someone wrote upon the wall these words, "Father, forgive." To this day when you visit Coventry Cathedral, it brings tears to your eyes to stand and gaze upon that pile of rocks and that old rugged and wooden cross.

But the people of Coventry were faced with a big decision after the air raid. Where they going to rebuild the old cathedral, or would they build a new cathedral?

The people of Coventry decided to build a new and modern cathedral, and they claimed as their verse these words from Habakkuk 2:9, "The latter glory of this house shall be greater than the former sayeth the Lord of Hosts."

Those people began to dream, and they began to build. This time they built a new and modern cathedral. Word got out, and donations poured in from all over the world. Interestingly enough, many of the donations came from Germany. Beautiful works of art were sent, and this day that art work adorns the walls of the new Coventry Cathedral. There is a large tapestry with the picture of Christ in a workman's apron with His hands outstretched as though He is saying, "Come unto me all ye that labor and are heavy laden, and I will give you rest."

While visiting Coventry Cathedral we had the privilege to worship in that modern edifice. We heard their boys choir sing. It was a moving worship experience. We then were inspired by words of a sharp young Anglican Priest who told us anew the story of Coventry Cathedral as I've shared it with you in this message.

While you worship in the new Coventry Cathedral, you never get away from the fact that right next door are the bombed-out remains of the old cathedral, and you constantly think about that old rugged cross that is in the chancel area and the words, "Father, forgive." You never get away from the power of God's redeeming and changing grace, and you are constantly reminded of what God can do.

Now, today maybe your experience is Durham. You've prayed, and God has covered you with the protective misty-cloud of His grace, and things are going great. I praise God for that, and I'm thankful for it.

Or perhaps your story today is not Durham, but it is Coventry. You prayed, the planes came and there was no misty-cloud cover, and the bombs fell; the bombs of disappointment, discouragement, defeat and despondency, and the result is a hurting heart.

May I challenge you to pick up the charred wood of your suffering, and the charred wood of your hurt, and you fasten them together and make a cross.

You then stand in the shadow of that cross, and you remember the One who died upon it. You recall that He did not stay upon that cross, and you remember the words of Charles Wesley when he wrote in that beautiful hymn of Christmas:

> Light and life to all He brings,
> Risen with healing in His wings.

And then you look to our God; the Lord we sang about a moment ago, "Our immortal, invisible, wise only God." You then put your hand into the nail-scarred Hand of your Savior, and you move out of the old and into the new. And as you move, you believe those words of Paul from the New Testament when he writes, "If any person be in Christ, he is a new creation. Old things have passed away and all things have become new."

And then like the people of Coventry, you claim those words of Habakkuk from the Old Testament, "the glory of the latter days shall be greater than the former." And with His grace you can master and find healing and wholeness for your hurting heart.

HOW TO DISCOVER YOUR VOCATIONAL CALL

"It seemed good to me also, having followed
all things closely for sometime past..."
(Luke 1:3)
Part I

(This was the only study that was not presented during our Monday morning Bible Study to the coaches. It was preached in our church with several hundred University students present, including several members of the football team. The purpose of this study is to help students find their place of service and their vocation in life. Because my role with the Athletic Department, especially the football team, brings me in contact with so many college kids who are searching for their "God called job," and who will be reading this book, I have included the two parts of this sermon.)

The next sermon in this series is <u>How Can I Discover My Vocational Call?</u> As I've prepared, prayed and planned this message, I have realized it is going to be very difficult for me to say what I want to say in just one sermon. Because this is such an important subject, especially in a University church like this, I want to divide this message into two parts. We will look at the first part in this study, and then the second part will be in the following chapter. The title of the message is <u>How to Discover Your Vocational Call?</u>

Basically, there are three important decisions you must make. And while I am speaking largely to University students, I want these remarks to be inclusive of everybody; but basically there are three important decisions you must make.

One, who or what will be your <u>master</u>? Who or what is going to be that which Dr. Paul Tillich describes as "the ground of our being." What is going to determine your belief system? What is going to determine the ethical norm that will decide how you understand and interpret life – and how you treat people?

For something or somebody will control and govern your life. Somebody or something will be your master. There are many things that master the lives of people.

Some people are mastered by an addictive habit. Some people are mastered by power or money. Some are mastered by fame while others are mastered by another person.

It is my prayer that your Master will be our Lord and Savior, Jesus Christ, but one thing is for certain: you will not have two masters. For Jesus said, "No person can serve two masters..."

The second big decision you must make regards your <u>mate</u>. With what person are you going to spend the rest of your life? Who is going to be the mother of your children? Who is going to be the father of your children? The person you marry will be the second big decision of your life. Now, you may say, "George, my decision is not to marry or have a mate." That is perfectly fine, but that also is a major decision in itself.

And the third big decision will be your mission in life. What will be your <u>mission</u> in life? What are you going to do with your life? What are you going to choose as your vocation? These two sermons will attempt to answer these questions.

Our church at Auburn is unique in that we have several hundred University students worship with us each Sunday, and one of the real decisions you are dealing with during the college years is this very issue. What is going to be your mission? What are you going to do with your life? How can you discover your vocational call?

Now I know there are guidance counsellors who can render valuable assistance in helping you answer these questions. There are many areas to which you can go to find help, and I strongly recommend that you take the maximum advantage of these resources. But in these two sermons, I want to show you how your spirituality can benefit you immensely in answering these questions. I wish to share with you a Biblical model that I believe can assist you in a very positive way.

Luke was the author of the third Gospel and the Book of Acts. When Luke met his Lord, he made a career change. When Luke found his <u>Master</u> he also found his <u>mission</u> in life.

In the Book of Luke, chapter 1, verses 1-4 are a prologue to the Book. Those verses are a prelude to the book. <u>The New International Version Study Bible</u> describes the first four verses as "the preface" to the third Gospel.

In verses 3 and 4, Luke tells us how he discovered his vocational call. In these two verses he provides a model that can be helpful to us.

As I've studied these verses, I have found there are five principles that make up this model. I wish for us to look at two of the principles today, and we will look at the final three in the next sermon.

Let me share with you all five principles, and then we will come back to Luke 1:3, and I will lift up the verse that will undergird the first two principles that we will look at in this message today.

The five principles found in this model are:

I.   **The Principle of Satisfaction**
II. **The Principle of Skill**
III. **The Principle of Service**
IV. **The Principle of Sensitivity**
V.   **The Principle of Security**

Today as we look at the Principle of Satisfaction and the Principle of Skill, I want us to notice how these principles are taken from the first part of Luke 1:3 as Luke writes, "It seemed good to me also, having followed all things closely for some time past..."

I. The Principle of Satisfaction

Now, I want you to notice the first part of verse 3 as Luke says, "It seemed good to me also." In these words of Luke, you can sense his deep satisfaction within. Now, as you think about a particular vocation, there are two questions I wish to ask you. One, are you satisfied, and two, is God satisfied?

One, are you satisfied? As you think about a particular vocation, along with Luke can you truly say deep within your soul about that job, "It seems good to me also?"

I think the people for whom I feel the sorriest are those folks who are not truly satisfied with their jobs; those people who find no meaning, no purpose and no sense of real satisfaction in what they are doing. And there are more people in this situation than you might think.

Are you truly satisfied, and is it a satisfaction that transcends monetary reward?

A sharp young couple met while they were students in medical school. Both of them were deeply committed Christians, and they married. Upon graduation they did a residency together in a very specialized area of medicine.

Upon their graduation they prayed about where they would begin their practice. Both of them felt strongly led to become medical missionaries, and they went in this capacity to a third world country in West Africa. There they labored for their Lord, and they gave themselves to the task of alleviating human suffering in that part of the world. There they began, and they started to raise their family.

After several years, they came home on furlough. They were taking continuing education courses in tropical diseases in a teaching hospital in a medical school. One day he was at the hospital, and he was approached by one of his former medical school classmates who had gone on to become an outstanding surgeon. This surgeon was enjoying a very lucrative practice.

The surgeon saw the missionary doctor, and he asked him if he could have a word with him. The surgeon said to the doctor while standing in the hallway of the hospital, "I've heard about the work you and your wife are doing. I've heard that the work is very dangerous. I've also heard that the conditions under which you must practice medicine in that country are very primitive. I also understand that you had to ask churches to help you raise money to buy an airplane so your wife and you could fly into the "bush country" to help people there because there are no accessible roads. I was also told that while you were there, your lives were in great jeopardy."

Then the surgeon looked the missionary doctor right in the eye and shaking his head, he said to him, "Why, I would not do what you and your wife are doing for $10 million." The missionary doctor, with a full throat, a smile upon twitching lips and with misty eyes said to the surgeon, "Doctor, my wife and I would not do what we are doing for $10 million either."

Yes, is there that deep feeling of satisfaction within? Can you say along with Luke, "It seems good to me also."

Secondly, is God satisfied? Not only is there that sense of satisfaction deep within you, but do you know that it has the approval of your Lord, and He is truly satisfied also?

In his book, <u>A Man For All Seasons</u>, Robert Bolt writes of a young Cambridge scholar by the name of Richard Rich. Rich approaches Sir Thomas More, the great Roman Catholic leader who would later be martyred for his faith. In this book, Rich is trying to discover his vocational call, and he seeks out the advice of More. Rich is very ambitious, and he wants to rise to great heights in the world.

He seeks this advice from More, and More responds by saying, "Why not be a teacher? You'd be a fine teacher. Perhaps even a great one."

Somewhat contemptuously, Rich retorts, "And if I was, who would know it?" Sir Thomas More responds by asking, "Who would know it? Who would know it?" And then this classic line, "Why you, your pupils, your friends, God. Not a bad public, that."

And my friend, the fact that you know it and God knows it; the fact that you are satisfied and God is satisfied is, in the final analysis, all that really matters. The fact that you can say along with Luke from deep within your soul, "It seems good to me also."

And so, principle number one is the principle of satisfaction. Principle number two is:

II.   The Principle of Skill

Notice that verse 2 goes on to read, "It seemed good to me also, having followed all things closely for some time past..."

And what Luke is saying in the second part of this verse is "from the past up until now, I have carefully followed, evaluated and investigated (some versions actually translate the verb form in this verse as investigated) my skills and where they can best be utilized."

You see, God has given to all of us certain gifts, graces, talents and abilities, and like Luke, we need to take inventory and see where our skills are aligned with vocational opportunity.

For you see, we all have an innate ability to do some things well. There are some things we don't do well. If you are like I am, there are a whole lot of things we don't do well.

For example, I knew at an early age that the good Lord did not want me to be an engineer or a mechanic because I don't know anything about machinery or tools. Some people have an affinity for these things, but I do not.

I have not yet learned how to work the VCR connected to our television set. I've been trying real hard for three years, but I just can't figure out how that thing works. And if the truth were known, some of you adults who are smiling don't know how to work a VCR either. And if the truth were further known, most of the children here today probably do. But that is not my skill.

I have great difficulty changing a flat tire. To be quite honest, I have great difficulty even finding the spare tire in these new cars.

As a matter of fact, if I'm off somewhere and I have a flat tire, and my sweet wife is not there to change it, I just don't know what to do. But my skill is not tools or machinery.

When I graduated from seminary I was appointed to a little church, and I did not have a secretary. I really did not have much of anything, and I did it all myself.

One of my jobs on Saturday was to do the bulletin for Sunday. We had one of those old mimeograph machines. That was the biggest and bulkiest old thing I think I've ever seen. It took up half of a room. It made a lot of noise, and it used a dark blue ink that had the worst smell. There were many Saturdays that I got more ink on me than I did on the 50 bulletins I was trying to do for the Sunday service.

Some people looked upon that mimeograph machine as an instrument of the church. There were times when I viewed it as a tool of the Devil. The phrase, "the Saturday night bath" took on a new meaning for me. It was not a phrase, it became a reality, and I like not to have ever gotten that ink off me. I often thought of all the courses I took in seminary, and the one that probably would have helped me the most would have been a course on how to operate that machine.

But again I say, machinery and tools are not my skill. But God has called me to a certain task, and I try to do the best I can with that. And you need to take the initiative and see where the skills God has given you will fuse into the vocation He has planned for you.

In closing, how do we sense this satisfaction within, and how do we align this skill without? I have a firm conviction that we understand and implement these principles through prayer. That is why it is so important that we create an atmosphere that is vibrant and holy with God's presence, and it is characterized by a receptivity to His call.

You see, we are at one place, and it could be that God's vocational call for our lives is at another place. The way the two are connected is through the medium of prayer. Prayer becomes the conduit through which God expresses to us His Will and plan for our lives.

It was during the early days of World War II. England stood alone. The United States had not yet come into the war. The King of England was making a broadcast to his people over the BBC. A wire broke. An alert technician quickly picked up the wires, and he spliced them together. Thus, the people were able to hear the important message of their King.

The message of our King is important because it contains His Will and His plan for our lives, and prayer is the means by which that call is connected and conveyed from Him to us. And so through prayer, I trust that we can implement the principles of satisfaction and skill, and we will be on the road to discovering our vocational call.

Chapter 11
<u>Helpful Hints On How To Live</u>

HOW TO DISCOVER
YOUR VOCATIONAL CALL

"It seemed good to me also, having followed all things closely for some time past, to write an orderly account for you, most excellent Theophilus, (verse 4) that you may know the truth concerning the things of which you have been informed."
(Luke 1:3-4)
Part II

This is the second part to the message, <u>How to Discover Your Vocational Call</u>. As I've said earlier, our church at Auburn is unique in that we have several hundred University students worship with us each Sunday, and while you as students are dealing with many important issues, you are especially wrestling with the issue of your "lifetime job." What are you going to do with your life? How can you discover your vocational call?

I know there are guidance counselors, placement services and personnel assistants who can be very helpful in dealing with this decision, and I encourage you to utilize these resources to the maximum; but in these two sermons I want to show you how your spirituality can benefit you. I want to share with you a Biblical model that I believe can be very helpful.

When Luke found his Lord, Luke found his vocation. When Luke found his <u>Master</u>, it was then that Luke truly found his <u>mission</u> in life.

Luke knew in that day what Cardinal Newman was to write some nineteen hundred years later, "Fear not that your life shall come to an end, but rather that it shall never have a beginning." When Luke found his vocation, it was then that Luke truly began to live, and I am not sure we are truly alive until we discover that purpose for which God has put us into this world.

This past Friday evening Rev. Jim Dannelly spoke to our Emmaus Group, and he said, "There are two important dates in the life of every great person. One is the date <u>when</u> that person was born, and the second is the date that person realizes <u>why</u> he was born."

Luke wrote the third Synoptic Gospel. If you study the Book of Luke, you will discover that verses 1-4 are a prelude to the Book of Luke. The New International Study Version of the New Testament describes the first four verses as "the preface" to the book. My good friend, Dr. Jim Dawsey, in his book, <u>The Lukan Voice</u>, describes the first four verses as "the prologue" to the book.

These verses are unique not only in that they are immensely helpful because of their theological content, but also because of the Greek in which it is written.

Dr. William Barclay, in his <u>Commentary on Luke</u>, describes the first four verses in Luke 1 as "the best bit of Greek in the New Testament."

Dr. Dawsey writes of Luke 1:1-4, "It stands in the best tradition of classical Greek."

It is interesting to note that Luke uses the same style of introduction as the great classical Greek historians such as Herodotes.

But it is in verses 3 and 4 of Luke 1 that Luke tells us how he discovered his vocational call. It is in these two verses that Luke also provides a model that can be very helpful to us.

Now, there are five principles that make up this model. In our last message we discussed the first two, and in this sermon I want us to look at the next three principles. They are:

I.   **The Principle of Satisfaction**
II.   **The Principle of Skill**
III. **The Principle of Service**
IV.   **The Principle of Sensitivity**
V.   **The Principle of Security**

Let us look again at our text, and then we'll study particularly Principles III, IV & V.

Luke writes, "...and it seemed good to me also, having followed all things closely for some time past, to write an orderly account for you, most excellent Theophilus, (4) that you may know the truth concerning the things of which you have been informed."

Principle I is the <u>Principle of Satisfaction</u> as Luke begins verse 3 by saying, "and it seemed good to me also." You can sense the deep satisfaction of Luke within as he makes this statement. As you think about a specific vocation, there are two questions I challenge you to ask under Principle I. *One*, are you truly satisfied? Can you say along with Luke, "it seems good to me also." *Secondly*, is God satisfied? Does it have the stamp of God's approving satisfaction upon it?

Principle II is the <u>Principle of Skill</u> as Luke goes on to say in verse 3, "...and it seemed good to me also, having followed closely all things for some time past." And what Luke is saying is, "from the past up until now, I have evaluated, investigated and taken inventory of my gifts, graces, abilities and talents, and this is where my skill aligns itself with a vocational opportunity." And as you think about your vocation, ask yourself the question, "Is my God-given skill aligned with this particular vocation?"

Now, let us continue as we look at the final three principles.

III. The Principle of Service

As we continue to read in verse 3, I especially want you to notice the last part of verse 3 as Luke writes, "...it seemed good to me also, having following all things close-ly for sometime past, to write a orderly account for you, most excellent Theophilus."

Now, as we think about the Principle of Service, there are two questions I want you to ask under this principle. They are: *One*, does this vocation <u>serve</u> other people, and *two*, does this vocation <u>serve</u> God?

One, does this vocation serve other people. Again I ask you to note the last part of verse 3 as Luke says, "...to write a orderly account for you, most excellent Theophilus." Now, we are not real sure of the identity of this person, Theophilus. Luke also wrote the Book of Acts, and in Acts 1:1 he begins that book by directing his thoughts to and lifting up this name, Theophilus.

Now, it is very possible that Theophilus was an actual person. It is a Greek name, and of course, Luke was a Greek. If it was an actual person, it was a person of equestri-an status because Luke describes him as "most excellent Theophilus." It is possible he was directing this Gospel to a leader in the Christian community, one who was deeply respected and admired for his devotion to God because the word "Theophilus" is a combination of two Greek words, <u>Theo</u>, derived from the noun, ***theos***, which means God, and <u>philus</u> which is a corruption of the Greek word for "brotherly love," ***philia***.

It is possible that this word Theophilus was simply a literary device that Luke was using in the third Gospel and the Book of Acts.

Or this word could have simply been an Apocalyptic collective noun that Luke was using in the First Century to address a specific community of people.

While we are not certain who Theophilus was or what he represented, we are certain that Luke was writing this letter for the purpose of <u>serving</u> the one whom this name rep-resented. Service is so very important.

Dr. Albert Schweitzer, while serving as a medical missionary in the Lamberene For-est, wrote just before he died, "I don't know what your destiny will be, but one thing I do know; the only ones among you who will be really happy are those who have sought and found how to serve."

Yes, service to others is so very important, and I ask you the questions, "does this vo-cation serve others, and will it make a difference in the life of somebody?"

Several months ago, Rick Hagans, who is the Director of "Our Place," a home for "homeless men" in our area, spoke at our United Methodist Men's breakfast, and he shared this story. He told of a man who was walking along the beach. This man was picking up starfish, and then he was throwing them back into the ocean.

Another fellow saw him and asked, "What are you doing?" The man replied, "I am throwing these starfish back into the ocean so they can live." The other fellow some-what caustically replied, "Why, what difference will that make?" The man lifted one little starfish up, and as he pointed to it, he said to the fellow, "Friend, to this little starfish, it makes all the difference in the world."

As you think about this particular job, does it make a difference in the life of somebody? Will it make this world a better place in which to live?

I recently read where an outstanding entertainer said, "Life's greatest success will be to come to the end of the way, look back, and know you made a positive influence upon the emotional life of somebody in some way."

Does this vocation serve others, and will it make a difference in the life of somebody, even if it is in a small way?

Secondly, does it serve God?

The Westminster Shorter Catechism begins with this question, "What is the chief end of man?" The answer is, "To glorify God and to enjoy Him forever." And I believe one of the ways we glorify our God is by serving Him.

Dr. Wallace Chapell told of a pedestrian who was walking down the street, and he noticed three men working at construction under the hot sun. He said to them, "What are you men doing?" The first man said, "I am working to make $8.00 an hour." The second one said, "I am putting in an eight (8) hour day." The third man with a smile of confidence upon his face proudly replied, "I am a building a church. I am working to build a more stately mansion where people can come and worship my God, the Lord God Jehovah!"

Three men doing the same job? Hardly! For two men it was an ordinary job, but for the third man it was a divinely called vocation where he was serving his God.

Does this vocation truly serve other people, and does it serve God?

IV.   The Principle of Sensitivity

Luke begins verse 4 by saying, "That you may know the truth..."

Now, what does Luke mean by the truth? The word we translate "truth" is an interesting word in the Greek. The word that is nearly always translated truth is the Greek word *alatheia*, but the word used here (in this phrase along with the term, *asphalian*) is the word *logon*. It is a form of the second declension noun, *logos*, which means "word." And so, I believe what Luke is referring to here is the truth of his call.

How can we know the truth of our call? I believe this is known through the Principle of Sensitivity.

Tell me, are you so sensitive to the whisper of God's Spirit that you can sense His calling and leading you?

Now, in the title of our message, there are two words I want you to note. One is the word "call." As a part of the Community of Faith, I believe your vocation is a divine call from God. The second word is "discover." Now, if our call is a divinely inspired call from God, then it is our responsibility to discover this, His call, for our lives; and I believe this discovery is made through this principle of sensitivity.

Late one afternoon a little boy asked his dad if he could go into the back yard to play.

The father told him he could, but he also instructed him to come immediately when he called him for dinner. The little fellow went into the back yard, and he started to play.

He then wandered out of the yard, across the street and into a little friend's yard. The lad's father, immediately before dinner, went to the back porch and starting to call his son. He called his name several times very loudly, but the little boy could not hear because he had wandered too far from his father's house.

My dear friend, is it possible that God has called or is calling you to some task or vocation, and the reason you have not heard is not because He has not called, but it is because you have wandered too far from the Father's House, and you have not heard?

Oh, I can tell you from personal experience, it is so easy for us to live out the words to the old Gospel hymn:

> *Prone to wander, Lord I feel it.*
> *Prone to leave the God I love.*

Yes friend, we hear His call through the principle of sensitivity, and that is why it so important that we cultivate and nurture this principle on a daily basis.

Now, how do we cultivate and nurture this sensitivity?

One, we cultivate it through our faithfulness in our worship in God's House. Many times we hear the call of God while we are in His House in a service of worship.

This was certainly the case of Isaiah when he went into the temple, for Isaiah heard God say, "Who will I send, and who will go for me?" And Isaiah answered, "Here am I, Lord, send me." And I remember it was in a service of worship when I unmistakably felt the call of God upon my life to become a Methodist preacher. Three summers ago Monteigne and I were at the Indian Springs Camp Meeting, and I was approached by a Methodist minister in the South Georgia Conference. He knew who I was, and he said, "I did my undergraduate work at Auburn. I was attending Auburn United Methodist Church one Sunday. Before the service started, I was sitting in that beautiful sanctuary listening to the lovely strains of organ music, and it was during that precise time that I felt God calling me to go in to ministry." Yes, we cultivate this principle through our faithfulness in worship.

Secondly, we cultivate it through our daily prayers.

Thirdly, we cultivate it through our daily study of the Scriptures.

Fourthly, we cultivate it through our daily study of the lives of the Saints of the Church.

And, *fifthly*, we cultivate it through our daily acts of compassion, kindness and goodwill to all people we meet everywhere.

Luke wrote, "...that you may know the truth," and it is my conviction that we discover and know this truth through the principle of sensitivity.

V.   The Principle of Security

I want you to notice again verse 4 as Luke says, "...that you may know the truth concerning the things of which you have been <u>informed</u>."

Now, while Principle IV (the Principle of Sensitivity) tells us <u>how</u> we discover the truth of our call, Principle V (the Principle of Security) tells us <u>what</u> the truth of this call can do for us. It can provide security as we seek and discover the truth of our call.

When Luke speaks, "...concerning the things of which you have been informed," it is my conviction that he is speaking of information that provides insight into Christ Jesus our Lord through this third synoptic gospel.

We gain insight into Christ through the parables, the miracles and the other inspired data that is recorded; and through the eyes of Luke we see the person of Christ, the purpose of Christ, the power of Christ, and we also see the pervading presence of Christ throughout this gospel.

It (His presence) begins in Chapter one, and it is the silver thread that runs through the fabric of the entire book, finding culmination in the two men on the Emmaus Road, in Luke 24, as Christ was present with them in such a real way.

So, our Lord wants us to know His presence today, and when we know His presence we gain the security that only He can bring.

One of my heros of the faith was a man by the name of Dr. Reuben Robinson. Many people don't know him as Reuben Robinson. Most people know him only as "Uncle Bud" Robinson.

Uncle Bud Robinson was an ordained Elder in the Church of the Nazarene, a denomination that is a part of our Wesleyan tradition. I have many good friends in the Church of the Nazarene, and they speak his name with a reverential hush.

Bud Robinson had very little education, and when he first felt God's call to go into the ministry, he could hardly read or write. In addition he was afflicted with many illnesses. He suffered from epilepsy, and he had a speech impediment that was so severe that at times it was hardly intelligible. He spoke with a pronounced lisp.

It was at a camp meeting in Texas that he felt God's call upon his life to go into the ministry.

He was a member of the old Methodist-Episcopal Church, South, and he went to his pastor to share with him his call. When his pastor brought Uncle Bud before the Quarterly Conference, they nearly turned him down because of his lack of qualifications. It was only through the insistence of his pastor that he was granted an "Exhorter's License."

Upon reception of this license, he was eager to preach. He had a burning desire to proclaim the Good News of the Gospel, but because of his lack of education and his speech impediment, no ministers would invite him to preach in their pulpits.

So, he rode his pony across the prairie there in Texas, and he invited people to come to an old school house to hear him preach his first sermon that night. That evening, the little school house was filled with people, and Uncle Bud stood up to preach. He opened his mouth, but no words came. He tried again, but he could not say anything.

He then felt that by reading The Bible he would be able to speak, so he picked up a Bible and started to read from the Sermon on the Mount. As he read, he read with that pronounced lisp, and he stuttered and stammered. Some little children on the front row started to giggle. Then some older adults started to chuckle, and then laughter rippled through the congregation. Uncle Bud realized that they were laughing at him, he bowed his head and he started to pray.

With tears rolling down his cheeks, Uncle Bud shared with his Lord that he was but a weak vessel, but he was also confident that God had called him to preach the Gospel. While he had very little in the way of physical and ministerial gifts, he was <u>secure</u> in the fact that God had called him, and he believed that since God had called him, He would not let him fail. He prayed for God to use his lisping, stammering tongue. Uncle Bud then prayed for God to do in the spirit that which he could not do in the flesh.

He then started to sing "Amazing Grace." As he sang with tears rolling down his cheeks, God's blessed Holy Spirit fell upon that school meeting house, and scores of people were converted to faith in Christ.

And as one biographer says, "Thus began the illustrious career of one of God's good and great men;" a man who was <u>short</u> on native gifts, but he was <u>secure</u> in the truth of his divine call. And from that night on God used Uncle Bud Robinson in a mighty way to touch the lives of thousands of people and lead them to faith in Christ.

God took away the stuttering and the stammering, but He left the marked lisp that became a hallmark of his ministry. It was a way of preaching that affectionately endeared him to the hearts of scores of people. Yes, with confidence, Uncle Bud Robinson was <u>secure</u> in his call.

And, my friend, when you are secure with God's presence and the truth of your call, you can go anywhere, and you can do anything because your Lord is with you. He promises, "I will never leave you nor forsake you. I will be with you until the end of the age."

HOW TO OVERCOME ENVY

"Wrath is cruel, and anger is outrageous;
but who is able to stand before envy?"
(Proverbs 27:4)

Our text is taken from the Book of Proverbs as it simply says, "Wrath is cruel, and anger is outrageous; but who is able to stand before envy?" We notice that in this verse the writer of Proverbs lifts up three negative emotions. He speaks of the cruelty of wrath, the outrageousness of anger, but when describing envy he appears to be at a loss for words. He simply says, "... who is able to stand before envy?"

Some time ago, my wife and I had the opportunity to attend the Larger Church Consultation at Epworth By the Sea in St. Simons, Georgia. This was a gathering of the ministers of the largest churches in our denomination in the Southeast.

On Thursday evening of that week, we enjoyed a banquet together. The speaker for the banquet was Bishop Bevel Jones who was the Bishop of the Charlotte, North Carolina, area. I was especially inspired by his message. He made one statement that particularly touched me. Bishop Jones said, "Ninety percent of the problems in ministry are caused by envy among ministers." And then with deep emotion in his voice, he said to the group that was exclusively composed of Methodist ministers and their spouses, "Guard yourselves! Guard yourselves!"

I may be wrong, but I've got a feeling that envy is not consigned exclusively to the ministry. It also affects coaches, doctors, lawyers, professors and neighbors. It is found in every walk of life. It could well be a problem right where you work. It could well be a problem right where you live.

Envy is a sin that separates us from God and other people. As we study this personal problem and its scriptural solution, I want us to understand envy in three ways. I want us to understand:

I. **The Definition Of It**
II. **The Destructiveness Of It**
III. **The Direction Of It**

I. **The Definition Of It**

How would you define envy? Charles Swindoll says it is, "...a team member that plays in the same backfield with profanity, suspicion and conceit."

Shakespeare simply refers to it as, "the green sickness."

One beloved minister simply called it, "A cancer that destroys the very essence of love and meaning in relationships."

While we were in England I heard several times the name of Philip Bailey, an eloquent poet of Britain who lived many years ago. Bailey describes envy as, "a coal that comes hissing hot from Hell."

Many people confuse envy with jealousy. We need to realize that envy and jealousy are distinctively different. Theologically and Biblically speaking, they are not the same. At times, jealousy can be good. Envy is never good.

At times, jealousy can be helpful. Envy is always hurtful. At times, we are taught to even pursue jealousy, but we are always taught to steer clear of the evil of envy. The Bible even says, "We are to be jealous after good works."

Jealousy is even a characteristic of divinity. When Moses was on Mount Sinai, the Lord God Jehovah thundered down the Decalogue to him, and said, "Thou shalt have no other Gods before me for I the Lord thy God am - (what?) - a jealous God." Yes, jealousy can even be an attribute of divinity. We need to understand that while jealousy, at times, can be good, envy is always very evil.

Now, how can we determine if we are envious people? Perhaps the first reaction of most people as they hear these words is, "I am not a envious person!" We think of people such as Troy Aikman, and we say, "I'm not envious of Troy Aikman. I was happy for him when he played such a good game in the Super Bowl.

I am not envious of Ted Turner and his communications empire. I'm happy for Ted. I'm not envious of the astronauts. I am happy for the astronauts. I am not envious of Roy Rogers, Dale Evans or Trigger." When I preached this message in my church at Auburn, a person came to me afterwards and said, "You'd better not be envious of Trigger because he is stuffed and mounted."

Please allow me to say that using names and people like those aforementioned is a very poor criterion to base your comparison and your judgement. If you want to know if you are an envious person, do not use people like those I've mentioned. Think of people who are in your realm. Think of people who are in your domain. Think of people who have jobs similar to yours. Think of your peers.

If you are a secretary, think of another secretary. If you are a student, think of another student – maybe someone in your sorority or fraternity, or someone with whom you have a class. If you are a teacher, think of another teacher. If you are a lawyer, think of another lawyer. If you are a minister, think of another minister. If you are an engineer, think of another engineer. If you are a merchant, think of another merchant in your line of business.

Then ask yourself these questions: Do I get upset when I hear that person praised for something he or she has done? Do I some how vicariously feel that person's gain is my loss? Do I cringe and become upset when I hear that person has accomplished something significant or attained some goal?

When that person is blessed or prospers in some way, do I rejoice with that person, or down deep, do I actually resent it? Do I inwardly wish that person well, or at best, am I ambivalent about that person; or at worst, do I wish that person harm? Do I resent that person having what he or she has?

In I Corinthians 13:4 Paul gives an insightful understanding of envy. In this beautiful "Love Chapter" Paul tells us that envy is the very antithesis of love. He simply says, "Love envies not."

Dr. William Barclay has a wonderful discussion of the word envy in his commentary on this particular selection of Scripture from I Corinthians. Dr. Barclay points out there are actually two types of envy in the Greek. One type of envy is an envy that simply covets the possessions of somebody else. It carries with it the idea that you possess something, and I want it. For example, suppose I am out playing tennis one day. I'm using my cheap racket that I normally use. I look over on the next court and I see a fellow attired in the latest tennis fashion. He has on an Izod shirt, silk Shark skin shorts and brand new Reeboks. He is using a custom built, fiberglass and technicolored racket like Andre Aggasi. I look at that fellow's racket, and I become envious for that racket. He possesses that racket, but as I covet that racket I am becoming envious of him because I want that racket to belong to me. Now, that is one type of envy, according to Dr. Barclay.

Dr. Barclay goes on to say there is a second type of envy that is much worse. This is a type of envy that simply begrudges you from having what you have. I don't really want it; I just don't want you to have it!

And of this type of envy, Dr. Barclay indicates that human personality can go no lower and the human spirit can become no meaner. This is the type of envy we are speaking of in this message, and are attempting to define.

Many people say Socrates was the wisest man to ever live. I do believe Socrates was one of the six or seven wisest persons to ever live. You remember, Socrates set forth the idea that ultimate truth can be established by reason. Aristotle and Plato built many of their philosophical ideas upon the philosophy of Socrates.

Socrates was a very wise man, and he said this about envy, (this is a rough translation from the Classical Greek of Socrates' day), "Envy is the daughter of pride. Envy is the author of murder and revenge. Envy is the beginner of secret sedition. Envy is a venom. Envy is a poison. Envy is a quick-silver. Envy consumes the flesh, and envy dries the marrow of the bones."

The writer of Proverbs said essentially the same thing as Socrates in Proverbs 14:30, "Envy is the rottenness of the bones." And so these definitions give us insight into the meaning of envy, and they naturally lead us to the second way we are to understand it as we study the destructiveness of envy.

II.   The Destructiveness Of It

We need to realize that envy is destructive, and envy is an evil force. Envy has within it absolutely no redeeming value or quality. The ultimate purpose of envy is to destroy.

I was reading about a parasitic plant that grows in South America. This plant begins to grow at the base of a tree. It gradually wraps its vines around the trunk, and in so doing, it suffocates and destroys the tree. It gradually grows, and then when it reaches the top of the tree, it blossoms forth in a flower to crown and celebrate its conquest. This plant is called "the Matador." Matador means "killer."

Envy is a killer. Envy takes root within the heart of a person, and it gradually wraps its deadly tentacles around a life and ultimately destroys it. Like "the Matador," it begins in a simply and seemingly harmless way, but its ultimate destiny is destruction.

I believe envy is destructive in two ways. *One*, it destroys the object of its evil influence. You see, when I am envious of somebody, that envy will naturally bring out the worst in me as I refer to and speak of that person of whom I am envious. Envy can prompt one to say ugly and vicious things about another person, and eventually those words can lead to actions. Words and actions combined can literally destroy a person.

Did you know envy even can lead to murder? In Genesis, the Book of Beginnings, Chapter four, we have the account of Cain and Abel. You remember, Cain was a tiller of the soil and Abel was a keeper of livestock. Both of them made their offerings to their God. Cain gave to God the first fruits of the land, and Abel gave to God the first hireling from the flock. God was pleased with the gift of Abel, and He accepted it. He had no regard for the gift of Cain. Because of this, Cain was consumed with envy, and he eventually murdered his brother, Abel. Envy is so destructive it leads to murder.

The first king of Israel was Saul. He was the son of Kish, and from the tribe of Benjamin. He towered over a land that was united. Saul was enjoying a crest of popularity, and he reveled in his acclaim by the people.

Then David came on the scene. David fought Goliath in the Valley of Elah, and he slew the giant. When David returned home, the people lined the streets, and they said, "Saul has slain his thousands, but David has slain his tens of thousands." Saul could not take this comparison. Envy began to set into Saul, and it ultimately consumed him. Saul was so driven by envy that he set out to murder David. The interesting thing as we study I Samuel is - I sincerely believe David really loved Saul.

Upon one occasion while Saul was seeking to find David to kill him, David slipped into the cave where Saul was sleeping and left a spear by his head. It was David's way of saying, "Saul, I want you to know that I care for you. I could have killed you, but I want to be your friend." Upon another occasion, David slipped in and cut off a piece of Saul's shirt. But the real tragedy of the story is that Saul could not see David's love because he was totally blinded by envy. That is precisely what envy does. It blinds us, and it leads to destruction. It was envy that eventually killed Saul.

Yes, envy leads to murder. We remember how the King of Israel was envious of the vineyard of Naboth. It was out of this envy that the King plotted that murderous scheme. Envy is destructive, and it can destroy the object of its influence.

Secondly, envy can destroy the one who is envious. This destructiveness not only goes outward, but it also turns itself inward. You see, envy is like a deadly acid. It will not only destroy that upon which it poured, it will eventually destroy the container that holds it.

Do you remember the fable of the eagle and the hunter? There was an eagle resting upon the low branch of a tree. This eagle was envious of another eagle that had a wider wing span, was prettier and could fly higher. The eagle in the tree was consumed with envy for the other eagle. He plotted to destroy the other eagle. He said to a hunter with a bow and arrow, "Why don't you shoot with your arrow that beautiful eagle that is soaring through the sky. It would make a lovely trophy for your den." The hunter said, "That is a good idea. I will destroy that eagle." The hunter shot an arrow into the sky toward the eagle, but it fell short. The eagle in the tree then plucked one of the feathers from its wing and gave it to the hunter.

The eagle said, "Attach this feather to your arrow, and it will go higher." The hunter attached the feather to the arrow, and he shot a second time. This arrow also fell short of the mighty bird.

The eagle in the tree then plucked two more feathers from its wing and gave them to the hunter with instructions to try again as those feathers would make the arrow go even higher. Again he tried, and again the arrow fell short of the mighty eagle in the air. The eagle in the tree then plucked three other feathers from his wing and gave those to the hunter. The hunter shot that arrow into the air, but it fell just short of the eagle soaring above.

Then the eagle in the tree plucked four more feathers from its wing and gave them to the hunter, and that arrow fell short also. As that arrow with the four feathers floated back to the ground, the mighty eagle spread his wings wider and soared into the heavens and out of sight. The hunter, then very distraught and disappointed, looked at the eagle in the tree and said, "I must have an eagle as a trophy for my den. If I can't have that one, I will have you!" The eagle in the tree said, "You will never get me!" He spread his wings, and he attempted to fly. But with the ten feathers missing from his wings, he went crashing down to the ground. The hunter then destroyed that eagle and took him as his trophy.

Now my friend, the simple point is this: The feathers that were intended to destroy the other eagle were the very ten feathers that actually brought about the destruction of the envious eagle itself.

That is precisely what envy is capable of doing. It can destroy the one who is envious. The writer of Proverbs said in 26:27, "He who digs a pit will fall into it, and a stone will come back upon him who starts it rolling."

The reason envy is so evil is because it is destructive. It destroys the object of its evil influence, and it eventually destroys the one who is envious.

III.   The Direction Of It.

By that I simply mean how can we direct envy to a redemptive solution? How can we direct it to a redemptive cure. Is there a cure for it?

One of the wisest men of antiquity was Marcus Aurielus. Many folks remember Marcus Aurielus as the Emperor of Rome and as a military leader. But he was also a very wise philosopher, and Marcus Aurielus said, "I've studied Greek, Hebrew, Caldean. I've consulted with many wise men, and I've concluded there is no cure for envy." Well, maybe from Marcus Aurielus' point of view, he is right. But the Good News of the Gospel is there is a solution to it.

Very quickly, let me share the scriptural solution to a personal problem that affects more people than we sometimes realize. I think the solution is found in two realizations and one application.

First, we need to realize what causes envy. Why are people envious? Basically, psychologically speaking, there are two reasons.

Number one is discontent. You see, if I'm not content with what I have and I see what somebody else has, I become envious for that. But there is a second cause. Not only is envy caused by discontent, but it is also caused by insecurity. And it is insecurity that leads to the second type of envy alluded to by Dr. Barclay. The realization of the causes of it.

The second realization is, we need to realize how powerful envy is. Envy is a very powerful emotion. When a person is envious, that person expends a lot of energy.

But the verse I shared with you from I Corinthians 13:4 is the use of the word "envy" in a verb form. The word that is used there is the word *zeali*. And that is the word from which you will immediately recognize that we get such a high energy word as "zeal, zealous, zealot." Envy is a very powerful emotion. We need to realize the causes of it. We need to realize the power of it. Two realizations and one application.

The application is that we need to direct that envy to the transforming grace of God allowing Him to apply His grace, and through His grace we become new creatures in Christ Jesus our Lord.

The scriptural text here is II Corinthians 5:17, "If any person be in Christ, he is a new creature: old things have passed away, and all things have become new." We become new creations in Him as we allow His grace to apply itself to the negative emotion of envy. And with His grace, it then becomes powerful energy that can be used for His glory.

I want you to notice, when you take this scriptural solution, it addresses both of the causes. Number one, it addresses my discontent, because when I proclaim the sovereignship of God over my life I am able to say along with the Apostle Paul in Philippians 4:11, "I've learned in whatsoever state I'm in to be content." I'm not envious of you because I am content with who I am, where I am and what I am.

But I want you to notice it also addresses the second cause - that of insecurity. For when I become a new creation in God through Jesus Christ, it is then that my insecurity is addressed, because my sense of worth and self-esteem is undergirded by the fact that I know I am loved by God; and when I know that I am loved by God, I no longer have to be insecure.

A Benedictine Brother said, "As I look back over my 70 years, I see clearly the secret of my inner happiness. The secret of my inner joy, peace and contentment rests in the fact that I know I am infinitely loved by God." That's the direction to it.

It was many years ago when the writer of Proverbs penned our text, "Wrath is cruel, anger is outrageous." And it is as though the writer of Proverbs had no words to express envy, "...but who can stand before envy?"

The definition of it. The destructiveness of it. The direction of it. Bishop Jones said, "Brothers and Sisters, guard yourself." And it could be where you live, where you work, where you are right now, you need to heed these words that are so applicable: "Guard yourself!"

Chapter 13
Helpful Hints On How To Live

HOW TO SLEEP SOUNDLY ON
A STORMY NIGHT

"I laid down and slept, and then I
awakened for the Lord sustained me."
(Psalm 3:5)
(Psalm 3:3-6)

As we look at Psalm 3:3-6, I especially want us to note verse 5 as it is our text for this study. You will note that our text is surrounded by three great promises of God that are found in verses 3, 4 and 6, but verse 5 is our text as the Psalmist says, "I laid down and slept, and I then awakened for the Lord sustained me." Let us pray:

Our Father, when we rest our faith upon your promises there is strength for the day, and there is sleep that is sweet and sound for the night. Today, help us to rest upon these promises. Amen.

How to sleep soundly on a stormy night! I remember what was perhaps the stormiest night of my life, and I might add that on that night I did not sleep a wink. I remember that night for four reasons.

One, on that night, September 12, 1979, Hurricane Frederick, one of the worst storms in the history of the Gulf Coast, slammed into Mobile and Baldwin Counties reeking unprecedented damage.

Secondly, I remember that night because at the time our daughter was only six months old, or younger.

Thirdly, I also remember it because at that time I was serving in a volunteer capacity as the Chaplain to the Police Department in the community where we lived. The Police Chief was and is one of my very best friends. He called me late that afternoon and said, "George, we are anticipating a long night. With this hurricane there could be some fatalities. We are going to need you, and if you will, we want you to spend the night and stay at the Police Station all night." I told Chief Pridgen that I would do anything I could to help, and I spent that evening with the Police Chief.

Fourthly, I remember that night because prior to the hurricane striking, I drove from the Police Station over to check on my wife and daughter. I wanted to have a prayer with them. They were spending the night with some dear friends from our church.

I remember how eerie and calm it was just before the hurricane hit. I believe mine was the only car on the roads in Mobile County at that time. When I got to where they were staying, both of them were sound asleep. They had already gone to bed, and they were sleeping.

The next morning after the hurricane, the Police Chief drove me back over to where they were staying to check on them as the telephones were out and there were no means of communication. I remember how his patrol car negotiated through the debris.

When we arrived at the home where they were staying, they both were still sound asleep. They had slept through the entire storm. Now, the reason our daughter slept was because I reckon a little six month old baby is supposed to sleep. But I know why my wife was able to sleep. The reason was that she was not anxious and worried on the outside because of what she believed, felt and knew on the inside.

And that was the precise case with the writer of the third Psalm. He was able to cope outwardly because of what he believed inwardly. He believed in three great promises of God, and because of his awareness of and belief in these promises, he was able to lay down and sleep, and his Lord sustained him in the midst of the storm.

And my friend, I would say to you that when the wind blows, when the lightening flashes, when the thunder crashes and when the storm comes, you rest your faith upon these same three promises that surround our text. The Psalmist was aware of and believed in:

I.   **The Protection of God**
II.   **The Presence of God**
III. **The Peace of God**

I.   **The Protection of God**

Notice the Psalmist says in verse 3, "But you, oh Lord, are a shield about me."

During the 20 years we lived in Mobile we had to contend with hurricanes, and I learned a great deal about those storms. I discovered that prior to a hurricane hitting land, there is always a stillness before the storm. I also realized that in the midst of the hurricane there is the "eye," and in that eye there is an almost perfect calm.

And my friend, when you are held in the protective palm of God's unchanging hand, there will be a stillness about you. There will be a calm within you, and there will be the protective shield of God's grace above and about you.

I think Isaac Watts, the great hymn writer of yesteryear understood this when he wrote that beautiful hymn we normally sing on the first Sunday of the year:

> *Oh God our help in ages past;*
> *Our hope for years to come.*
> *Our shelter from the stormy blast;*
> *And our eternal home.*

Osborn Gregory tells the story of a family that lived in the backwoods during the frontier days of our country. A little boy lived with his mother and dad. A school was opened several miles from where the lad lived.

The quickest way to get to the school was through a thick patch of woods. The father insisted that the little boy walk alone through the woods each morning to school, and then return alone by the same route. The father was brave and courageous, and he wanted his little boy to grow up to be brave also. The boy wanted to be brave like his dad, and he especially wanted to make his father proud of him.

So each morning the boy walked through the woods all alone, and in the afternoons he returned by the same route. One afternoon while the boy was walking home he encountered a big grizzly bear on the pathway. The little fellow looked at the bear, and he became alarmed. He turned and thought about running, but he knew there was no way he could outrun the bear. He started to cry.

The big bear growled and glared at the boy, and as the bear prepared to attack, a shot rang out, and the big bear keeled over dead.

Then the boy's father emerged from behind a bush. He put his arms around the boy, and he wiped the tears from his eyes. He said to him, "It's alright, Son, I've been with you all the time. Every morning I have followed you to school, and every afternoon I have been in the shadows watching you. I kept myself hidden from you because I wanted you to learn to be brave."

Yes, that father was hiding behind the trees and the bushes protecting his child whom he loved. And how comforting it is to know that our Lord is standing in the shadows keeping watch over His own.

It matters not how dark the forests of life may be; it matters not how large the big ugly bears of life may loom; and it matters not how dangerous the treacherous storms might become, we simply need to rest our faith upon the promise that our God is watching over us and protecting us. Along with the Psalmist we can say, "But you, oh Lord, are a shield about me."

II. The Presence of God

The next verse, verse 4, the Psalmist says, "I cried unto the Lord, and He answered me..."

Now the reason the Psalmist prayed unto the Lord, and the reason his Lord answered him was because he knew that his Lord was present right there with him.

I believe the Psalmist knew then what Christ Jesus was to say many years later, "I will never leave you nor forsake you," and "I am with you always even to the end of the age."

Over the years I have greatly admired Billy Graham and his fine organization. He has had a big impact and influence upon my life. I also greatly appreciate his son, Franklin. I recently went over to Columbus, Georgia, with friends, to hear Franklin preach in the Greater Columbus Crusade, and his message greatly blessed me.

In December of 1994, a moving article by Franklin Graham appeared in *Decision* magazine. In this article, Anna Warner, a Missionary in Africa, told of how hard it was to get medical teams into an area to help the Rwanda refugees.

Because of this difficulty, the missionaries went into rebel controlled areas just north of the Capital of Rwanda. While there, they set up a make-shift hospital, and they were given over 62,000 people to care for. Within ten days this number escalated to 100,000. In addition to dealing with disease, many of the people were suffering from machete cuts and gun shot wounds.

Then to exacerbate an already complex and complicated situation, 900 children who were orphans were thrust upon them.

It was while they were in the town of Byumba caring for these orphans that they noticed one little girl who was standing apart from the other children. She was a beautiful little girl with big brown eyes, and she was about seven or eight years old. She had an old tattered blanket in her arms, and she was clutching it tightly to her body. The little girl was also singing a song in French, rocking back and forth on her feet as she sang.

Standing close by was a rebel guard with a cigarette dangling from his lips and a Russian made machine gun strapped over his shoulder.

One of the missionaries asked the guard who the little girl was and what she was singing. The guard said, "She's just like all the others – an orphan." They then asked, "What is she singing?" He replied, "I don't know. Something about Jesus." They then asked the rebel soldier, "What are the words that she is singing?" The man listened very attentively, and then he replied, "She is saying something like 'Jesus loves me! This I know.' And she just keeps singing it over and over."

They then learned that the little girl had watched as her entire family was murdered. They were killed with the standard form of execution there, dismembered with razor sharp machetes.

That little girl stood there with her only two possessions: one, a ragged and tattered blanket that perhaps mystically reminded her of her family – her mother, her father, her brothers and sisters.

And two, a song in her heart that reflected a childlike faith that told her she was not alone, but there was One greater than she who was present with her. And that Presence was articulated in the words to that little children's song, "Jesus loves me. This I know..."

Just as the Psalmist knew that his prayers were answered through the presence of Yahweh, the Lord God of Abraham, Jacob and Isaac. And just as that little girl knew that Christ Jesus was present with her through the words of that simple song, so we need to rest our faith upon the promise that our God, through Christ Jesus, is present with us now through the presence, person and power of the third person of the Trinity, the Holy Spirit.

III.   The Peace of God

As we read on in verse 6, we notice that the Psalmist says, "I am not afraid of 10,000 people." Now, the reason he was not afraid was because he had the peace of God within his heart and mind. You see, the opposite of fear is peace. In direct antithesis to fear is peace.

Paul wrote to Timothy and said, "God has not given us the spirit of fear, but of power, love and a sound mind." And a sound mind is a peaceful mind.

The reason many people are not able to lead productive lives during the day or sleep at night is because their minds are filled with fear.

In I John, there is a little verse that says, "Fear worketh torment." Shakespeare said, "The minds of men are filled with dread (or fear)."

Now the reason the Psalmist was able to retire and repose was because his life was void of fear, and it was filled with this peace of God.

It is interesting that the Old Testament word for peace is **shalom**. We do not have an equivalent word in the English. It is a word that means more than the absence of war. It means the deep abiding presence of God.

Isaiah spoke of this peace when he wrote, "Thou shalt keep him in perfect peace whose mind is stayed upon Thee."

And Jesus picked up on this theme and developed it further in the New Testament when He said, "My peace I give unto you." And the peace our Lord Jesus gives is a peace that, one, this world does not know; two, it is a peace this world cannot give; and three, it is a peace this world cannot take away.

And when we have this deep abiding peace within, then we are not affected by the fightings and fears without.

One of the great spiritual classics is a little volume entitled, The Saint's Everlasting Rest. It was written by Richard Baxter in the 1600's. If you are familiar with your English history you know that it was written during the time of the English Civil War, and it is important to note that while the winds of war were fiercely blowing all about, Richard Baxter spoke of an everlasting rest and peace that God has for his saints and His children within.

And isn't it wonderful to know that when we have this peace within, then we are able to rest, retire and repose.

Alfred Lord Tennyson lauded Queen Victoria with these words, "Her court was pure; her life serene; God gave her peace, her land reposed." And when we allow God to grant us this peace it is then that we will repose and know the joy of productive living during the day and sound sleep at night.

And the way we experience this peace is by putting our trust in God. That is precisely what the Psalmist did in Chapter three, and that is what we must do if we want our lives to be filled with God's peace.

John Benjamin Figgis was a part of the Wesleyan movement in 18th Century England. He was greatly influenced by the Countess of Huntingdon. Figgis, in speaking of God's peace, wrote, "If the basis of peace is God, the secret of peace is to trust in God." And it is only when we put our trust in Him totally that we completely understand and experience this blessed peace.

How do you sleep soundly on a stormy night? We follow the example of the Psalmist and rest our faith upon these three promises. The promise of: His protection; His presence, and His peace.

We sing the old Gospel hymn,

> *Standing on the promises of Christ my King,*
> *Through eternal ages let His praises ring.*
> *Glory in the highest I will shout and sing;*
> *I'm standing on the promises of God.*

And we need to stand upon these three promises of God. We need not only to stand upon them during the day, but we need to sleep, and we need to rest upon them at night.

And when the storm comes, we need to remember the words of Dave Nicholas who assuredly said, "God's promises are like the stars. The darker the night, the brighter they shine."

Chapter 14
Helpful Hints On How To Live

HOW TO WATCH YOUR WORDS
"Set a guard over my mouth, oh Lord,
keep watch over the door of my lips."
(Psalm 141:3)
(Psalm 141:1-3)

In this study, I want us to think about this subject, How To Watch Our Words. Our text is taken from Psalm 141:3 as the Psalmist, who in this instance is David, says, "Set a guard over my mouth, oh Lord, keep watch over the door of my lips."

I may be wrong, but I believe the good Lord knew exactly what He was doing when He gave us two feet, two legs, two hands, two arms, and especially two ears, two eyes and only one tongue.

The unrestricted movement of the lower jaw has broken more hearts, destroyed more homes and ruined more lives than any one thing I know.

One of the things I enjoy so much about my ministry here in Auburn is serving as one of the Chaplains to the Auburn University football team. I especially look forward to being on the sideline with our team and coaches. It is exciting, but it can also be a little dangerous.

I remember at the Independence Bowl in Shreveport when we were playing Army. An Army running back was making an "end sweep" when he was tackled by our great linebacker, Takeo Spikes. I looked to the left, and I saw the running back. It looked as if he was running right towards me. I looked to the right, and I saw Brother Takeo coming from that direction. It looked as though he was heading right for me also. I did what any good Chaplain would do under such circumstances; I bowed my head, prayed, and I jumped back. Brother Tekeo tackled him right on the sideline, and he nearly tackled me too. One of the cleats on the bottom of Tekeo's shoe hit me in the shin, and it caused my leg to bleed. That could have been my most exciting moment in college football. Since that game, I've enjoyed showing that place on my leg to people, and I proudly tell them it is from the shoe of Tekeo Spikes. I kind of hate to see the place getting well because I am so proud of it.

But when players are on the sidelines, they normally hold their helmets under their arms until the coach sends them in. They then put the helmets on their heads. In front of the helmet is a face guard, and attached to the face guard is a mouth guard. When those fellows get ready to go into the game and do battle, they allow that guard to protect their mouths.

And the same is true for us when we go into the game of life and prepare to do battle. Paul tells us in the Book of Ephesians that we are to put on "the helmet of salvation," and David tells us that we are "to set a guard over our mouths," and we are to let God "keep watch over the door of our lips."

Now, why do we need to let God set a guard over our mouths? Why do we need to let Him keep watch over the door of our lips? Why do we need to learn to watch closely and carefully the words we speak? I believe there are three reasons. We need to watch our words because:

I.   Words Break Down

II.   Words Build Up

III.   Words Bring In

I.   Words Break Down

First of all, we need to watch our words because words break down. Proverbs 18:21 says, "There is death in the power of the tongue."

Proverbs 15:1 says, "Grievous words stir up anger."

Yes, words can break down, and words can hurt; and many people are very careless with the words they speak.

I heard about a lady who went to the newspaper office to pay her bill. She inadvertently wandered into the wrong room. She entered the printing press room where they had all the fresh type carefully laid out. This dear lady accidentally backed against some fresh type. Two words were imprinted in big, black and bold letters on the back of her dress, and they were **"Daily News."**

This lady made her way to the office, and as she paid her bill the people laughed at her behind her back. She turned around and gave them a dirty look. The woman then left the newspaper office and started for home. As she made her way down the sidewalk, she noticed that people were giggling as she walked by.

When she got home, in a huff she said to her husband, "Husband, everywhere I have been today people have looked at me from the rear, and they have snickered. I want you to look on the back of my dress and see if there is anything there that ought not be there."

Her husband looked on the back of her dress, saw the words, and he said, "No ma'am, nothing at all!"

Yes, people are very careless with the words they speak, and there are some folks who even intentionally use words to hurt other people.

A man was not feeling well, and he went to the doctor. The doctor examined him, and then looking at the fellow he very seriously said to him, "Mister, I don't know how to tell you this, but you have rabies."

The man was taken back, but he took out a notebook, and he started to make a list of names. The good doctor said to him, "Sir, are you making out your will?" The man said, "No, I'm making out a list of the people I plan to bite!" And there are some people who are just like that. They use words to intentionally hurt, and they use words to break down.

Morgan Blake was a sports writer for the Atlanta Journal, and he said this, "I am more dangerous than the screaming shell from the Howitzer. I win without killing. I tear down, break hearts, and ruin lives. I travel on the wings of the wind. No innocence is strong enough to intimidate me. No purity strong enough to daunt me. I have no regard for truth, no respect for justice, and no mercy for the defenseless. My victims are as numerous as the sands of the sea, and often just as innocent. I never forget – and seldom forgive. My name is gossip!"

Yes, Proverbs 18:21 says, "Death is in the power of the tongue," and Proverbs 15:1 says, "Grievous words stir up anger."

I heard the story about a little boy who had a bad habit of saying unkind things about people. He was very harsh with some of the words he spoke.

His father wanted to find a way to address the problem and teach his son a lesson. He got a big white post and put it in the backyard. He said to his son, "Now, every time you say something ugly about somebody, I'm going to have you go into the backyard, take a knife and carve a notch in that white post. That will graphically show you how ugly your words are and the frequency with which you speak them.

It wasn't long until the little fellow had the white post filled with notches. He then came into where his dad was and with big tears running down his cheeks he said, "Dad, I never realized how ugly were my words. Is there anything I can do to make up?"

The father very thoughtfully said, "Yes there is." He said, "Every time you say something good to somebody or about somebody, you can take this bucket of white paint and paint over each of the notches, and perhaps it won't be long until the post will have a coat of white again."

The little boy immediately went out and started to do and say nice things to everybody with whom he came in contact. Each time he did, he painted over one of the notches with white paint. It was not long until the post was covered with a coat of white again. But when he looked at it, he began to cry.

He came into where his dad was and said, "Dad, I feel that I've made up for the ugly things I've said. I've painted the post white again, but I want you to go out and look at it. The scars are still there. You can still see them, and they are so very ugly!"

And my dear friend, that is exactly the way it is with the words we speak. We can go back, and we can try to make amends, but once a word is spoken in a negative and ugly way, the damage has been done. The hurt is there. The scar is there. The pain is there. Yes, the brokenness is still there.

Words break down.

But, words also build up.

II.   Words Build Up

Yes, words do build up in a powerful way. I call your attention again to the two verses that I read a moment ago. Proverbs 18:21 does say, "There is death in the power of the tongue," but that verse also says, "There is <u>life</u> in the power of the tongue," for there is death and <u>life</u> in the power of the tongue.

Proverbs 15:1 does say, "Grievous words stir up anger," but that verse also says, "A <u>soft answer</u> turns away wrath and anger." Yes, a soft answer does turn away wrath while grievous words do stir up anger.

Yes, words can be negative, or they can be positive. Words can break down, or words can build up.

And words can hurt, or words can help make this world a better place in which to live.

I think of poets like Wordsworth, Tennyson, Shelley, Keats and Browning, and how they can weave words together and build beautiful poetry.

I think of writers like Thomas Hardy, Charles Dickens, Robert Lewis Stevenson and Edgar Allen Poe, and how they can lace words together, build intriguing tales and wonderful stories.

I think of preachers like John Chrysostom, Martin Luther, John Wesley and E. Stanley Jones, and how they can use words to build powerful sermons that can influence and even change the lives of people.

I think of musicians like Hayden, Handel and Bach; and hymn writers like Isaac Watts, Charles Wesley and Fannie J. Crosby, and how they can take words, put them to melody and then build hymnody and music that will last for eternity.

I think of a kind person who can take a positive word, drop that word into the life of another and build that persons self- respect, self-esteem and self-confidence.

Mark Twain reflected the feelings of most of us when he said, "I can go a long ways on a sincere compliment."

A favorite verse of my mother's is Proverbs 25:11. It simply says, "A word fitly spoken is like apples of gold in pictures of silver." Isn't that a beautiful verse? Doesn't it remind us how words can so beautifully build people up?

Yes, words break down, and words build up; but they also bring in.

III.   Words Bring In

Words bring in. They bring the virtues of God in to our very being and in to our spirituality. Yes, words bring in.

With words, <u>through prayer</u>, we experience God's grace.

There are many ways to pray. We can pray silently, privately, meditatively and contemplatively. We also can pray in public gatherings like lifting up Pastoral prayers during services of worship. Also, in prayer gatherings with others, we can lift up our prayers of petition. But there is another type of prayer that we can practice in private, and that is when we pray verbally, and those words can bring in to our spirituality God's grace.

Through prayer, we can experience God's saving grace that redeems. We can experience God's sanctifying grace that empowers us. We can experience God's serving grace that enables us to reach out and help others. We can experience God's strengthening grace that undergirds us, and we can experience God's sustaining grace that gives to us the courage to go on.

Yes, with words through prayer, we can experience God's grace.

Also, with words, through praise, we experience God's cleansing.

Praise is a very important component part of worship. When we incorporate praise into our worship in a very significant way, it simply means that we glorify and honor the name of our God.

The shorter Westminster Catechism says, "The chief end of mankind is to glorify God and love Him forever." And just as prayer is important in our worship and our prayer time, we also need to realize that a by-product of praise is a cleansing effect it has upon our spirits.

Proverbs 27:21 says, "The refining pot is for silver, and the furnace is for gold, but so is a man to his praise." For me, that means praise refines and cleanses our spirits.

True praise burns away the chaff of despair. Sincere praise singes away the dross of disappointment, and when we praise God, it lifts our spirits in a very powerful and significant way.

Also, with words, through proclamation, we experience God's gladness.

Proverbs 12:25 says, "Heaviness within the heart of a person makes it droop, but a good word makes it glad."

You see, a good and positive word can bring gladness to your heart. You can actually talk yourself into being a happy person.

A coach in any field of athletics can use words to motivate a team and turn them from losers into winners.

A deadpan salesman with positive words can transform herself into a go-getter.

Yes, a good word can instill within us a spirit of gladness and joy.

And so, in this message we see why words are so important, and we especially see why David tells us that we need to set a guard over our mouths, and we need to let God keep watch over the door of our lips.

It is my prayer that this week we can learn how to live life more effectively as we realize the important place words have in our daily relationships, and how we can see, on a daily basis, they can truly build up, break down and bring in; and I pray that we will use them in a positive way to truly build up others and bring into our lives God's grace, God's cleansing and God's gladness.

Jaret Holmes is a blessing to my life with his witness for Christ. He attends our church regularly.

Victor Riley is smiling in this photo because I've just given him some good advice on how to block.

Jimmy Brumbaugh is an inspiration to me with his durability and work ethic. He's also become a great friend.

Antwoine Nolan and I have become really good friends. I like the fact that we have the same color hair.

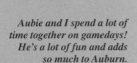

Aubie and I spend a lot of time together on gamedays! He's a lot of fun and adds so much to Auburn.

I showed this photo to a friend of mine who said it reminded him of Beauty and the Beast. You know, I was offended by him calling those lovely ladies beasts!

Here's a photo of Buddy Davidson and me on the sidelines in Columbia, SC. I don't know of a more caring person than Buddy. He looks after all the arrangements related to the football team's travel, and that's not an easy job.

Here I am with Assistant Coach Joe Whitt and Melvin Owens of the Auburn University Police, two great friends of mine. I like to say that Melvin protects the team and I protect Melvin. Joe's faith is an inspiration to me.

My friend Rick Trickett, who coaches the offensive line, doesn't appear to be too happy in this photo. Brother Rick has a knack for getting his point across to his players!

Here I am giving Brother Bob Baggott a good Methodist illustration to preach in his Baptist Church on Sunday.

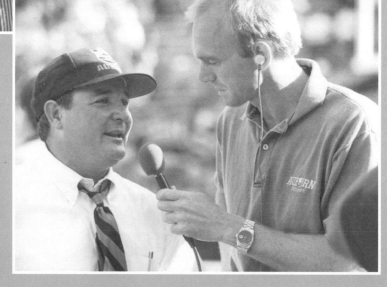

Here is Rowdy Gaines interviewing Coach Bowden for an Auburn Network telecast. Rowdy is an Olympic Gold Medalist swimmer and is a great representative of Auburn.

My good friend Rob Pate came in as a freshman and made an immediate impact in the secondary. He's a fine Christian young man.

Here's Hicks Poor celebrating a touchdown reception. He walked on at Auburn and, through hard work and determination, earned a scholarship and became a great receiver for the Tigers.

Terry is one of the closest friends I have in this world. I admire him as a coach but more as a Christian gentleman. He and his family are active members of our church in Auburn.

Over the years, Dameyune and I have become great pals. He has been such a joy to watch on the football field and has done some amazing things. I have come to really love and appreciate him so much.

Larry Edmondson is the newest addition to the coaching staff. He and his family attend our church regularly.

HOW TO GROW OLDER GRACEFULLY
"Surely goodness and mercy shall follow me
all the days of my life..."
(Psalms 23:6a)
(Psalms 23:4-6)

Our text is found in the last verse of the 23rd Psalm as David says, "Surely goodness and mercy shall follow me all the days of my life."

When I read these words I am reminded of the country fellow who named all of his children after people in The Bible.

He had four sons, and he named them Matthew, Mark, Luke and John.

He had twin boys, and he named them Paul and Silas.

His wife then had triplets, three girls, and he named them "Shirley, Goodness and Mercy."

His pastor came to visit with him and said, "My brother, those are not names in The Bible." The farmer said, "Oh yes they are: 'Shirley, Goodness and Mercy!' David said, 'they will follow you all the days of your life.'"

Now, that is not my interpretation of our text, but I do believe it means that God's grace and goodness and His love and mercy will completely encircle and encompass us as we walk down the pathway of life, as our text suggests, "all the days of our life."

Now, when we define age, we normally do it with numbers and years. I am not so sure that is the best way.

Sometimes I think we ought to define age by state of mind.

For example, this very day, I know some people who are in their 20's, and they are bored, decrepid and tired way beyond their years.

On the other hand, I know some people in their 80's, and they are excited, enthused and fresh way beneath their years.

Now, it is interesting how we think about time.

Bernard Baruch said, "To me, old age is always fifteen years older than I am."

And quite often we are very secretive about our age. A husband was standing next to his wife as he was admiring a very beautiful lady. He said to his wife, "Isn't it remarkable how Gertrude has kept her age?"

"It surely is," replied his wife rather dryly, "She has not changed it in ten years!"

There was a wife who was usually very caustic in her conversation with her husband. One day he asked her, "My Dear, will you still love me when I am old and ugly?"

She immediately replied, "My Dear, you may grow older, but you could never get any uglier!"

But the truth of the matter is that we are all getting older, and the question is: "How can we grow older gracefully?"

I believe we grow older gracefully when we take three disciplines, and always keep them as we walk down the pathway of life, as our text suggests, "all the days of our life."

We need to:

I.   Keep An Expanding Mind
II.   Keep An Enthusiastic Spirit
III. Keep An Ever-Growing Faith

And so, we need to:

I.   Keep An Expanding Mind

Sometime ago, my father preached in our church at Auburn, and he reminded us that with our years we are spending our days as a book that is being written. He based his Scripture on the last part of verse 9 of Psalm 90 when the Psalmist said, "We are spending our years as a tale that is being told," (KJV) and that is precisely what we are doing with our lives everyday that we live.

In that chapter, three verses down, the Psalmist says in verse 12, "So teach us to number our days so that we may apply our hearts unto wisdom," and what that means is this: as we grow in years, we also need to expand our minds and grow in wisdom and knowledge.

We are never too old to <u>stop</u> learning, and we are never too old to <u>start</u> learning.

When Cato, the Roman Philosopher, was 80 years old he decided that he wanted to learn Greek. Actually he not only wanted to study and learn Greek, but he wanted to master the language.

Somebody said to him, "Cato, why are you beginning your study of Greek at this advanced age?"

He immediately replied, "Because it is the earliest age available to me."

We are never too old to start learning, and regardless of our age we should always be growing and expanding our minds.

The Benét's (Stephen and Rosemary), in their beautiful poem on Lincoln, end with these descriptive words:

Lincoln was the green tree,
Lincoln kept on growing.

We are never too old to stop learning, and we are never too old to stop expanding our mental capacities.

100

I think of Tennyson. He was 83 when he wrote, "Crossing the Bar."

Goethe was 80 when he wrote the second part of "Faust."

Amos Alonzo Staggs was forced to retire at the age of 70, but he continued to coach for 14 more years at the University of the Pacific, and at 81, he was voted National Coach of the Year.

Benjamin Franklin was 81 when he helped frame the U.S. Constitution.

Golda Meir was 71 when she became Prime Minister of Israel.

My wife is an artist, and she told me that Michelangelo was 71 when he finished painting the top of the Sistine Chapel. I told her that I bet his back hurt when he got through. She told me that he did it by lying on his back on a scaffold, looking up and painting. I told her that Michelangelo was not only a good artist, but he was also a smart one.

The pianist, Arthur Rubinstein, gave one of his greatest recitals at the age of 89.

Jessica Tandy was 80 years old when she won an Oscar for her performance in "Driving Miss Daisy."

At the age of 90, Pablo Picasso was still painting, and it is said that some of his latest works were among his most innovative.

Henry Ford, Albert Coe, Toscanini, Oliver Wendell Holmes, and Hubert Hoover attained some of their greatest heights of success after the age of 80.

Our golden years can be among our most productive years. Once a young man said to the 89 year old poet, Dorothy Duncan, "Why, Mrs. Duncan, you have lived a full and productive life."

She immediately retorted, "Young man, don't you past tense me!"

As we grow older, there may be some physical limitation to our bodies, but we can still think with our minds, and we can still dream with our hearts.

When J. C. Penney was 91 years of age, he said, "My eye-sight is getting weaker and decreasing, but my vision is getting stronger and increasing!"

In 1864, Robert Browning wrote a magnificent poem entitled "Rabbi Ben Ezra." There are 32 stanzas in the poem, but I think the first two lines encapsulate and remind us of the hope of life as those lines simply say,

> *Grow old along with me,*
> *The best is yet to be.*

And we experience the very best when we expand our minds, and when we grow in wisdom and knowledge everyday.

II.   Keep An Enthusiastic Spirit

It is so important to retain our enthusiasm all through life.

Henry Threoau said, "None are so old as those who have outlived their enthusiasm."

We all start out with enthusiasm and a passion for life, but quite often, some where along the line, our enthusiasm wanes and our passion grows cold. The key to growing older gracefully is to learn to keep our enthusiasm.

Thomas Huxley said, "The secret of genius is to carry the spirit of the child into old age.

Sir Edward Appleton was a Scottish Physicist and a Nobel Prize winner who helped make world-wide broadcasting possible.

He was asked the secret of his achievements, and he immediately replied, "Enthusiasm! Enthusiasm! Enthusiasm is the secret of achievement, and I even place it above professional skill."

This past week I was reading about a man who has lost his enthusiasm. This man is a minister, and he lives in the midwestern part of the United States. He is 77 years of age, and if anybody asks him how he is doing, his standard and patent answer is always lethargically expressed in this statement, "I am 77 years of age, and I am fading fast."

One day this minister was walking across the street at a busy intersection and a fellow walking next to him politely spoke and asked how he was doing. The minister stopped, looked the fellow in the eye and said, "I am 77 years of age, but I am fading fast."

The fellow then looked at the minister and said, "Well, if you don't get out of this road you are going to fade a whole lot faster because there is a car heading directly towards us!"

This minister has no enthusiasm, and he is truly fading fast. Several years ago he felt that his church hurt him. He tells of how his denomination let him down and how his ecclesiastical superiors disappointed him.

His enthusiasm has faded, and over the years he has become negative, bitter, and cynical about life. He is very critical when he talks about other people, especially other ministers, and his conversation is marked by a sarcasm that borders on being mean-spirited. Yes, that man is fading fast, and he is getting old everyday.

Let me tell you about another minister. This minister is not 77, but he is 87, and he is not fading fast. Everyday he is growing, going and glowing.

He awakens every morning, and as he bounces out of bed, he quotes these motivating words of the Psalmist, "This is the day the Lord has made, I will rejoice and be glad in it," and he lives every minute of everyday with a sense of excitement, a sense of expectancy and a sense of enthusiasm.

This minister has a little radio devotion that he presents five mornings a week, and he helps the people in his community begin the day on a positive note.

On Monday morning of each week, he has a short devotion on a widely watched television station at 7:00 am, and he helps even more people in that part of the county and state begin their day on an enthusiastic note.

Also, he is the Chaplain for four different businesses in that city; which means that four mornings a week, he goes to those places of business and helps those employees and employers begin their day with an encouraging and motivating word.

He goes to the hospitals there just about everyday. He goes for two reasons: one, because he simply enjoys being with people, and two, because he gets a 20% discount on his lunch each day.

He is the past president of his civic club, and in that county he has served as President and leader of the American Cancer Society, the American Lung Association, the Salvation Army and numerous other boards and agencies in that community.

Last year he preached in 67 churches in denominations ranging from Pentecostal to Episcopal.

Like many retired people, he lives in Florida. He lives in Panama City, Florida. He has lived there for over 31 years, and the interesting thing is that nearly everybody in that county knows him and loves him.

Sometime ago, the leading and largest newspaper in that county, the Panama City *News Herald*, did a survey, and they named this man as one of the six most popular, most beloved and most respected persons in Bay County. It was not just in Panama City or on Panama City Beach, but in ALL the county; and they affectionately gave to him the title "The Chaplain of Bay County."

I happen to know that man. He is my father.

He preached for us three times last Sunday morning, and following the third service, he went down to Panama City Beach where he began a week-long revival.

This morning he is preaching in the Methodist Church in Bonifay, Florida. This afternoon he will drive up to Montgomery, and tonight he will preach in the Delraida United Methodist Church. After the evening service, he then will drive nearly 200 miles back to Panama City where he has a full week beginning early in the morning.

Next Saturday he will drive back here to Auburn, and he will lead the singing in the three morning worship services as we begin our revival. That Sunday afternoon, he will preach at Wesley Terrace, and then he will do some visiting with me. On Sunday evening, he will lead the singing again in our revival.

Now, how is he able to do all that he does? How is he able to maintain such a schedule and keep going? Oh, I know the answer, and it is very simple. You see, one, he loves his Lord. Two, he loves people, and three, he loves life; and he is enthusiastic about all three.

He is not growing old, but he is growing older gracefully each day with an enthusiasm for living.

And so, the way to grow older gracefully is to keep an expanding mind and keep an enthusiastic spirit.

III. Keep An Ever-Growing Faith

Don't ever become stagnant in your faith, but always continue to grow.

Peter, in the last verse of the last chapter, in his second letter, writes, "Grow in grace and in the knowledge of our Lord and Savior Jesus Christ."

This past week, in preparation for this sermon, I read a delightful book entitled, Outwitting Your Years. The author is a physician by the name of Dr. Clarence Lieb. Before his retirement, Dr. Lieb specialized in treating diseases of older people.

In this interesting book, he tells us how to stay alive physically, mentally, emotionally and spiritually.

He then points out that the supreme alchemy in outwitting your years is to have a faith and belief in God, and to cultivate and nurture that faith on a daily basis.

Yes, a growing faith is a vibrant and vital faith that enables us to grow older gracefully.

Somebody once asked John Adams this question: "How are you doing?"

"John Adams is quite alright, thank you," came the youthful answer.

"Of course, the house in which he is living is a bit dilapidated. The walls are tottering on their foundation, and the roof is in great need of repair."

And then he continued with these poignant and revealing words, "I think he will soon have to move out of this old house into a new house, a house not made with hands, eternal in the heavens. But Mr. Adams is quite alright, thank you!"

A person with such a faith never grows old. Praise His Name!

HOW DOES GOD ANSWER OUR PRAYERS?

"Ask, and it will be given to you; seek, and you will find;
knock, and it will be opened to you."
(Luke 11:10)
(Luke 11:9-10)
Part I

This is the first of two chapters on the subject, How Does God Answer Our Prayers?

Over the past several months there has been a veritable explosion of interest on the subject of prayer.

"Sixty Minutes" and "20/20" both did prime time pieces on the subject of prayer.

I do not subscribe to **Reader's Digest**, but someone gave to me a recent edition, and in it was an article entitled, "Does Prayer Heal?"

I have a very simple faith, and one of the basic tenets of my faith is a belief that God answers prayer.

I agree with the poet who wrote,

> *I know not by what methods rare,*
> *But this I know, God answers prayer.*
> *I know not how He sends the word*
> *That tells us fervent prayer is heard.*
> *But I know the answer comes.*

Now, I am sure there are times when we all wonder if God truly answers our prayers.

Someone has well said that the two most prevalent and asked questions in the area of prayer are: One, "Lord, I've prayed and prayed and prayed; why haven't you answered?" Two, "My child, I've answered, and answered and answered; why haven't you listened?"

Now, for me, our text is simply a Scriptural confirmation that God does answer our prayers.

For it says, "Ask, and you will receive; seek, and you will find; knock, and it will be opened to you."

In teaching about prayer, our Lord emphatically states to us that God does answer our petitions and requests that we direct to Him.

Now, it is important that we understand how God answers our prayers, because if we do not know how He answers our prayers then we may get the idea and have the notion that God does not answer our prayers at all. I believe God answers our prayers in at least four ways. In this message, we will look at two of the ways, and in the next study we will consider the other two. His answer is sometimes:

I.   **Direct**
II.   **Different**

Yes, sometimes His answer is:

I.   Direct

Two Old Testament references scripturally buttress this point. In Jeremiah 33:3, we hear the voice of God speaking through His Old Testament Prophet as He says, "Call unto me, and I will answer you, and show you great and mighty things which thou knowest not."

And again, God is speaking through the pen of Isaiah as He says in Isaiah 65:24, "...before they call, I will answer..."

Yes, sometimes God's answer is direct. We will lift up a prayer to Him concerning some need, some relationship, some hurt or some concern, and He directly answers it just like we want Him to answer it.

Probably, every person reading these lines has experienced answered prayer like this where you have prayed for something and God directly answered it. And how wonderful it is when we receive an answer like that. It happens now. It happened in the days of the New Testament, and it happened in the days of the Old Testament.

In Genesis, Chapter 24, Isaac's servant was trying to find a wife for Isaac. This faithful servant was praying for God to supply a bride for his master.

In a little village, he came to a well of water, and before the servant finished praying the prayer, God directly answered it and furnished Isaac with a wife.

Now, if you are single, and you are praying for a husband or a wife, you study Genesis 24 and see how that fellow did it. I don't guarantee that God will answer it directly like He answered the prayer of that man, but there are times when God does answer our prayers directly.

But there is a second way that God answers our prayers. Sometimes His answer is:

II.   Different

There are times that we will pray to God and He does not answer our prayers in a direct way, instead His answer is different from what we expected.

Now, I believe there are three ways His answer can be different.

One, sometimes He gives to us far more than we expect.

Secondly, sometimes He gives to us far less than we expect.

Thirdly, sometimes He doesn't necessarily give us more or less than we expect, but

He answers our prayers altogether differently than what we expect.

Let's look at these three ways that God answers our prayers differently.

One, sometimes His answer is different in that He gives to us far more than we request or expect.

When I was in seminary I served five little country churches that were spread over three counties in South Alabama. I did not have a parsonage, so that meant I had to drive down from Atlanta (I was a student in seminary at Emory University), preach, visit my people and then drive back to Emory on Sunday night. It made for a very long day.

At that time, Monteigne was a senior at Florida State University in Tallahassee. We were engaged, and she would drive up with two of her sorority sisters on Saturday. She would spend Saturday night with her cousin who lived in Atlanta, and I would go by and get her at 4:00 AM in the morning.

Now, keep in mind we were not coming *in*! We were going *out* at 4:00 AM! That is an early hour to have a date, and our date was to church. Most of our dates were to church.

We have a lot of students worship with us here at AUMC, and I can tell you from personal experience that it is a whole lot more inspiring to take your date to church. I can also tell you from personal experience that it is a whole lot cheaper to take your date to church.

But I would pick her up at 4:00 AM in the morning, and we would drive over 200 miles down to South Alabama. I would preach at Carr's Chapel at 9:00 AM. I would preach at Pleasant Hill at 11:00 AM, and we then would spend all Sunday afternoon visiting. I would preach at Perote at 7:00 PM that Sunday night, and then we would drive back to Atlanta.

When we got back to Atlanta late Saturday night, Monteigne would meet two of her KD Sorority sisters, and they would drive back to Tallahassee. That was when I knew my wife really loved me, when she did all that riding and driving just to be with me.

But I remember that on Sunday afternoons around 6:00 PM I would start to get really hungry. I was getting ready for the evening preaching service at Perote, and there were no fast food stores in Perote where I could get something to eat on Sunday afternoon. As a matter of fact, there was not anything <u>fast</u> in Perote. Everything moved at a kind of slow pace. Actually, there were not even any stores in Perote.

While I served as the Pastor of that church, I became close friends with a dear lady by the name of Mrs. Harrison. She was the Matriarch of the Perote Charge. She especially took the young student ministers under her wing and cared for them. She was one of the sweetest ladies I've ever known. She died a little over a month ago, and that saintly lady has made heaven all the more lovelier with her presence.

Mrs. Harrison lived in a little frame house at the top of a hill. Living with her was her bachelor son, Gene. Gene became one of my closest friends, and during the six years I served that little country circuit, we would go to Auburn football games on Saturdays in the fall. I truly learned to love Mrs. Harrison and Gene.

But I called Mrs. Harrison and told her how hungry I would get on Sunday afternoons along about 6:00 PM. I was really trying to make her feel sorry for me. I said, "Mrs. Harrison, after I've driven so far, preached twice, and spent the whole afternoon visiting, I get so hungry. Would you please fix a sandwich for me tomorrow afternoon about 6:00 so I'll have the strength to preach at Perote and then drive on back to Atlanta?"

I'll never forget her answer. Very warmly and graciously she said, "Brother George, (that is what she called me) I would be so honored for you 'to take' supper with Gene and me tomorrow night." I remember that was the first time I had ever heard it referred to as "take supper," but I was deeply touched by that phrase because of the love and warmth with which she shared it and because of what it meant.

That next Sunday afternoon, I drove up the hill to her little house. I parked the car and walked up on the front porch. Through the front screen, I caught a whiff of something and I knew it was far better than a sandwich. She then led me into the dining room, and when I walked through that door, what I saw nearly made me weep with joy.

I can see now what was spread over that dining room table: fried chicken, fried okra, creamed corn, fresh squash, tomatoes recently picked from the garden, big cat-head biscuits, homemade churned butter, field peas (and I don't mean those little green English peas; I mean those delicious and sumptuous field peas that came out of her garden, and like they grow only in Perote.) and a big chocolate pie.

When I saw that, I thought I had died and gone to heaven.

Now, the simple point I want to make is this: it took boldness on my part to make a request to Mrs. Harrison in the first place. But I did it. I asked for a sandwich. Now, she answered my request, but she responded with so much more than that for which I asked. She gave me so much more, and she did it because she loved me.

And there are times when God answers our prayers exactly like that because He loves us.

We make a request to God, and He opens up the windows of Heaven and pours out His blessing upon us in such a magnificent manner that we can hardly receive it. He gives us far more than we request, and at times, that is the way He answers our prayers. I've experienced answers like that, and I know you have too.

And may I parenthetically say right here that so often we restrict God by our reluctance to ask God. With our limited faith, we ask for little, and we are surprised when we receive much. God wants so much to bless us. He wants to bless us as individuals, and He wants to bless us as a church. He longs and desires to pour His blessing out upon us.

There is a line in an old Methodist Camp Meeting song that simply says,

And James says, "The effectual fervent prayer of a righteous man availeth much." And James goes on to say, "You have not because you ask not."

I believe God wants us to honor Him by asking Him to do, as the hymn suggests, "great and marvelous things for us."

Once a Frenchman approached Napoleon and made a huge request. To the surprise of everybody, Napoleon granted the request. One of Napoleon's lieutenants said to him, "Emperor, why did you give that man everything for which he asked?" And Napoleon answered, "Because he honored me by the enormity of his request. Yes, he greatly honored me by the magnitude of his request."

And sometimes, even without our asking, God answers our prayer by giving far more than we request.

Secondly, He answers our prayer differently in that at times He gives us less than we request.

There are those times we pray and God answers our prayers by giving us less than we request.

For example, when we get sick, we go to the doctor. Our physician will prescribe for us antibiotics to combat and arrest the infection. Now, we may feel that we need more medicine than he prescribes for us so we can get well sooner. But the good doctor knows the exacting amount that is needed to make us well. He also knows that too much medicine can be detrimental to our health, so he measures out to us just the right amount to make us whole.

Now, His answer may be less than we expect, but we need to remember that His answer is always to help us and it is never to hurt or hinder us.

And in answering our prayers, He metes out the divinely right answer, and it is always in accord with His Will, and it is within the context of Romans 8:28, "And we know all things work together for good for those who love the Lord; for those who are the called according to His purpose."

Thirdly, sometimes His answer is not necessarily more than we expect or less than we expect, but it is altogether different from what we expect.

Again, there are times when God's answer is totally different from any answer we expect, but again we must remember that God is answering it against the background of His omnipotence, omnipresence and omniscience, and it is always for our very best.

Following the second bloody day at the Battle of Gettysburg, a prayer was found upon the body of a dead Confederate soldier. This young soldier realized that God sometimes answers our prayers in a totally different way than we might expect, but He always does it for His glory and our good. The prayer found in the pocket of the soldier reads:

109

I prayed to God for strength,
        that I might achieve...
I was made weak,
        that I might learn humbly to obey.
I prayed for health,
        that I might do greater things...
I was given infirmity,
        that I might do better things.
I prayed for riches,
        that I might be happy...
I was given poverty,
        that I might be wise.
I prayed for power,
        that I might have the praise of men...
I was given weakness,
        that I might feel the need of God.
I prayed for all things,
        that I might enjoy life...
I was given life,
        that I might enjoy all things.
I got nothing that I asked for,
        but everything I had hoped for.
And in spite of myself,
        My prayers were truly answered.
I am among all people, most richly blessed!

Yes, sometimes God's answer is different than what we expect.

In closing, let's pick up our text, take it home with us today, and then carry it through the week with us, and when we lift up our prayers let us always remember these words of our Lord, "If you ask, you will receive; if you seek, you will find; and if you knock, it will be opened unto you." And let us remember that God always answers our prayers.

HOW DOES GOD ANSWER OUR PRAYERS?

"Ask, and it will be given to you; seek, and you will find;
knock, and it will be opened to you."
(Luke 11:10)
(Luke 11:9-10)
Part II

I have a minister friend who shared with his congregation some statements by important people that might be a little hard to understand:

- Former Michigan governor George Romney said, "I didn't say that I didn't say it. I said that I didn't say that I said it. I want to make that very clear."
- Former President Gerald Ford said, "Things are more like they are now than they have ever been."
- Former Vice President Dan Quayle said, "I support efforts to limit the terms of members of the Congress, especially members of the House and the Senate." • A Clinton staff member said, "If we don't make some changes, the status quo will remain the same."
- President Bill Clinton said, "I believe that this country's policies should be heavily biased in favor of non-discrimination."
- Senator Barbara Boxer said, "Those who survived the San Francisco earthquake said, 'Thank God I'm still alive.' But, of course, those who died, their lives will never be the same again."

We need to speak up and be clear with what we are saying.

Some time ago my brother, John Ed, was preaching in a little church in the country. When he stood up to preach, he saw this note attached to the pulpit, "When you preach, Brother, please speak up. The agnostics in this place are terrible."

Well, in this second study on prayer, I want to speak up so you can clearly hear what I am attempting to say, and I hope that these thoughts will be helpful to you.

And so, I want to talk some more about prayer.

Alfred Lord Tennyson said, "More things are wrought by prayer than this world dreams of."

We need to learn to pray.

And we need a time to pray. We need to set aside a time each day to nurture those deep spiritual recesses of the soul.

The Bible says that "Jesus rising up a great while before day..." went out to pray. And like our Lord, we need a definite time to pray each day. We need a place to pray.

The Bible says, "Jesus went to the desert...He went to the sea...He went to the mountains...He went to the garden..." and there He prayed.

An ancient legend tells of when Zacchaeus was an elderly man. It is said that he would go to a certain tree in Jericho, and there he would gently caress it and tenderly touch it. Somebody said to him, "Why do you come to this same tree day after day?" With a lump in his throat, the old man said, "Because it was from this tree that I first saw my Lord, and I come back each day to this place to meet Him again and again."

And we need, as the old gospel hymn suggests, *A place of quiet rest nearer to the heart of God; a place where sin cannot molest near to the heart of God."*

And so, when we learn to pray, and when we have a time and a place to pray, it is then that we discover that God does answer our prayers.

And it is then that we find and lay claim to the truthfulness in the words of our text, "Ask and ye shall receive, seek and ye shall find; knock and it shall be opened unto you."

Now the title of the message is <u>How Does God Answer Our Prayers?</u>

You see, it is important that we know how God answers our prayers, because if we do not know how He answers our prayers we may have the notion and embrace the idea that God does not answer our prayers.

And we need to remember that God answers our prayers in several ways. He is the God of diversity and infinite variety. He doesn't answer our prayers in just one way, but there are several ways.

In the first study we said that God answers our prayers in two ways:

One, sometimes His answer is <u>direct</u>.

Sometimes God directly answers our prayers.

In Jeremiah 33:3, we hear the voice of God through the pen of Jeremiah as God says, "Call upon Me and I will show you great and mighty things which you do not know." And how wonderful it is when God does answer our prayers in a direct way.

And I dare say every person reading these lines or hearing this sermon can point to those times when God directly answered a specific prayer; and in the wake of such a beautiful experience, all you can do is just lift your hand to heaven and say, "Blessed be the name of the Lord."

Secondly, sometimes His answer is different.

Sometimes when we pray our prayer might have to do with a relationship or an illness or asking God to meet a specific need, and He answers that prayer in a <u>different</u> way than we expected.

One, sometimes God in His providence gives to us more than we ask.

Secondly, sometimes God in His omniscience and all embracing knowledge and wisdom gives us less than we request because He knows less is best for us.

And *thirdly*, sometimes His answer is altogether different from anything we expected, but we need to remember that His answer is always in accord with His divine Will, and it is ever couched in the context of Romans 8:28, "And we know that all things work together for good for those who love the Lord; for those who are called according to His purpose."

Now, in addition to these two ways, God also answers our prayers in two other ways. Sometimes His answer is delayed, and at other times His answer is <u>denial</u>.

And so, another way is...

III.   Delayed

Let me share with you a verse of Scripture that can help you in your prayer life. It is Isaiah 30:18. It says, "The waiting of God is gracious to you."

Now, think about that verse for a moment. God delays His answer sometimes so <u>you</u> can more fully know <u>His</u> <u>grace</u> and <u>others</u> can more completely and clearly see <u>His</u> <u>glory</u>.

May I say that again? God delays His answer sometimes so <u>you</u> can more fully know <u>His</u> <u>grace</u> and <u>others</u> can more clearly and completely see <u>His</u> <u>glory</u>. There are many illustrations, but I wish to share with you one example that illustrates this fact.

In John 11, Lazarus was very sick. His sisters, Mary and Martha, prayed to the Lord. Their prayer was definite, direct and distinctive.

But I want you to notice how Jesus answered their prayer. They prayed for Him to come and touch their brother. Jesus answered the prayer, but He delayed His coming for three days, and when the Lord got there, poor Lazarus was dead. You can imagine how disappointed and distraught were those two sisters.

Jesus raised Lazarus from the dead, but in my opinion, that is not the important lesson that is taught in this story.

More importantly, God revealed a higher purpose in His delay, for notice that John 11:4 says, "This sickness is not unto death, but it is for the glory of God."

And so, sometimes God delays His answer so you can more fully know His grace and others can more clearly see His glory in you and your sweet Christian witness.

And a fourth way God answers our prayers is...

IV.   Denial

Sometimes God denies our requests. There are those times when God says no, but we need to remember it is always for a reason.

You see, God always answers our prayers even if our prayers appear to be foolish, and at times that answer is denial and no.

One of the great missionaries of the Church was Amy Carmichael. As a little girl, she had big beautiful brown eyes. She was also a little lassie with extraordinary faith.

As a youngster, for some strange reason, she wanted to have blue eyes. One night she got down by her bed, and she prayed with all the faith that was in her that God would change and make her brown eyes blue. She prayed so hard until she actually wept herself to sleep kneeling by her bed.

When she awakened, she immediately ran and looked into the mirror. She was disappointed because her eyes were still brown. She had prayed and made a request to God, and God said no.

Years later, Amy went as a missionary to India. Many missionologists attest that she was one of the greatest missionaries to ever serve in that country. Her name is spoken with the same affection and admiration as is the name of E. Stanley Jones in India.

Amy later said that the one thing that caused the dear people in that country to accept her; and the one thing that prompted her to have such an effective ministry there; and the one thing more than any others, that prompted them not to look upon her as a foreigner was the fact that she had brown eyes.

Yes, God sometimes answers our prayers with a no. But it is always for a reason.

I have a dear friend whom I deeply admire and respect. He shared with his Sunday School class that the one dream of his life as a young man was to receive an appointment to the U.S. Naval Academy. In Junior High and High School, that was the one great goal of his life, and he took courses to direct him to that end and help him attain that goal.

In addition to that, he prayed that God would allow him and permit him to receive an appointment to the U.S. Naval Academy. The appointment never came. My friend was crushed.

He then heard about the U.S. Air Force Academy which at that time had not been in existence very long. He applied for an appointment there, and he received it.

The rest is history. He graduated, having established an exemplary record. He rose rapidly within the ranks of the Air Force, and he served with distinction. Not too long ago he retired with great honor having reached the high rank of General.

Now if you were to ask my friend, "Did you pray?" He would immediately tell you, "Yes." If you were to ask him, "Did God answer your prayer?" He would answer, "Yes, but He said, no." And then my friend would quickly tell you that God said no for a reason. He would tell you that God said no and God closed one door so He could open another door – an even better door.

There are those times when God answers our prayers with a no.

God even said no to His own dear Son in the Garden of Gethsemane. Remember that Jesus had a dualistic nature. He was divine, but at the same time He was human. In His divinity He could forgive sin, but in His humanity He hurt and identified with our need. And as He knelt in the garden, I believe the human part of His nature cried out when He prayed to His heavenly Father, "Father, if it be Your will, let this cup pass from me."

You see, the human part of Jesus did not want to suffer and die upon the cross. And Jesus prayed for God to take away that bitter cup of suffering. But God refused to remove it, and God said no to His prayer, and Jesus endured the agony of the crucifixion and died upon the old rugged cross for you and me, for there was no other way our salvation could be consummated without His atoning death upon Calvary's cross.

Yes, there are times when God answers our prayers with a denial and a no.

I close with this little essay that is simply entitled, "And God Said, No."

I do not know the author, but it underscores this final point so well.

"And God Said, NO."

I asked God to take away my pride.
And God said, "NO."
He said it was not for Him to take away,
But for me to give up.

I asked God to make my handicapped child whole,
And God said, "NO."
Her spirit is whole.
Her body is only temporary.

I asked God to grant me patience.
And God said, "NO."
He said that patience is a by-product of tribulation;
It isn't granted, It's earned.

I asked God to give me happiness.
And God said, "NO."
He said that He gives blessings.
Happiness is a choice.

I asked God to spare me pain.
And God said, "NO."
He said suffering draws you apart from worldly
Care and brings you closer to Me.

I asked God to make my spirit grow.
And God said, "NO."
He said I must grow on my own
But He will prune me to make me fruitful.

I asked God if He loved me
And God said, "YES."
He gave me His only Son who died for me
And I will be in Heaven someday because I believe.

I asked God to help me to love others
As much as He loves me,
And God said,
"Ah, finally you have the idea."

And so this week when you pray, please remember that God always answers your prayers, but He answers them in different ways.

Build your faith upon our text from Luke and remember that if you ask, you shall receive, but you will receive what God has in store for you.

Seek and you will find, but you will find in God's answer to your prayer that which is best for you.

Knock and it will be opened, and remember God will always open the door that He wills for your life.

SECTION II
Looking For Leaders

LEADERSHIP BY EXAMPLE AND WITH EXPECTATION

*"And what you have heard from me before many witnesses,
commit to faithful people who will be able to teach others also."*
(II Timothy 2:1)
Part I in Series on "Leadership"

With this chapter, we begin a study on the theme of "Leadership." Winners are leaders.

Aside from Jesus, I think the greatest leader in the New Testament was the Apostle Paul. He founded all of those churches. He organized those many missionary journeys, and he directed and led many people into the ministry.

Among them was a young man by the name of Timothy. He wrote two letters to Timothy giving him instructions.

In the second letter, the second chapter and the second verse, Paul said to him, "The things I have taught you, I want you to commit to others so they can teach too." In other words, Paul was saying, "Timothy, as I've taught you to be a leader, so I want you to teach others so they can lead also, because there is a real need for leaders."

Now, just as there was a need for leaders in the First Century, so there is a need for leaders in this day in which we live.

There is a need for leadership in the home. I heard about a wife who was looking to her husband to give direction and leadership on some matters in the home, but the husband would simply waffle on every issue. Finally she looked at him and said, "Herman, are you man or mouse?" And then she said, "Squeak up, Herman, squeak up!"

Leadership is needed in the school.

Leadership is needed in the Church.

Leadership is needed in athletics. You show me a great athletic team, and I will show you a great leader.

Leadership is needed in business. You show me a successful business, and I will show you an outstanding leader. Leadership is needed in the government and the military. I think one of the greatest military and presidential leaders of the 20th Century was President Dwight D. Eisenhower. In World War II, General Eisenhower assumed the position of Supreme Commander of the Allied Forces in Europe, and he led the Allies to victory over Nazi Germany.

President Eisenhower was a great president. It is said that he would bring all of his Cabinet members and leaders into a conference room, and he would place a piece of string on the table. He then would look at them and say, "There are two ways to move this string. You can get behind it, and you can push it. When you push it, there is chaos and confusion. But, if you get in front of it and pull it, there is precision and order, and the rest of the string will follow behind." He then said, "Leaders never get behind and try to push. They always get in front and lead, and people follow."

Now, how can you get people to follow? How can you become an effective leader? I believe there are several principles that are vitally important, and I also believe these principles must be understood and they must be implemented.

In this series we are going to study these different principles. I want us to look at two of them today, and we will look at the others in the following chapters. First, I want us to consider the principles of:

I.   The Principle of Example
   (A leader leads by example.)
II.   The Principle of Excitement
   (A leader leads with excitement.)

In the next chapter we will look at the principles of Ex-pectation and Excellence. A leader leads through expectation and a leader leads towards excellence, but for this study, the principles of Example and Excitement.

I.   The Principle of Example
   (A leader leads by example.)

If you are going to be an effective leader, people have got to know that you know where you are going.

One of my dear friends in our church is Mr. Homer Turner. Sometime ago, Homer shared a cute little story with me about a good man who died, and they buried this good man in a cemetery – which is a good place to bury a good man. It is a good place to bury any dead man whether he is good or bad. This good man had requested that these words be inscribed on his tombstone.

> *Please tip your hat as you walk by,*
> *For as you are now so once was I,*
> *And as I am now soon you must be,*
> *So, my friend, prepare yourself to follow me.*

Homer said that a young wag came by, saw the inscription, and he wrote with chalk these words on the bottom of the tombstone:

> *To follow you, my friend, I'm not content*
> *Until I know which way you went!*

You see, it is very difficult to lead where you are not going, and it is absolutely imperative that you embody those principles which you wish to instill within other people.

It was near Valley Forge during the American Revolution. It was misty, and a slight rain was falling. Several Private foot soldiers were desperately trying to push a wagon up a steep and muddy incline.

A Corporal was barking out orders to the Private foot soldiers. A rider approached upon a horse. Because of the rain, the rider's hat was pulled over his eyes, and a raincoat covered his uniform and insignia. The rider said to the Private foot soldiers, "What are you fellows doing?" They responded, "We're trying to push this wagon up this incline." He then said to the Corporal, "Why aren't you helping them?" The Corporal rather condescendingly replied, "The reason I am not helping is because I am a Corporal and they are Privates. I am the one giving the orders."

With those words, the rider dismounted, and he made his way to the wagon with the foot soldiers. He put his shoulder to the wagon and with a big push he helped them get the wagon up the incline.

He then turned to the Corporal and said, "Corporal, if I can help you in any other way, please feel free to call upon me. You can find me at Commandant Headquarters in Valley Forge."

The Corporal said, "And for whom might I ask?"

As the horse reared-up and the rider pulled the bridle turning the horse's head to the side, he then saluted the Corporal and said, "Just ask for Washington, General George Washington!"

Is it any wonder that George Washington was such a great military leader? Is it any wonder that he was such a great presidential leader during the embryonic stage of our country's existence as a nation?

Yes, a leader leads by example.

Our Lord Jesus led by example. You remember, James and John came to Jesus and said, "Lord, when you come into your glory, you are going to remember us, aren't you? We want to sit at your right hand and at your left hand in glory."

Jesus did not respond by preaching a sermon to them. He did not say anything, but with His example He led them as He took a basin of water, a towel, and He got down before them and started to wash their dirty feet.

While they were arguing about the top, Jesus taught them an important lesson about humility and that true service begins at the very bottom.

Yes, a leader leads by example, and the interesting thing is there are many times when a leader is not even aware of his example.

Dr. Lovett Weems is President of Saint Paul School of Theology in Kansas City. It is one of our United Methodist Seminaries.

Dr. Weems did his undergraduate work at Millsaps College in Jackson, Mississippi.

While a student there, he tells of becoming friends with an older student who shared with him how a particular Philosophy Professor profoundly impacted his life, influenced him and ul-timately changed his life.

He went on to tell Lovett how that particular Professor, in a course he taught that year, had caused him to change his views on virtually every major issue of the day.

Lovett was intrigued, and he asked his friend what argumentation or rationale did the professor use.

The student replied that those issues never came up in class. Weems asked him to explain how the professor impacted his life in such a significant way.

The student then said, "Every time I went into that professor's class, I realized that I was in the presence of someone whose values, ideals and commitments were so much richer, deeper and broader than mine that I was challenged to the very core of my being. Who this professor was and what this professor represented became a challenge to all my littleness, narrowness and bigotry. My life was changed, and this professor may never know it."

That professor, by example, led that student in the most important area of life: his belief system, his thinking and his formulation of opinion.

Yes, a leader leads by example. And for a good leader it can become so instinctive that he is not even aware of it.

II.   The Principle of Excitement
(A leader leads with excitement.)

You see, a group, a team or an organization can be at one level. A goal can be at a higher level. Now, they are trying to get to that higher level and reach that goal. If they are excited and enthused about doing it, then two things will happen. *One*, they will attain the goal much more quickly, and *two*, and it will be a whole lot more fun in the process.

A leader knows how to get his followers excited and enthused about what they are doing because he knows excitement and enthusiasm lead to success.

He understands well the words of Ralph Waldo Emerson when he said, "Nothing great in this word was ever accomplished without enthusiasm!"

Lance Moore reminds us that the reason Euro Disney has not been as successful as Disney World is because they have great difficulty getting the French employees to smile, and if you've ever visited Disney World you know that excitement, enthusiasm and smiles are a major part of their success. A real leader knows how to get his people excited, and he knows how to put a smile upon their faces.

It was in the closing months of the American Civil War. General William Tecumsah Sherman's mighty Army of the Ohio was moving southeast towards Atlanta. They had fought and won battles at Chattanooga, Lookout Mountain and Chickamauga. They then proceeded to move through such places as Adairsville, Allatoona, Cassville, Buzzard's Roost and Reseca.

They then came to a seemingly impregnable natural barrier just northeast of Atlanta called Kennesaw Mountain.

To complicate things even more for the Union was the fact that some of the Confederacy's outstanding Generals were in that particular theater.

Generals like Joseph Johnston, or as he was so well known to the enemy as "Little Fighting" Joe Johnston.

Bishop Leonidas Polk, the Episcopal Bishop who had graduated from West Point, who had served as Rector of Saint Luke's Episcopal Church in Atlanta and who would fall and be killed at Kennesaw Mountain.

The native of Ireland, and great Corp Commander, General Patrick Cleburne.

There were also many other outstanding Generals such as General William Hardee and General John Bell Hood.

As one Historian described it, "At Kennesaw Mountain, the Confederates had the position and fire power."

But there was one part of the Union Army that attacked with a reckless abandon and an unrelenting resolve, and they sang with excitement as they attacked. Because of the attack, and especially because of the flanking movements of the Union, the Confederates fell back into Atlanta.

Then this Historian makes this interesting and arresting observation, "The Confederates had the position and the power, but the Union had the spirit and the song." And ultimately, spirit and song win out over position and power every time.

With his followers, a leader knows how to put a song within their hearts, a smile upon their faces, and spirit into their very beings.

A spiritual leader knows how to make his followers feel and know they are a part of God, and God is a part of them, and together there is no limit as to what they can do. For Jesus said, "With God all things are possible."

Yes, a spiritual leader knows how to make his people realize that they are a part of God and God is a part of them, and together they can win any battle, overcome any obstacle, and accomplish any task with excitement and enthusiasm.

The word enthusiasm is an interesting word. It is built from two Greek words, en which literally means "in," and theus which is a corruption of the Greek word theos, which means "God." And so, enthusiasm literally means to be "in God," and when you are in God and God is in you, it is amazing what you are capable of accomplishing. A spiritual leader makes his followers aware of this excitement and this enthusiasm that is deep within. Yes, a leader leads with excitement.

How can you become an effective leader? A starting point is to study and understand the principles of example and excitement, and then by God's grace learn to implement and make them a part of your leadership style.

It is my prayer that our example will reflect the spirit and mind of Christ, and our excitement will be a deep joy, placed by God and welling up within.

When we thus lead by example and through excitement, then we will become the leaders for whom God is looking.

Chapter 19
Looking For Leaders

LEADERSHIP THROUGH EXPECTATION AND TOWARDS EXCELLENCE
"And what you have heard from me before many witnesses,
commit to faithful people who will be able to teach others also."
(II Timothy 2:2)
Part II in Series on "Leadership"

With this chapter we continue our series on the theme of "Leadership." The title of the series is <u>Looking For Leaders</u>.

As we pointed out in the last chapter, aside from Jesus the greatest leader in the New Testament was the Apostle Paul. He founded all those many churches in the New Testament. He organized numerous missionary journeys, and he led and directed many men and women into full time Christian ministry. One person upon whom he had a tremendous influence was a young man by the name of Timothy. He wrote two letters to Timothy giving to him instruction and showing him how to be a leader.

In the second letter, the second chapter, the second verse, Paul says to Timothy, "The things I have taught you, I want you to commit to others so they can teach also." And what Paul was saying to Timothy was this, "Timothy, just as I have taught you to lead, so I want you to teach others to lead so they can in turn teach others because the church is beginning to grow, and there is a real need for leaders."

And just as there was a need for leaders in the First Century, so there is a need for leaders in this day in which we live.

Leaders are needed in the home.

Leaders are needed in the school.

Leaders are needed in the church.

Leaders are needed in the business sector.

Leaders are needed in athletics.

Leaders are needed in government.

Yes, there is a real need for leaders in this day in which we live, and people will follow a leader.

My Brother, John Ed, told of a minister in Florida who conducted a funeral on a Saturday afternoon. Following the funeral service, the Director of the Funeral Home asked the minister if he would mind leading the procession from the funeral home to the cemetery. He shared with the minister that he had two other funerals on that Saturday afternoon, and it would be a great help to him. Since the minister had conducted several funerals there before, he told the Director that he would be glad to help him in that way.

Following the funeral, the minister pulled out of the funeral home parking lot leading the procession of 49 cars.

He pulled onto the by-pass, and the funeral procession was making its way toward the cemetery. John Ed said the minister then reached down and turned on the radio. It was the Saturday afternoon of the Auburn/Florida game, and he became wrapped up in the ball game. He momentarily forgot about the funeral procession.

He then looked over to the right, and he saw a Wal-Mart. He remembered that his wife had told him to pick up some things at Wal-Mart, so he immediately turned into the Wal-Mart parking lot. All of those cars followed along behind him. Have you ever seen a funeral procession of 49 cars with their lights on trying to weave through a Wal-Mart parking lot on a Saturday afternoon? Yes, people follow when someone leads.

But the key is not for us just to be leaders, but for us to become effective leaders. Now, how can we become effective leaders? I believe if our leadership is going to be effective then there are certain principles that must be understood, learned and implemented. In our last chapter we looked at the first two principles. I want us to look at two others today, we will consider two in the next message, and then two in the final study. In the way of review, allow me to say just a word about the two principles we discussed in the last chapter.

Principle one is the Principle of Example. A leader leads by example. If you are going to be a leader, then people have got to know that you know where you are going because it is very difficult to lead where you are not going, and it is absolutely imperative that you embody within yourself those principles which you wish to instill within other people. A leader leads by example.

The second principle is the Principle of Excitement. As I pointed out last week, you can have a group, a team or an organization on one level. A goal is on a higher level. The purpose of that organization is to attain that goal. Now, if the organization and team members are enthused and excited about what they are doing, then two things will happen: *one*, they will attain the goal a whole lot more quickly, and *two*, it will be a whole lot more fun in the process.

Yes, a leader leads with excitement. With his/her followers, a leader knows how to put a smile upon their faces, a song within their hearts, and spirit into their being. Yes, a leader leads with excitement and enthusiasm.

In addition to these two principles, the two principles I want us to consider in our message today are:

III.   The Principle of Expectation
A leader leads through expectation.
IV.   The Principle of Excellence
A leader leads towards excellence.

125

III. The Principle of Expectation
(A leader leads through expectation.)

A leader knows how to instill expectant hope within the minds of his followers. A leader know how to instill expectant hope within the hearts of his followers.

A leader understands well the words in the Book of Proverbs when the wise writer says, "Where there is no vision, the people perish." A leader not only has a vision, but he is able to share that vision with others and then allow others to gain ownership of that vision with him.

Someone once said to Helen Keller, that dear lady who was enshrouded in a world of darkness because of her blindness, "It must be awful to be blind. I cannot think of anything any worse!"

Helen Keller said, "Oh, there is something worse than blindness, and that is to have eyes and not be able to see." It is to have eyes and have no vision.

A real leader not only has eyes, and he not only can see, but he can also get others to see with him.

I have a good friend who does the music at the Epcot Center in Disney World. He was present the night that Epcot opened a few years ago. He had the privilege of sitting in the booth with Mrs. Walt Disney. It was the first time that laser light show had ever been presented to the public. It was a phenomenal experience.

People came from all over the world to those opening ceremonies. They watched in awe and amazement for they had never seen anything like it.

Afterwards, Derrick Johnson overheard a reporter say to Mrs. Disney, "This is unbelievable! None of us ever dreamed you could see something like this." And then he said, "There is one thing I regret. I am so sorry that Walt died, and he never got to see it."

Quick as a flash, Derrick said that Mrs. Disney responded to him and said, "Oh, Walt did see it. Walt saw it 20 years ago, and if Walt had not seen it 20 years ago, we would not be seeing it tonight." Yes, a leader is a visionary, and a leader leads with expectant hope.

I said earlier that Paul, aside from Jesus, was the greatest leader in the New Testament. I believe Moses was the greatest leader in the Old Testament. We remember Moses in the Book of Exodus and how those many plagues came upon Egypt. Moses led the children of Israel through the Red Sea and into the wilderness. They spent 40 years in the wilderness, and during that time they were very hungry, and they were very tired. The Bible says they ate "manna" and "quail" in the wilderness. But through that pilgrimage and through that journey, Moses kept before them the expectant hope of a land that "flowed with milk and honey."

I can understand why the Hebrew children were hungry if all they had to eat was manna and quail. I don't know that I've ever eaten any manna, but I have eaten quail, and that is about as near nothing as anything I've ever eaten.

I was preaching in a revival once, and the dear people had quail for supper. I looked at that little quail on my plate, and that was the poorest and least looking little bird I think I've ever seen. I struggled, labored and toiled trying to get some meat off that bony little bird, but I had very little luck. I may be prejudiced because I'm use to eating fried chicken, but I just didn't get much to eat that night. Now, I am aware that there are some quail that perhaps provide more meat, but I did not get much that night.

So I can understand why they were tired and hungry. But all through that pilgrimage, Moses kept before his people the expectant hope that just ahead, just over the Jordan River, there was "a land that flowed with milk and honey."

And a leader knows how to lead his people through expectant hope.

IV. The Principle of Excellence
   (A leader leads towards excellence.)

I remember reading Peters and Waterman's book, In Search of Excellence. The book is the result of an indepth study that the authors did in over 40 of the leading companies in Corporate America. From that study they gleaned eight principles which they contend are essential to and germane for success in the corporate world.

When you read that volume and other similar volumes such as A Passion For Excellence, The Effective Executive, and other like books, the over-arching dynamic I find is this: "If an organization or a corporation is going to be successful, there must be a leader who is committed to the principle of excellence!"

I remember when I was ordained into the United Methodist ministry. I vividly remember standing before the bar of the Annual Conference, and I recall the questions the Bishop asked me along with the other ordinands. Two of the questions were, "Are you going on to perfection?" and, "Do you expect to be made perfect in love in this life?" Those are questions that are deeply rooted in our Methodist tradition and in the theology of John Wesley, and I suppose they have been asked of every Methodist minister since the time of Wesley.

But I remember when the Bishop lifted those questions up to us. I'll be honest with you. I was not real sure how to answer them. In our church here, we have a number of ministers, and I would be interested to know how they answered those questions. "Are you going on to perfection?" As I stood there, I knew I had to tell the truth. The good Lord, the Bishop and all the District Superintendents were there looking at us, and I could not tell a lie. I felt as though they all were looking directly at me. That is a somber experience.

I'll tell you what I thought about when he asked that question. I remembered the words of the philosopher when he said, "Know thyself!" And I knew myself, and I knew I was a long ways from being perfect, and I knew I had a lot of work to do if I was ever going to attain that goal.

I also remember that I looked around at some of the other ministers standing there, and I hoped to gain a little help from them. I remember how serious and solemn they looked, and I thought to myself, "They look like they are well on their way to perfection." I remember I saw one or two who looked as though they had already made it to perfection.

I don't know what the others said, but I remember I sort of smiled to myself and said under my breath, "I am going to do the very best I can."

But after several years in the ministry, I have realized those questions are not matters to smile about because they are very serious. We should all strive for perfection everyday. Jesus said, "Be ye perfect even as your Father in heaven is perfect," and if we are not striving for perfection in ministry then we will be satisfied with mediocrity in ministry. And my friend, what is true in ministry is true in every walk of life – your job, your vocation, your studies – if you are not striving for perfection, then you will settle for mediocrity because strival for perfection is at the very basis of a purposeful and meaningful life.

Sometime ago I was visiting in the office of a dear friend. I noticed as I walked into his office that there was a big sign on his wall that read, "Perfection is our goal, but we will settle for excellence." I like that: "Perfection is our goal, but we will settle for excellence." For unless our goal is to be the very best then we will never be all that we are capable of becoming.

I think one of the great professional football coaches and leaders was Tom Landry. You remember, he coached the Dallas Cowboys, and many people looked upon them as America's team. In the 1972 Super Bowl, the Dallas Cowboys beat the Miami Dolphins by a score of 24-3. Following the game, a reporter was talking with Nick Buoniconti, the great middle linebacker for the Dolphins. Buoniconti said, "I can't understand why we lost! From the first day of camp our goal has been to reach the Super Bowl. Then we came here and lost." Buoniconti then later said, "Maybe the Cowboys won because our goal was the reach the Super Bowl, but their goal was to win the Super Bowl."

Yes, at the beginning of the season the goal of the Dolphins was to get to the Super Bowl. The goal of the Dallas Cowboys was to win the Super Bowl, and that made all the difference in the world. Don't you see, there is a difference, and that difference is excellence. And a true and effective leader will help you see that difference and work toward attaining that goal of excellence.

If you ever visit the British Museum in London, you will see Thomas Gray's masterpiece, "Elegy Written in a Country Churchyard." I think it is one of the most beautiful poems that has ever been written.

When we did our pulpit exchange in England, we not only served the Roundhay

Church in Leeds, but I also preached once a week in the little country village of Thorner just outside of Leeds. My wife and I would drive out two or three times a week to preach and to visit the members in that little country village. I always looked forward to going out there. Most of the members were quite elderly, and I was so amazed with their knowledge and recall of British history. We would sit and talk with them for hours about the history of England.

Like many little villages in England, there is an Anglican church right in the middle of the community. It appeared to me that most of them were constructed from a dark red brick, and most of them were surrounded by quaint cemeteries and church yards. I enjoyed walking through the church yard of that Anglican cemetery and reading the names on the head stones. Many of the stones over the sleeping bodies dated back to the 19th and 18th Centuries. I remember, when I walked in that quaint and shady cemetery, I thought to myself that this is the very type of place a poet would yearn to come, sit, reflect and write his poetry. I think I felt something of what Thomas Gray felt many years ago.

Yes, as I said, "Elegy Written in a Country Church Yard" is one of the most beautiful poems that has ever been written. As a preacher and communicator, I am very much interested in words, and when you read this beautiful poem, it appears that every word was carefully, almost perfectly chosen.

When I first read the poem I thought that perhaps Gray just sat down and in one sitting wrote it. But when you visit the British Museum, you discover that was not the case. Gray wrote the first draft, and he was not satisfied. He then wrote a second draft, then a third, then a fourth and on and on. He wrote for eight years, and he finally completed it with the 75th draft. There in the British Museum on display, you can see all 75 copies in succession. All of them were penned by hand.

As you stand there, it makes cold chills run up and down your back. It is a moving experience to stand there and think of eight years and 75 manuscripts, but that long and winding road led to the goal of excellence for Gray.

A leader, an effective leader, a true leader will take you by the hand, lead you down that same road, no matter how winding and long, and not be satisfied until you have attained the goal of excellence.

Yes, Paul wrote to Timothy and said, "As you've learned from me, so I want you to teach others so they in turn can lead others because we are looking for leaders." And just as there was a need for leaders in the First Century, so there is a need for leaders today. There is a need for effective leaders who will lead by example, with excitement, through expectation and towards excellence. I'll challenge you today – will you be that leader?

Chapter 20
Looking For Leaders

LEADERSHIP BY EMPOWERMENT AND WITH ENCOURAGEMENT

"And what you have heard from me before many witnesses,
commit to faithful people who will be able to teach others also."
(II Timothy 2:2)
Part III in Series on "Leadership"

Today we continue our study on the theme of "Leadership." It is entitled Looking For Leaders.

As we have said previously, aside from Jesus, the greatest leader in the New Testament was the Apostle Paul. Paul founded those many churches. Paul organized numerous missionary journeys, and Paul directed and led many men and women into full time ministry.

One young man upon whom Paul had a profound influence was Timothy. Paul wrote two letters to Timothy giving to him words of inspiration and instruction. In the second chapter, the second letter, the second verse, we find the words that we are using as our text for this entire series of sermons as Paul says, "And what you have heard from me before many witnesses, commit to faithful people who will be able to teach others also."

And what Paul is saying is this: "Timothy, the Church is starting to grow. As I've taught you to be a leader, so I want you to teach others to lead so they in turn can teach even others because there is a need for leadership within in the Church." And just as there was a need for leadership in the First Century, so there is a need for leadership in this day in which we live.

Now, I might point out that there is not just a need for leaders, but there is a need for effective leadership. How can a person be an effective leader? I believe there are certain principles that must be understood, learned and then implemented if our leadership is going to be effective. In the first two studies we discussed four principles of leadership. In the way of review, allow me to say just a brief word about them, and then we will consider two other principles in this message.

One, a leader leads by example. You see, it is difficult to lead where you are not going, and it is absolutely imperative that you embody within yourself those principles which you wish to share with other people.

Two, a leader leads with excitement. With her followers, a leader knows how to put a smile upon their faces, a song within their hearts, spirit into their being and spring into their step. A leader leads with excitement.

Three, a leader leads through expectation. A leader knows how to instill expectant

130

hope within the hearts and minds of his followers.

Four, a leader leads towards excellence. A leader will lead his people towards the lofty, noble and worthy goal of excellence because he wants the very best for them.

Now, in addition to these principles, I want us to consider Principles V and VI.

V. The Principle of Empowerment
A leader leads by empowerment.
VI. The Principle of Encouragement
A leader leads with encouragement.

V. The Principle of Empowerment
(A leader leads by empowerment.)

And when I speak of the Principle of Empowerment, I simply mean a leader knows how to delegate responsibility and then empower the person to discharge that responsibility.

Now, there are many types of leadership. As I've researched and prpared this series of studies, I've attempted to read every-thing I could find on the subject of leadership, and there are many styles of ecclesiastical leadership and corporate leadership. They range from the laissez faire style to the autocratic style, with varying styles in between. And the experts tell us that each style has its own merit, and each style is good in itself depending upon the personality of the individual who leads.

My style of leadership as a Senior Minister is to surround myself with the very best people possible, show them what they are supposed to do, give them the authority to do it, and then get out of the way and let them do it. And I will let you in on a little secret. If you surround yourself with great people, it will make you look like you are a great leader whether you are a good leader or not.

I have a friend who is a minister in another Annual Conference, and we were discussing styles of leadership, and he said, "George, I totally disagree with you."

He said, "I am a nuts and bolts type person. I run a tight ship. I have all of my leaders submit to me an outline, in memorandum form, any ministry they wish to implement or any money they want to spend. My Staff-Parish Relations Committee, my Finance Committee, my Trustees, and all of the Work Areas are required to do this. I require the same of all our salaried staff from our nursery workers right up to our janitorial people. I attend all the meetings, and I know everything that is going on in my church."

When this friend made that statement, I thought of an observation my Brother, John Ed, made when he said, "If you know everything that is going on in a church, it usually means that you do not have a lot going on in a church."

This minister went on to say, "I am even more stringent with my Program staff. But I have them all submit to me in memorandum form what they want to do. I ask them to share with me the theological justification as well as the ministerial objective of the expenditure of that money or the implementation of that ministry. I then will take the memorandum, and I will spend a great deal of time studying it and praying over it. One, I will see if it has ecclesiastical integrity, and secondly, I will see if it parallels my theological flow of ministry. If I feel comfortable with it, I then will initial it and give to that respective committee or person the 'go ahead.'"

Now, I am sure that is a very effective and valid style of leadership. But I will share with you three observations about this particular minister. *One*, he moves every two to three years to another church. *Two*, he has a big turnover in staff. And *three*, he is all the time sitting in his office with his door closed studying and reading memorandums.

You see, the corollary to the Principle of Empowerment – or the key to the Principle of Empowerment is trust. A leader must trust the people who are a part of his organization, and the trust level must be very high. A wise leader recognizes this, and a wise leader will trust his people, and he will constantly let them know that he trusts them and believes in them.

And so, the Principle of Empowerment is very important.

In their book, Leading and Managing Your Church, George and Logan remind us of the account in Exodus, chapter 18, when Moses was leading the Hebrew children in the wilderness. Moses was having a difficult time getting all those people organized and leading them.

Then he was approached by his father-in-law, Jethro. Aren't we thankful for our fathers and our father-in-laws? I imagine Jethro put his arm around Moses and said something to this effect, "Moses, son, you are going to kill yourself trying to lead all of these people by yourself. You organize the people on one level and make them accountable to leaders on another level. You then make those leaders accountable to other leaders on another level, and then let those leaders be accountable to you."

George and Logan refer to this in Biblical leadership as "The Jethro Principle," and in actuality it is simply this Principle of Empowerment, trust and delegation. And so, a wise leader leads by empowerment.

VI. The Principle of Encouragement
   (A leader leads with encouragement.)

And a wise leader will never embarrass his people in front of a large group because a wise leader knows that chastisement and castigation lead to humiliation and discouragement, while encouragement results in productivity and a build up of confidence.

Now, to be sure, there are times when a correction is called for or a reprimand is needed. In this case, a wise leader will meet with the person either one-on-one or in a small group to address the problem, and the approach will always be to help and not hurt. It will be to build up and not break down. It will be to encourage and not discourage.

And so, a leader leads with encouragement.

I believe a leader leads with encouragement in two ways. *One*, at times that encouragement will be characterized by spirit, robust spirit, and at other times it will be characterized by sensitivity, reflective sensitivity.

One, an effective leader will encourage with spirit, with robust spirit.

It was the 1950 NFL Championship game. The Cleveland Browns were playing the Los Angeles Rams. The Browns were trailing by one point with less that two minutes left in the game. They were in Ram territory. Cleveland had one of the best field goal kickers in the game, a fellow by the name of Lou Grozza. They called him "Lou the toe" Grozza.

They were close enough for Grozza to kick a field goal, but the quarterback, Otto Graham, an All-Pro, decided to try another running play. By attempting another running play, he could move the ball further down field, nearer the center of the field, and he also could eliminate some time on the clock. But guess what happened? You're right, he fumbled, and Los Angeles recovered the ball.

When Otto Graham came off the field he was met by his coach, Paul Brown. Coach Brown, with spirit, encouraged Otto Graham as he said to him, "Don't worry, Otts, we're still going to get them." As Coach Brown spoke to Graham, Graham felt that his coach knew he could still win the ball game for them.

Brown told them that their defense would hold, Graham could lead them back down the field and they could win the game.

You study the record. The defense did hold. Otto Graham did lead them back down the field, and Grozza kicked a field goal to give the Browns a 30-28 victory.

Afterwards, Otto Graham would say, "Paul Brown knew when to kick you in the pants and when to pat you on the shoulder. If he had glared at me, we would have lost. His encouragement gave me so much confidence, and I passed on that confidence to my teammates in the huddle, and we went right down the field and got three points. That is a part of coaching that people don't understand."

Yes, Otto Graham felt that if his coach had belittled or demeaned him it would have destroyed his confidence. But when he supported him with those spirited words of encouragement, Otto Graham knew right then that he wanted to win that game not only for himself, not only for the Browns, not only for the Cleveland organization, but also for his coach – his leader – who believed in him.

Yes, it was the spirited encouragement of that leader that led the team to victory.

Yes, a leader leads with spirited encouragement.

Many Georgians are familiar with the name of Bob Strickland. He served as Chairman of the Board of Trustees at Emory University. He died the day before he was to step down as Chairman of the Board of Trustees at Emory. He was one the outstanding community and state leaders in Georgia.

Bob Strickland's next-door neighbor was Joseph R. Bankoff, an Atlanta attorney. Following the death of Bob Strickland, Joseph Bankoff wrote these moving lines in a memorial tribute about his dear friend that appeared in the *Atlanta Constitution*.

Bankoff said, "What made him special, however, was that he could sell people on themselves. He could see potential in others that they did not see in themselves. He could find opportunities in what others saw only as problems. I don't think he was so much smarter than others; he was just so sure that his friends and colleagues could rise to any challenge. He didn't mean that they could do it; he was sure that they would. After they finished the simple service for Bob Strickland they rolled his casket down the aisle. We all stood and knew that one of our best cheerleaders was passing by."

Bob Strickland was a great leader. Bob Strickland knew how to lead with spirited encouragement.

Secondly, a leader encourages with <u>sensitivity</u>, reflective sensitivity.

You see, an effective leader understands human nature. There are times when a leader encourages as a cheerleader, but there are other times when a leader encourages as a confidante.

There are times when an effective leader encourages with robust spirit, but there are other times when he encourages with reflective sensitivity.

I heard a minister share this story. It occurred several years ago.

An elephant was shipped from India to England. He was sold to the circus, and he immediately became the showpiece of the circus. They named him Bozo.

He was a gentle and loving elephant, and people, especially children, came from all over England to see him. It is said that as each child gave him a peanut, Bozo seemed to smile at that child as he swallowed the peanut that was given to him.

Then one day Bozo's temperament radically changed. He charged the person who was cleaning his cage. He then bellowed in a mean-spirited way at the children standing around, and he made them cry.

The owner then made the decision that Bozo would have to be exterminated. The owner decided to sell tickets to the execution. It is a sad commentary, but the tickets immediately sold-out.

The day of the killing arrived, and the arena was filled to capacity. Every place was taken as the people with a sadistic glee anticipated the execution. There below them in a huge cage sat Bozo all alone. Bozo was shifting his eyes to each side sensing the eery and sinister feeling in the air.

Three men with high powered rifles were placed in selected and strategic positions around the cage. At the appointed time, the owner was to raise his arm to give the riflemen the signal to shoot. Just prior to the signal, a stranger walked down from the crowd and approached the gate. He rattled the gate, and then he said to the owner, "Sir, Bozo is not a bad elephant. Please let me go in and stand by him."

At first, the owner refused, but then he realized that the presence of the man in the cage would simply add to the sensation of the event. He then told the stranger that he would permit him to go into the cage if he would sign a waiver absolving him of any responsibility. The stranger signed the waiver, and then he started to make his way towards the center of the cage.

All eyes were focused upon the stranger as he started to walk towards Bozo. When Bozo realized that somebody was in the cage and walking near him, Bozo then rared up on his hind legs. He lifted his trunk, and he trumpeted loudly.

The stranger continued to walk towards Bozo, and then he started to speak in a strange and unusual language. The sound was almost mystical in its presentation. As the stranger got closer to Bozo, the more clearly Bozo heard the language.

Bozo then came down upon all four feet. He fell to his knees, and then he gracefully laid down upon his stomach.

Bozo started to tremble. He almost playfully started to wave his trunk back and forth. Then those who were there said Bozo started to cry.

The stranger stood next to Bozo, and he gently patted him on the forehead. Then the stranger placed his cheek against the face of Bozo, and he put his arms out and held the elephant.

It was a moving scene as tears came to the eyes of the people in the arena.

The stranger then guided Bozo to his feet, and he led Bozo around the arena. Notice, he led Bozo.

He then led Bozo to the owner. The stranger said to the owner, "Sir, Bozo is a good elephant. But you must realize that he is not from England. He is from India. He is homesick for a language that he can understand."

By the way, that stranger's name was Rudyard Kipling.

In my opinion, Rudyard Kipling was a great leader. He was a great leader because he knew how to speak a language that could be understood, but he was also an effective leader because he knew how to lead with encouragement that was characterized by sensitivity and understanding.

And an effective leader knows the value of encouragement. Whether it's leading an animal, a person or an organization, a wise and effective leader knows when to encourage with reflective sensitivity and when to encourage with robust spirit. But an effective leader always knows the power of the Principle of Encouragement, and he leads with encouragement.

Yes, Paul wrote to Timothy and said, "Timothy, the Church is starting to grow, and there is a need for leaders." Just as there was a need for leaders in the First Century, so there is a need for leaders in this day in which we live.

Looking for leaders. Leaders that will lead by example. Leaders that will lead with excitement. Leaders that will lead through expectation. Leaders that will lead towards excellence. Leaders that will lead by empowerment, and leaders that will lead with encouragement.

It is my prayer that you will be that leader.

LEADERSHIP WITH ENDURANCE AND BY ENDUEMENT

"And what you've heard from me before many witnesses,
commit to faithful people who will be able to teach others also."
(II Timothy 2:2)
Part IV in Series on "Leadership"

This is the fourth and final study in our series on the theme of "Leadership" to a close. The title of the study is <u>Looking For Leaders</u>.

As we've said previously, the second greatest leader in the New Testament was the Apostle Paul. As a leader, he founded those many churches. As a leader, he organized those many missionary journeys. As a leader, he directed and led many men and women into full-time ministry.

One person upon whom he had a tremendous influence was Timothy. He wrote two letters to Timothy, and in these letters he gives to him instruction on how to be an effective leader. In the second letter, the second chapter, the second verse, we find the words that we've used as a text for this entire series of studies.

In this verse, Paul says, "The things I have taught you and the things you have heard from me, I want you to commit to others so they can teach too."

And what Paul was saying to Timothy was this, "Timothy, as I've taught you to be a leader, so I want you to teach others so they in turn can teach others to lead also, because the church is starting to grow, and there is a need for leaders."

Now, just as there was a need for leaders in the First Century, so there is a need for leaders in this day in which we live.

Yes, leaders are needed on all fronts, and there is a need not only for just leaders, but the need is for effective leadership. The need is for leadership that is a careful balance between competence and character.

One of my closest friends in Auburn was Burl Galloway. Burl died in March of this year, and I miss him. I loved Burl so much. He was very interested in this series on leadership because he presented corporate seminars on leadership around the nation. He shared with me one of his work manuals in which he quotes General Norman Schwarzkoff in a speech to the Corps of Cadets at the United States Military Academy. General Schwarzkoff said,

> "I've met a lot of leaders in the Army who were very competent, but they
> didn't have character. And for every job they did well, they sought reward
> in the form of promotions, in the form of awards and decorations, in the
> form of getting ahead at the expense of someone else, in the form of another

piece of paper that awarded them another degree – a sure road to the top. You see, they were competent people, but they lacked character.

I've also met a lot of leaders who had superb character but who lacked competence. They weren't willing to pay the price of leadership, to go the extra mile, because that's what it took to be a great leader."

You see, competence and character are the twin oars that row the boat of leadership. Competence and caring are the banks upon which the river of effective leadership flows. Now, how can a person lead with competence and character?

I personally believe there are certain principles that must be understood and learned. And leadership is not something we are born with, but it is something we learn. Shakespeare said, "Everyone is born a baby, not a leader." And so, I believe these principles must be: *one*, understood; *two*, learned; and *three*, then implemented and applied.

As I've created and developed these principles, I've arranged them so that each builds one upon the other. I want you to notice their progression as they develop. I also want you to notice that leadership begins with the Principle of Example, and it concludes with the Principle of Enduement.

Since the principles build upon each other, in the way of review allow me to say just a brief word about each.

One, a leader leads <u>by example</u>, and this is where leadership begins,for you see, leadership is in actuality and expression of who you are and what you are, and what you believe and represent. It is very difficult to lead where you are not going, and it is absolutely imperative that you embody those principles which you wish to share with other people.

Secondly, a leader leads <u>with excitement</u>. With his followers, a leader knows how to put a smile upon their faces. He knows how to put a song within their hearts. He knows how to put spirit into their being, and he knows how to put spring into their step. Yes, a leader leads with excitement and enthusiasm.

Thirdly, a leader leads <u>through expectation</u>. A leader knows how to instill expectant hope within the hearts and minds of his followers. A leader is a visionary, and he knows how to get his people not only to share the vision, but even more importantly, he knows how to get them to claim ownership of the vision.

Fourthly, a leader leads <u>towards excellence</u>. An effective leader always leads towards the high, lofty and noble goal of excellence because a leader wants the very best for his people.

Fifthly, a leader leads <u>by empowerment</u>. The three parts of this principle are *one*, trust; *two*, delegation; and *three*, empowerment. An effective leader will trust his people, and because of this trust he will delegate responsibility to them. He then will empower them to discharge the responsibility that has been delegated to them.

Sixthly, a leader leads with <u>encouragement</u>. An effective leader encourages with spirit and with sensitivity. An effective leader understands human nature, and at times a leader will encourage with robust spirit and at other times with reflective sensitivity, but an effective leader always leads with encouragement.

The Kisi people in Liberia, West Africa, define encouragement in this proverbial statement: "When a man steps into the center of the circle to dance and no one claps, he will soon tire and sit down; but if everyone claps, he will dance all night." An effective leader knows how to encourage his followers to dance all night. And this naturally leads us to Principle VII.

VII.   The Principle of Endurance
   (A leader leads with endurance.)

Yes, a leader leads with endurance. When I was in seminary I became dear friends with a minister by the name of Fred Lofton. Fred and I corresponded afterwards, and he would always sign by his name this verse of Scripture, "Those who endure to the end shall be saved."

That is a powerful verse of Scripture, and I would go on to say, "Those who endure to the end also endure to the end because they are led by an effective leader."

You see, to endure means you have to constantly stay with it.

Bishop Moore told the story of a little boy with a small shovel who was trying to dig through a big bank of snow. He was laboriously engaged in the task when a man passed by and saw the lad. He said to the little boy, "Son, what are you doing?" The little boy replied, "Mister, I am digging through this bank of snow!"

The man then asked, "How is a little boy like you with such a small shovel ever going to dig through that huge drift of snow?" The little boy, without stopping, glanced out of the corner of his eye and said, "By giving it all I've got, and by staying with it, Sir; by staying with it!"

And that is the philosophy of an effective leader. An effective leader "gives it all he's got, and he stays with it, Sir, he stays with it."

Yes, an effective leader stays with it even when things aren't going well. An effective leader stays with it even when he loses some of the battles.

This past week I was reading about George Washington's military career. This article pointed out that Washington lost more battles than he won, but he stayed with it, he endured, and he ultimately won the war, and in the final analysis that is what really counts.

At the surrender ceremony in Yorktown, when the British General Cornwallis gave to Washington his sword, which was the gallant custom in that day, his first words to Washington were, "Sir, I salute you as a great leader."

Many people consider Abraham Lincoln as the greatest leader of our nation, but you study his political career and you will discover that he lost his first several political battles. You study his military career as Commander in Chief of the Union Army, and you will discover he lost many Civil War battles; but Lincoln stayed with it, issued the Emancipation Proclamation which was one of the first real steps forward in social justice, held the Union together, and he ultimately won the war. He endured to the end.

To be sure, there will be times when we lose some of the battles. There will be times when we are interrupted, but an effective leader works through those interruptions, stays with it and endures to the end.

One of the great leaders in Alabama Methodism was Dr. Ed Kimbrough. While he was minister of the Trinity Methodist Church in Birmingham, he suffered a heart attack one Sunday morning while he was preaching. He was out of the pulpit for several months. On the Sunday he returned, those who were present said that as he ascended to the pulpit to preach, his first words were, "As I was saying when I was interrupted." Now, that is the mark of a great leader.

Yes, A great leader sees interruptions as temporary, and he always sees those interruptions not as stumbling blocks that cause us to falter and fail, but as stepping stones that lead us upward and onward to the lighted heights of glorious and productive living.

Yes, an effective leader endures and stays with it until the job is done. He stays with it until the task is completed. He stays with it until the goal is reached; and he stays with it until the victory is won.

I am impressed with leadership principles in the military, and I especially like the spirit of the U.S. Coast Guard.

A ship at sea encountered a terrible storm. A Coast Guard Clipper received orders to go into the storm and rescue the people on the ship. When the Captain told the sailors aboard where they were going, a young sailor approached the Captain and said, "Captain, if we go out, we may not come back." The Captain looked at the young man and said, "Sailor, we are members of the U.S. Coast Guard. We have orders to go out. We have to go out, but we don't have to come back!"

That is the enduring spirit in which an effective and great leader leads.

A leader leads with endurance.

VIII. The Principle of Enduement
(A leader leads with enduement.)

Now, when I speak of the Principle of Enduement I simply mean a leader lets his people know that they are not alone. An effective leader lets his people know they are led by someone greater than the leader himself, and that someone is our God.

Now, the reason I used the word enduement is because it is a good Bible word.

We began this series of studies by saying that Paul was the second greatest leader in the New Testament. Now, that could be debated as there are some who would consider Peter the second greatest leader in the New Testament, but the greatest leader in the New Testament is not debatable because we all agree it was our Lord and Savior Jesus Christ.

After the resurrection, in Luke 24:49, Jesus instructed his followers to go to the City of Jerusalem and wait there "until they were endued with power from on high."

The word endued is an interesting word in the Greek. It is one of those words we have transliterated, almost bodily, from the Greek into the English, and it is no wonder that many translators have taken advantage of this linguistical link to render the verb simply as <u>endued</u>.

Professor Detzler points out that the Greek term *enduo* means "to clothe." Literally it means "to draw on," but in the Greek New Testament, its reference always is to "clothing oneself."

As a matter of fact, the <u>Amplified New Testament</u> renders this verse from Luke to read, "But remain in the city until you are clothed with power from on high."

Now, what does this mean for a leader, and how is it applicable to the subject of leadership?

One, it means we are <u>clothed</u> in God's great power. Notice in the verse, Luke 24:49, that they were instructed to go to Jerusalem and wait until they were endued. With what were they to be endued? "Wait until you are endued with <u>power</u> from on high."

A leader lets his people know that they are clothed with God's great power. From a Christian perspective, a leader lets his people know they are operating on the level of a power that exceeds their own, for it is the power of our omnipotent God.

John Killinger told of when Dr. Perry Biddle was preaching in a church in Scotland. He took as his text the verse, "The Lord God omnipotent reignt." He read the text at the beginning of the sermon, and he quoted those words throughout the message. Towards the end of the sermon he got so blessed as he shared those words until he shouted them.

After the sermon, as in the custom in Scotland and England when a guest minister preaches, one of the officials of the church went with Dr. Biddle to the back of the church to greet the members of the congregation as they left. Two elderly women approached Dr. Biddle, and the church leader explained that both of them were nearly deaf and could hardly hear. One of the women took Perry by the hand and said, "I didn't hear anythin' you said today, Minister, except 'The Lord God omnipotent reignt!'" And then as she turned to leave she quickly added with a twinkle in her eye, "But that's all that really matters, isn't it?"

It <u>is</u> all that really matters, and because our Lord God omnipotent does reign, He also rains down His power upon His children to be His people about His business.

And so, the Principle of Enduement means we are clothed with His great power.

Secondly, it means we are <u>carried</u> with His great strength.

Now, I want you to get the picture that a Christian leader should paint for his followers. We have God's great power above us and upon us, and we have His great strength beneath us carrying us.

This is reflected in the words of the Gospel song that we sing:

What a fellowship, what a joy divine,
Leaning on the everlasting arms.

How firm a foundation ye saints of the Lord,
Is laid for your faith in his excellent word!
The soul that on Jesus still leans for repose,
I will not, I will not desert to its foes.

Yes, we have God's power clothing us from above and His mighty arms carrying us and strengthening us below.

There was a husband, a wife and a little girl. The little girl was crippled and she could not walk a step. One afternoon the father came home, and he had in his arms a gift for his wife. He walked into the den, and he said to his little girl who was sitting there, "Honey, where is your mother? I have a gift for her."

As the eyes of little girls tend to do, they brightened at the thought of a gift for her mother. She said to her dad, "Mother is upstairs in her room." Then the little girl said to her father, "Daddy, would you please let me take the gift to Mother?"

The father looked at his little crippled daughter, he swallowed hard and said, "Sweetheart, you cannot walk a step. You cannot take this present up the stairs to your Mother."

The girl then said, "I know, Daddy, but I can take the gift from you, and I can carry it in my arms. You then can take me, and you can carry me in your strong arms, and I then can give the gift to Mother."

And my friend, whether you are delivering a package, sharing a gift, making a sale, attempting to win some type of victory, or if you are simply a member of the team or organization, a wise leader will let you know that you are not doing it alone, but you are carried in the strong arms of your God, and He can enable you to accomplish any task.

Yes, the Principle of Enduement means we are clothed in His spirit, we are carried by His great strength, but it also means we are:

Thirdly, it means we are capable of accomplishing great things.

William Carey, the highly effective missionary from England, said, "Expect great things from God, and attempt great things for God!"

An effective leader lets you know, that because of this great power from above and this great strength from beneath, that you are capable of accomplishing great things around about you. An effective leader lets you know that with God's grace your potential is unlimited, the sky is the limit, and you are capable of accomplishing great things because of Him.

Yes, Paul wrote to his friend Timothy and said, "Timothy, there is a need for leaders." And just as there was a need for leaders in that day, so there is a need for leaders in this day.

Looking for leaders. Looking for leaders who will lead by example, with excitement, through expectation, towards excellence, by empowerment, with encouragement, with endurance, and most importantly, with enduement.

My challenge to you today is to be that leader.

Put your hand into the hand of our great God and sing from the depths of your heart and live with your life these words:

> *He leadeth me, He leadeth me,*
> *By his own hand he leadeth me;*
> *His faithful follower I would be,*
> *For by his hand he leadeth me.*

SECTION III
The Tunnels In Life

THE TUNNEL OF DESPAIR
"When you pass through the waters I will be with you;
and through the rivers, they shall not overwhelm you;
when you walk through fire you shall not be burned,
and the flame shall not consume you."
(Isaiah 43:2)
(Isaiah 43:1-3)

This the first of three studies on the subject, <u>The Tunnels In Life</u>.

One of my good friends in the ministry is Reverend Bobby Holiday. Several years ago, I remember hearing Bobby tell the story about a little girl who had a morbid fear of tunnels. When she was travelling, whether it was in a car, a bus or a plane, if the vehicle approached a tunnel she would become rigid with fear, bury her face in her mother's lap and then cling tightly to her dress.

Several years later her attitude completely changed.

One day she was riding with her mother on the Pennsylvania Turnpike, and they approached a tunnel. The little girl became pleasantly excited, and the mother said to her, "Dear, I do not understand. You use to be so fearful of tunnels, but now when we approach and enter one you are pleasantly surprised. Why?"

The little girl responded with this profound answer as she said, "Because, Mother, I have discovered that a tunnel has light at both ends!"

And my dear friend, it will be a great day in your life when you make that same discovery.

Now, that little girl was simply articulating and echoing an important Scriptural truth, and that truth is our text.

Now, allow me to set the background for our text.

In 586, the Babylonians invaded Judah and took the Jewish people into captivity. There in that distant land they were under the oppressive yoke of the enemy. There they hung their harps upon the willow tree, and they raised the lamenting question, "How can we sing the Lord's song in a strange land?"

There they were in deep and troubled waters, and there they were in the midst of a dark and dismal tunnel. It was a tunnel of despair, defeat, doubt, disappointment and yes, even death.

It is here that we find the words of our text as God says through the pen of the Old Testament Prophet Isaiah, "When you pass through the waters I will be with you; and through the rivers, they shall not overwhelm you," and God promises to bring us safely to the dry shore on the other side. He promises to bring us out to the bright sunlight at the other end of the tunnel.

In this series of messages, I want us to look at several tunnels through which we must pass in life, and I want us to remember the words of our text. I also want us to remember that a tunnel has light at both ends, and our God will bring us through to the other side.

In this first part, I want us to think about the tunnel of despair.

I.   The Tunnel of Despair

Webster describes despair as "giving up all hope," and there are many people in today's world who have given up hope, and they are in this dark tunnel of despair. People experience this today, and folks have experienced it throughout history.

One of the greatest saints in Christendom was Saint John of the Cross. He and Teresa of Avila organized the Order of the Bare-footed Carmelites; and they did much to improve the religious and moral climate of 17th Century Spain and France.

John also wrote a book that is considered to be one of the classic devotional writings of the Church. It is entitled, <u>The Dark Night of the Soul</u>, and it describes that time in our lives when we feel that God is very far away. Our spirits are dry, and we tend to condemn ourselves. This little volume describes the tunnel of despair.

The early Church Fathers, in listing the seven deadly sins, described this as "the sin of sloth."

And many people have experienced this "dark night of the soul." Many people have experienced this "sloth of the spirit." Yes, many people have experienced this tunnel of despair.

People experience it today, and people experienced it during the times of the Bible.

I believe Job was in the tunnel of despair when he said, "How long will you look away from me, oh God?"

Isaiah was there when he said, "Woe is me, for I am undone. I am a man of unclean lips."

Jeremiah was going through this when he said, "Why is my pain perpetual and my wound incurable which refuses to be healed: will you be to me as a deceitful brook, as waters that fail?"

I believe David was in the tunnel of despair when he cried out, "No man cares for my soul."

I know the Psalmist was there when he said, "Oh God, how long will you hide your face from me?"

Even our blessed Lord when He prayed in the garden in Mark 14, was greatly distressed and in despair as He said, "My soul is very sorrowful, even to death..."

Yes, the tunnel of despair is very real, and we all pass through it at some time. Every week ministers talk to lay people who are bogged down in this tunnel of despair. There are even times when ministers find themselves in this tunnel.

One of my closest friends in the ministry is not in my denomination. He is a pastor in another tradition, and he recently shared with me an experience that occurred in the life and ministry of one of his friends.

He shared with me how this friend pastored one of the great churches in their denomination. He was highly respected, and all was going well in his church.

This minister also had a wonderful family. One son held a PhD and taught in a mid-western university. A second son was a successful insurance salesman in Florida, and his daughter, along with her husband and three beautiful children, lived in the community where he served and they were all active in her Dad's church.

Then it happened. All of a sudden this minister went from the top to the bottom. He went from the mountain to the valley, and it all happened with such suddenness. Usually, that is the way it happens. With just a snap of your fingers everything can change.

The son who taught in the university burned his degree, moved to the Rocky Mountains in Colorado and joined a commune.

The second son who sold insurance just up and left his family in Florida and moved to California.

His daughter, who was the darling of his heart and the apple of his eye, left her husband and children and moved in to live with a man who was married, thus breaking up his home in the process. The two of them, still married to others, began to live in open adultery in that community.

Then on top of that, on a Saturday morning, his wife came in and told her husband that she no longer wanted to be a preacher's wife. She said that because of the pressure in the community and the stress in the church, she could not take it any longer. She asked for a divorce.

The minister called the Chairman of his Board, and he requested an emergency meeting for that afternoon. The purpose of the meeting was for the minister to tender his resignation.

My friend shared with me that the Board was made up of a group of very wise and Godly, and spiritually sensitive and compassionate people. Before the Board met with the minister, the chairman assembled them together.

After they met, the minister came in and the Board Chairman said to him, "We know why you've called this meeting. It is to submit your resignation, but we want you to know that we, as a Board, have unanimously agreed not to accept it."

"You have been our Pastor for several years. You have always been there when we needed you. When our eyes were blinded by tears, you have always been there to help us wipe those tears away. When our lives were broken and shattered, you have always been there to help us pick up the fragmented pieces, put them together and, with God's help, try to get on with our lives. Yes, when we have needed you, you have always been there. You need us now, and we want you to know that we are here for you. We decided that we have an opportunity to be what the Church is really all about."

"We do not want you to make a hasty decision. We want you to take some time off: two weeks, a month, two months or even three months. You get away somewhere, spend some time in prayer and sort through some things. This church will take care of itself, and we will be here for you."

The minister threw some clothes in a suitcase, and he drove to a large city in a neighboring state. When he got to the city he made his way down a side street, and he checked into a second-rate hotel on that Saturday night.

Because there was no elevator, he climbed the stairs to his room. When he walked into the room he saw a mattress on an old cast iron bed, and he fell upon it, and as my friend said, "He prayed until he did not think he could pray anymore; and he wept until he did not think he could cry anymore."

Darkness fell upon the city and the bright and gaudy neon lights on the outside were flashing through the window and ricocheting off the inexpensive furniture in the little dingy hotel room. He got up, walked up to the window, opened it, and he looked out. He looked below and saw scores of people on the street. As he looked to the left and right he saw cheap nightclubs lining both sides of the street.

He then looked just to the left of the hotel, and he saw a store-front mission church with a big neon sign in the shape of a cross, and there were two words on the cross: "Jesus Saves," and that sign was blinking on and off. When he saw the sign, he shouted out above the heads of the people below, "Does He really save? Oh, does He? Does He?"

With his head hung in despair, he found his way back to the bed, and he fell asleep on that lonely and despairing Saturday night. He awakened several times during the night, walked over to the window and saw the sign.

The next day was Sunday, and for the first time in a long while, he did not go to church. He left the hotel room only to go to a fast food store to get a hamburger. That afternoon, he just sat in his hotel room and prayed and wept and wondered, "Does He really save? Does He?"

He then fell asleep, and about two o'clock Monday morning he awakened. He got up, he walked over to the window and looked out. There were no lights on. There were no people on the street. He looked at the cross, and it had been turned off. He shouted out over that empty corridor of the street, "Turn it, God. Turn it on." But God did not turn it on.

The next day was Monday, and as is the case in most communities, the ministers of that particular denomination were meeting at the old First Church downtown. This is a common practice in towns, and I know this may come as a shock to you, but preachers usually get together on Monday mornings to brag on themselves. He decided to go and meet with them. They met at 10:00 am, and he got there a little after ten o'clock. About fifteen or twenty of them had already gathered in a circle, and they were beginning to talk about the great spiritual victories that had been won and claimed on the day before.

The minister, very unobtrusive,ly walked in the door, and, without their noticing him, took a seat in a chair next to the wall. He just sat there and listened to them as they shared the victories of the day that we preachers do so well.

The pastor of First Church got up and said, "We had a great day at church yesterday. We had over 800 in worship. We had an offering of $45,000; and we received eight new members into the Church. All goes well at our church." He then sat down, and all the brothers and sisters said, "Amen!"

Then a second minister stood up. He was a balding minister, and he said, "We had a great day also. We had 400 in worship. We had a offering of over $20,000; and we had four new members join our church. All is well at our church." All the brothers and sisters in a chorus together registered their approval by saying, "Amen!"

Then another minister stood up and spoke of the wonderful day his people and he experienced. They went around the circle, and nearly all of them shared the marvelous victories that had been won the day before. Each one stood to speak.

Then the minister sitting in the chair next to the wall stood up. He walked over to the circle, and for the first time, they noticed him. Some of them knew him.

He said to them, "There are two things I wish to say to you. *One*, I want each one of you to know that I love you because 'beautiful are the feet of those who preach and teach the Gospel of Jesus Christ upon the mountain top.' *Secondly*, I want to ask you a question, but before I ask you a question, may I please share with you a story?"

He proceeded to tell them the story of his son the PhD Professor, and of his son who successfully sold insurance, and of his daughter whom he loved so very much. He then told them about his wife and their impending divorce.

And then he said, "In the light of what has happened to me, and in the light of what you have shared about your lives and ministries today, I wish to ask you this question." Then with his voice breaking he asked, "Is there any place in God's kingdom for a loser? Is there any place in God's kingdom for a fellow who's heart is broken? Is there any place in God's kingdom for someone who is bogged down in the tunnel of despair, and he can't seem to move?"

The minister then buried his face in his hands and sat down in one of the chairs. A strange eery silence pervaded the basement room, and no one spoke for two, three and then four minutes.

Then the pastor of the First Church stood and said, "It is true that we had over 800 in worship. It is true that we had an offering of over $40,000. It is true that we had several new members join the Church yesterday, but all is not well at First Church because all is not well in my home. My wife and I are seriously considering a divorce, and I want each one of you to pray for us. When you pray, please remember us by name, and please ask God to fan the flames of love that once burned so brightly in our relation-ship." His voice broke as he said, "Please pray for us."

Then the second minister stood and said, "It is true that we had a great day yesterday. We had wonderful attendance, a fine offering, and we had several new members join; but all is not well in my church because all is not well in my life. I'm having trouble with my son. Although my son has broken my heart, I still worship the ground upon which that boy walks. He is heavy into drugs, and he left home six months ago. We have no idea where he is. We are not even sure if he is even still alive. Every night my wife cries herself to sleep, and when you talk to the Good Lord, please ask Him to somehow lead our son to call us to let us know he is alive so we can reestablish com-munication with him." And then with a full throat he said, "Please pray that God will bring my boy back home to me."

And as they went around that room in the same order that they had stood a few min-utes earlier to share their victories, each person peeled back the cover of his heart and allowed the others to see the needs, hurts and despair that were so evident.

And that minister said to my friend later, "With every person who stood, I felt taller and taller because I realized afresh and anew that there is a place in God's kingdom for a loser. There is a place in God's kingdom for someone who is hurting, and there is a place in God's kingdom for one who is mired down in the midst of the tunnel of de-spair."

Now, maybe right now I'm speaking to somebody who is in the tunnel of despair. If so, in closing, there are four things I want to say to you.

One, God is with you. He is present with you in the midst of the tunnel. He is with you in the deep and troubled waters for our text says, "When you pass through the wa-ters I will be with you; and through the rivers, they shall not overwhelm you."

He was with Shadrack, Meshach and Abednego in the fiery furnace. He was with Daniel in the lion's den. He was with Paul and Silas in the Philippian jail, and He promises to be with you.

Secondly, He cares about you. I want you to know that your Lord truly cares for you. And because your Lord cares for you, that means your church cares for you because the Church is the extension of our Lord in this community, and this is more important than many people realize.

I recently read an interesting paper that was written by George Barna. Dr. Barna is one of the leading authorities in church planning and church growth. In this article Dr. Barna lifts up what he calls "several myths of the Church," and he then explodes these myths.

He says myth number one is: "People are looking for a friendly church." Dr. Barna points out that people are not looking for a friendly church. People can find friendly folks anywhere. They can find friendly people at a bridge party on Friday night. They can find friendly people at a football game on Saturday afternoon. They can find friendly folks in a bar on Saturday night. They can find friendly people on the golf course on a Sunday afternoon. Dr. Barna says people are not looking for a <u>friendly</u> church, but they are looking for a <u>caring</u> church. People want to be a part of a church where they feel they are truly cared for and loved. They are looking for a church where they can sense they are indeed loved and cared for by God and God's people.

And so, when we are in the tunnel of despair we need to know that our Lord and His Church truly care.

Thirdly, your Lord suffers and hurts with you. It is important for us to know that when we are in the tunnel of despair, our Lord is there with us and He is hurting there with us.

Scotland has given to us some of the greatest martyrs of the Church, but I think none were any more courageous than Agnes McLaughlin and Mary Wilson. Because they refused to retract their deep spiritual convictions, both of them were sentenced to be drowned in the Soulway tide.

They took both of them into the water, and they tied the older Agnes to a post. Then closer to shore, between Agnes and the shore, they tied Mary Wilson to a second post. As the tide quickly came in, the waters gathered around the knees of Agnes. The waters then rose to her waist, her shoulders, and then to the bottom of her neck.

The executioners then shouted to Mary, "Mary Wilson, what do you see now? Tell us. What do you see?"

And as Mary Wilson looked upon her spiritual mentor, her friend and her sister in Christ, she shouted with a voice choked with emotion, "What do I see? I see Jesus Christ suffering in one of His children."

And when we are in the tunnel of despair, our Lord is right there with us, hurting with us and suffering with us.

But, *fourthly*, He leads us. He is there with us. He does care about us. He does suffer with us, and He wants to take us by the hand and lead us through the tunnel to the other side. He wants to lead us out of the deep waters and place our feet upon the dry shore on the other side. He wants to lead us through the tunnel into the light at the other end.

So today, if you are in the tunnel of despair, won't you let Him lead you to the bright sunlight at the other end of the tunnel. You do not have to stay in the midst of it. He wants to lead us through with His grace.

As the words to old Gospel hymn go:

> *'Tis grace hath brought me safe thus far,*
> *and grace will lead me on.*

Yes, the tunnel of despair is not something to be feared because there is light at both ends. Praise His Name.

Chapter 23
The Tunnels In Life

THE TUNNELS OF DEFEAT AND DOUBT

"When you pass through the waters I will be with you;
and through the rivers, they shall not overwhelm you;
when you walk through fire you shall not be burned,
and the flame shall not consume you."

(Isaiah 43:2)

(Isaiah 43:1-3)

Part II

In this chapter I want to share with you the second part in our series on The Tunnels In Life.

In our last message I shared with you the experience that was told by my friend, Rev. Bobby Holiday. Bobby told of a little girl who had a morbid fear of tunnels. When she was riding with her mother, and when they would approach a tunnel, she would become rigid with fear, bury her face in her mother's lap and then cling tightly to her skirt.

Several years later the little girl's attitude about tunnels completely changed. Whenever they approached a tunnel, instead of being frightened she would become pleasantly excited.

Bobby told of how one day they were riding down the Pennsylvania Turnpike, and they approached a tunnel. The little girl became pleasantly surprised, and her mother said, "Honey, I do not understand. You used to be afraid of tunnels, but now you are joyfully excited when we approach one. Why the change?"

The little girl, with dancing eyes and a big smile, responded to her mother with this profound statement, "It is because, Mother, I have learned that a tunnel has light at both ends."

And my friend, it will be a great day in your life when you make that same discovery.

Now that little girl was simply echoing an important Scriptural truth.

Again, allow me to set the Scriptural background for our text: In 586 B.C., the Jewish people were taken into captivity by the Babylonians. There in that foreign land they were under the oppressive yoke of the enemy. It was there that the Psalmist describes how they "hung their harps upon the willow tree," and they lifted the lamenting cry, "How can we sing the Lord's song in a strange land?"

Yes, they were in the midst of a dark and dismal tunnel. They were indeed passing through deep and troubled waters.

And it is against this background that we find our text as God speaks through the pen of Isaiah and says, "When you pass through the waters I will be with you; and through the rivers, they shall not overwhelm you."

And God promised to bring them over safely to the dry shore on the other side; and our Lord promises to bring us through the tunnel to the bright light at the other end.

There are many dark tunnels through which we must pass in life. In the first study in this series we looked at the tunnel of despair, and that is a very real tunnel, and many people are stuck within that tunnel this very day.

In our last message we stated that Webster defines this tunnel as "giving up all hope." Yes, the tunnel of despair is a place without hope.

John of the Cross, the Church Father of the 16th Century describes it in his classic devotional writing as <u>The Dark Night of the Soul</u>, and it is a tunnel in which God seems far away, our spirits become very dry, and we tend to condemn ourselves.

The early church fathers identified this tunnel, and they listed it as one of the seven deadly sins; and they called it sloth.

Yes, the tunnel of despair is real, and many people have difficulty getting through it.

In this message, I want us to look at two other tunnels through which we must pass. I want us to think for just a few moments about:

I.   The Tunnel of Defeat
II.   The Tunnel of Doubt

I.   The Tunnel of Defeat

The tunnel of defeat is a tunnel through which we all must pass at some time or the other. It is a one of the inevitables of life because defeat is woven into the very fabric of life. We are going to fail. We are going to lose. It goes with the territory, but the real question is, "What do we do when we lose? What do we do when we experience defeat?"

I believe we can do either one of two things:

One, we can <u>be</u> <u>satisfied</u> with defeat, and many people are content with defeat. We can sit down in this tunnel under the dark cloud of defeat, and let it break open and rain down upon us its drops of negativism, ininitative and laziness; and we will find ourselves continuously mired and bogged down in this tunnel. Defeat and losing will become a way of life for us in every realm of our existance.

Dr. Norman Vincent Peale told of a time when his wife and he were in Hong Kong. They were walking down a street, and they were window shopping. They passed a tatoo parlor, and they were intrigued by the number of tatoos in the window that were available. One particular tatoo especially intrigued and fascinated them. It was a tatoo of three words: "Born To Lose." Dr. and Mrs. Peale went in the tatoo parlor, and they began to talk with the Chinese gentleman who owned the shop. Dr. Peale said, "Do you really tatoo those words, 'Born To Lose' upon people? Why would anybody want to be branded with such a gloomy statement?" The tatoo artist replied, "Do you see that man walking out the door?" And he pointed to a big burly fellow who was leaving his shop. He said, "I just tattooed those three words in big letters upon his chest." And then the man said, "But, Sir, the reason the people want to be branded with that statement goes beneath the surface of the skin. In every instance I've found that before the tatoo is placed on the body, the tatoo is always stamped on the mind."

Yes, defeat can become a way of life, and people accommodate themselves to it. They become satisfied with it.

But *secondly*, we can be smart and do something about our defeat. We can realize that defeat is but a temporary tunnel, and there is light at the end of that tunnel.

You see, the real measure of you as a person is not, will you fail? Will you experience defeat? The real question is, "What happens when you fall? What happens when you fail? What happens when you experience defeat? Do you wallow in self-pity and feel sorry for yourself, or do you pick yourself up, learn from defeat and try to move a little bit further through the tunnel? Those are the important questions to ask in the tunnel of defeat.

I think three of the greatest Professional Football Coaches of yesteryear were Tom Landry, Chuck Noll and Bill Walsh. It is interesting in that those three coaches won nine of the fifteen Super Bowl victories between the years of 1974 and 1989. That means those three coaches claimed nearly two-thirds of all the Super Bowls won during that fifteen year span. Something else interesting about those three coaches is this: all three of them had the worst records of first season head coaches in NFL history!

Oh, don't you see, they were in the tunnel of defeat, but they didn't stay there. They were smart. They learned from their defeats, they pressed on through the tunnel, and they came out to the bright light of Super Bowl victory at the other end.

This past week I was reading about one of my heros in American history. As I read about this fellow I thought to myself, he must have invented the tunnel of defeat. If he did not invent it, he certainly spent a whole lot of time there.

In 1832, he was defeated as he ran for the State Legislature in Illinois.

In 1852, he was defeated as he ran for the U.S. Senate.

In 1856, he was defeated as he ran for the Vice Presidency of the United States.

In 1858, he was defeated as he ran again for the U.S. Senate, but two years later in 1860, he came to the end of the tunnel of defeat as he was elected President of the United States.

And all of our lives have been inspired by Abraham Lincoln.

During the course of his life, and especially during the years of his Presidency, he made many insightful statements.

Some of the greatest thoughts he ever expressed were told to a group of young men when he said to them: "You boys must always thank the good God that you have been born in a country where, if you will lead a decent, clean life, trust God and work hard, you can rise, and the only thing that will limit you is your industry, your character and your brain." And it was that philosophy that enabled him to make it through to the end of the tunnel.

I do all of my studying in my office at home. Next to my desk is a picture of Abraham Lincoln that was drawn by my wife. I think it is the best picture of Lincoln that I've seen anywhere. On the canvass beneath the picture there are these three statements: "Work hard; lead a clean, decent life; trust in God."

Yes, that was the plan Abraham Lincoln used to make it through the tunnel to the light on the other side, and that plan still works 125 years later when we find ourselves in the tunnel of defeat.

II.   The Tunnel of Doubt

Just like despair and defeat, so doubt is a very real tunnel in life, and I believe we all pass through it at some time or another. Some of God's giants passed through the tunnel of doubt. I think of Thomas and how he said, "Except I put my hand into His side and my finger into the nail print, I will not believe!"

I believe our blessed Lord even doubted the presence of our Heavenly Father, for as He hung upon Calvary's Cross He cried, "My God, my God, why hast thou forsaken me?"

Yes, we all experience doubt. We all, like Walt Whitman have "felt those curious abrupt questionings stirring within us."

Doubt is one of the real tunnels of life, and I think one of the ways we can best get through this tunnel is to make an attempt at understanding why we doubt. Why do we doubt? I believe we doubt for several reasons.

First, a lifestyle that is inconsistent with a Spiritual conviction will sometimes cause doubt. If we have a deep spiritual conviction that is basic to our belief system, and then we engage in a lifestyle that is contrary to that belief, then there will be spiritual, emotional and mental conflict; and quite often that conflict expresses itself through doubt.

I remember reading of a minister who told of counseling with a college student. This young man came to the minister's office, and he began to share with the pastor his many doubts. He told the minister, "I no longer believe in God. I no longer subscribe to those moral and spiritual values that were taught to me by my family," and then he thus proceeded to continue with his litany of doubt and unbelief.

When he finished, this minister felt inspired to ask him one simple, but insightful and probing question. He asked, "Son, is your life pure? Is your life pure?"

Jesus said in the Sermon on the Mount, "Blessed are the pure in heart for they shall see God," and quite often a lifestyle that is inconsistent with what we truly believe can obscure our vision of God and cause us to doubt Him.

Secondly, a searching mind in the midst of an expanding world can cause doubt.

I am reminded of the words of the German Philosopher, Immanuel Kant who lived in the 18th Century. He is recognized as one of the Fathers of The Enlightenment. In his work, Critique of Practical Reason, Kant said, "Two things fill the mind with increasing wonder and awe, the more often and the more intensely the mind of thought is drawn to them: the starry heavens above and the moral law within me."

Yes, as we reflect upon the starry heavens high above us and the moral law deep within us, it can cause us to have doubts as we seek to thoughtfully live our lives in this world around us.

But as I think of this world, I am thankful for those who have doubted. I am thankful that Columbus doubted that the world was flat. I am thankful that somebody doubted that we would never find a cure for diphtheria. I am thankful that somebody doubted that we would never find a cure for polio. I am thankful that President John F. Kennedy doubted when somebody said, "We will never place a person on the moon during the decade of the 60's," and I am thankful for those who today doubt the pessimists who say we will never find a cure for Aids."

Yes, doubt can be caused by a searching mind that is consistent with an expanding world, and I am grateful for those who excerise doubt in this capacity and help make this world a better place in which to live.

Thirdly, a believing heart that is consistent with a searching faith can cause doubt.

The Christian faith is a journey of constant growth, and as we grow we gain new theological, spiritual and biblical insights, and as we seek to assimilate these thoughts into our belief system it sometimes causes us to doubt and question, but we need to realize that this is a part of the way we grow in our faith journey.

Augustine, the Church Father of the Fifth Century, said, "A free curiosity has more efficacy in learning than a frightful enforcement."

And so doubt is a natural part, not only of life, but also of faith, and it is often through our doubts that we gain certainty.

In his book, The Person Reborn, Dr. Paul Tournier, the Swiss Psychiatrist, points out that those who say they have never doubted, in all probability, have never truly believed because real faith is forged through honest doubt.

And so, when we find ourselves in the tunnel of doubt, it helps to understand why we doubt, and it also helps us to realize that quite often doubt is only temporary. We also need to embrace the certainties of the faith that we do believe and focus our attention upon them; and we then need to remember that our God is with us while we are passing through this tunnel, and He will bring us to the light of assurance, belief and confidence at the other end.

While my wife and I attended the World Methodist Conference in Rio de Janeiro, Brazil, we took off one afternoon and visited one of the most famous statues of the world.

They call it the "Christus." It is also called "Christ the Redeemer" as it as 100 feet tall statue of Christ that stands a top Mount Corcovada, a rising mountain that towers over 3,200 feet above the city of Rio. This huge representation of Christ with His arms stretched out to all dominates the skyline of the beautiful city. It is an awesome sight whether it is seen by night or day.

Rio is one of the most beautiful and lovely cities of the world. It is the home of Sugar Loaf Mountain, Ipenema Beach and the Bay of Guantanamero. It is also a place of abject and ugly poverty. It will break your heart to see the hundreds of little dirty-faced and malnourished street children that roam the city by day and night.

Those children, along with thousands of other people live in hundreds of ghettos on the steep slopes of the volcanic mountains that surround the city. The Brazilians call them "favellas," and it is in those places that the poor exist in crowded, germ-infested, and unsanitary conditions. On the backside of Mount Corcovada, where the statue of the "Christus" stands, there is one of the biggest favellas in Rio.

One of the speakers at the World Methodist Conference told about two young men who live in that particular favella. The first man who was an unbeliever looked up at the Christ and very angrily shouted, "Look, the Christ has turned His back on us. He cares nothing for the poor and the oppressed!"

The other person, a committed believer, responded, "No, my friend, I do not believe that Jesus has turned His back upon us. I believe He is leading us out of this place, but we have to decide that we want to follow Him."

And so today, this "Christus," this "Christ the Redeemer" does not wish to lead us <u>over</u> the mountain, but if we are in one of these dark tunnels, He longs to lead us <u>through</u> the mountain, to the end of the tunnel, and to the light at the other end.

I'll challenge you to let Him lead you out of the tunnels of despair, defeat and doubt, and into the sunshine of His possibilities. Will you make your prayer the words to the old Gospel hymn:

He leadeth me: O blessed thought!
O words with heavenly comfort fraught!
What-e'er I do, wher-e'er I be,
Still 'tis God's hand that leadeth me.

Lord, I would place my hand in thine,
Nor every murmur nor repine;
Content, whatever lot I see,
Since 'tis my God that leadeth me.

He leadeth me, he leadeth me,
by his own hand he leadeth me;
His faithful follower I would be,
for by his hand he leadeth me.

Chapter 24
The Tunnels In Life

THE TUNNELS OF DISAPPOINTMENT
AND DEATH

"When you pass through the waters I will be with you;
and through the rivers, they shall not overwhelm you;
when you walk through fire you shall not be burned,
and the flame shall not consume you."

(Isaiah 43:2)

(Isaiah 43:1-3)

Part III

I recently heard the cute story about a football game that took place between the big animals and the little animals. In the first half, the big animals were mercilessly defeating the little animals. They were leading by a score of 40 - 0. At half-time, the coach of the little animals gathered them in the locker room, and he attempted to encourage them.

The coach of the big animals gathered his team in the other locker room, and he said, "Alright, we've got those little animals down 40 to nothing. I want us to run the score up on those little critters and beat them 80 to nothing."

The second half started, and the big animals had the ball. On the first play from scrimmage a big buffalo tried to run over right tackle. A bunch of hands raised up, grabbed the buffalo by all four legs and threw him for a five yard loss. The poor buffalo limped back to the huddle, and they asked, "What happened?" He said, "That centipede!"

On the second play, a big bear tried to run the ball up the middle of the line, and a bunch of hands raised up and stopped the bear. They then picked him up and threw him back for a ten yard loss. The dazed bear stumbled back to the huddle, and they asked, "Where did those hands come from?" He said, "That centipede!"

On the third down, a big elephant tried to run around left end when a bunch of hands raised up and grabbed him by his trunk and hind legs and threw him backwards for a fifteen yard loss. The elephant made his way back to the huddle, and they said, "Where did those hands come from?" The elephant said, "That centipede!"

Then the coach of the big animals called time-out, ran across the field and said to the coach of the little animals, "Where was that centipede during the first half?" The coach of the little animals said, "He was in the locker room. Man! We were putting on his shoes!"

Now I'm glad you coaches laughed at that joke, because I had to explain it to the congregations in the 8:30 and 9:45 services in our church. A centipede is a little animal with a whole bunch of little feet. It's not quite as funny when you have to explain it.

Now, the reason I share that story is because today I want us to put our shoes on as we are going to continue our walk through the Tunnels of Life. This will be the third and final message in this series.

In parts one and two, I shared an experience that Bobby Holiday related about a little girl who had a morbid fear of tunnels. When she was riding with her mother, and when they would approach a tunnel, she would become rigid with fright. She would cling tightly to her mother's skirt and bury her face in her mother's lap.

Several years later the little girl's attitude completely changed. Instead of being afraid when they approached a tunnel, the little girl became pleasantly surprised.

One day they were riding down the Pennsylvania Turnpike, and they approached a tunnel. The little girl became excited, and the mother said, "Honey, I don't understand. You used to be so fearful of tunnels, but you are not any more. Why?"

And the little girl responded with this profound statement, "Mother, I have discovered that a tunnel has light at both ends."

And it will be a great day in our lives when we make that very same discovery.

Now, that little girl was simply echoing an important Scriptural truth, and that truth is our text for today.

To again set the background, the Jewish people were in captivity in Babylonia. They were under the oppressive yoke of the enemy, and they were in a distant place and in a foreign land.

They were indeed in the midst of a dark and dismal tunnel. They were passing through deep and troubled waters, and it is in this Scriptural context that we find the words of our text as God is speaking through Isaiah in chapter 43:2. He says, "When you pass through the waters I will be with you; and through the rivers, they shall not overwhelm you; when you walk through fire, you shall not be burned, and the flame shall not consume you."

Now, what I've attempted to do in this series of messages is share with you some of the tunnels in life through which we must pass. As we study these various tunnels, I want you to keep in mind the words of that little girl, "a tunnel has light at both ends," and the words of our text, "when you pass through the waters, I will be with you."

In the first two messages we spoke of, *one*, the tunnel of <u>despair</u>, and there are those times when we all are down.

Secondly, we spoke of the tunnel of <u>defeat</u>, and there are those times when we all experience loss.

Thirdly, we spoke of the tunnel of <u>doubt</u>, and there are those times when we all experience what Walt Whitman referred to as "those curious, abrupt questionings within."

In this final message, I want us to look at two other tunnels:

IV.   The Tunnel of Disappointment

V.   The Tunnel of Death

And so, Tunnel IV is:

IV.   The Tunnel of Disappointment

We all experience disappointment. Alfred Lord Tennyson said, "Never morning wears to evening but some heart did break," and that heartbreak takes place in the Tunnel of Disappointment.

You see, our life is interspersed with disappointments, and as we make our journey down the highway of life we are going to pass through the Tunnel of Disappointment. Some people pass through this tunnel many times, and there are some who never make it to the other end.

I think we basically experience disappointment in three ways. We experience it providentially, professionally and personally.

One, we experience it providentially. There are those times when we are disappointed with God. I believe the Psalmist was experiencing this type of disappointment when he said in Psalm 89:46, "How long, oh Lord, will you hide yourself forever? How long will your anger burn like fire?"

I remember when my Dad was pastor of the First Methodist Church in Opelika. We had revival services that were led by Dr. Charles Allen. At that time Charles Allen was probably the leading preacher in Methodism, and he served the Grace Methodist Church in Atlanta.

Dr. Allen shared with our congregation an experience that occurred while he was the minister of that church. He said on a recent Sunday morning he stood up to preach, and he noticed a lady sitting on the fourth row. When he saw that lady, he started to just sit down. In the words of Charles, he said, "I did not think I had enough that morning."

He shared how he had just recently conducted the funeral of her 26 year old son. Just prior to that he had presided over the funeral of her husband. Charles then told of how in the last five years he had buried her mother, her father and her sister who was also her very best friend.

All of the funerals were difficult, but the hardest by far was the service for her son. Charles told of how that mother, some 26 years prior to that date, dedicated her little baby boy to God. She prayed that God would use her son to help people and bring honor and glory to Him. She also vowed that her son would have an opportunity for the very best education, something she was denied.

The mother worked in a department store in downtown Atlanta. She literally saved her nickels, dimes and quarters to provide for the education of her boy. He was able to go to the finest high school in Atlanta, and he graduated Valedictorian. He then went to

Emory College where he made Phi Beta Kappa. He established an exemplary record at Emory Medical School, and he graduated second in his class.

He began his internship at Grady Hospital in downtown Atlanta. After serving there for three months he began to complain of chest pains. His doctor friends, his colleagues, discovered that he was suffering with lung cancer. He was placed in a hospital, and for six months he lay upon a bed in agonizing pain, and then he died.

That very week, Charles told of how that bereft mother had stood in his office, looked him in the eye and said, "Dr. Allen, I just want to ask you one question. Why has the Lord taken from me every person upon the face of this earth that I care anything about?"

Charles said he could not answer that question, but he could sense her deep disappointment in God.

Yes, there are those times when we are providentially disappointed.

Secondly, in this tunnel we experience disappointment <u>professionally</u>.

You see, our jobs occupy much of our time. They are constantly on our minds, and because of this, quite often our disappointment is job related.

For example, a man is in line for a promotion. He works hard, and he gives his very best to the company. He is certain he is going to be appointed to that position, and then he discovers that Corporate headquarters has passed over him in favor of a young person. That man is left in the tunnel of disappointment.

A professional woman sets high and lofty goals. She labors industriously to attain those goals, and then she falls short. She is left in the tunnel of disappointment.

Yes, we are disappointed professionally.

Thirdly, we are disappointed <u>personally</u>.

People disappoint us. People let us down.

I have a good friend who is an attorney in Mobile. He said to me one day, "George, I love being a lawyer. I love everything about the legal profession. The only thing I don't like is having to deal with people. They don't do what I tell them to do, and they make life miserable. People are contrary, inconsistent, and down-right peculiar." Now, I'm not so sure folks are all that inconsistent, contrary and peculiar, but I do know people will let you down.

I want to share with you the saddest verse in the Bible. I believe it is II Timothy 4:10. Paul wrote two letters to his friend Timothy, and in the second letter he simply says, "Demas has forsaken me having loved this present world." I don't know very much about Demas. His name is only mentioned three times in the New Testament, but there is one thing I do know about him. He disappointed Paul.

In Luke's Gospel, there is the account of Jesus healing ten lepers. Only one returned to say thank you. Jesus then raised this sad question, "Where are the nine?" I don't know what happened to those nine fellows. I don't know why those nine men did not come back and express their thanks. But there's one thing I do know, they disappointed the Master.

Yes, people disappoint us. I remember right before we moved from Mobile to Auburn, a lady came into my office to see me. She is a deeply committed Christian, and she has a wonderful family. They have a beautiful home in West Mobile, and she has lovely children. I could tell by the way she entered the room that something was deeply troubling her. She simply stood there, looked me in the eye and said, "Dr. Mathison, I discovered this morning that my husband is involved with another women. He is having an affair with her. He does not know that I know, and I don't know what to do."

I then asked her, "Are you angry?" She replied, "No, I am not angry. I am deeply hurt, and I am very disappointed."

Yes, people disappoint us, and in the tunnel of disappointment we experience this emotion providentially, professionally and personally.

V. The Tunnel of Death

Now there is some question as to whether we will pass through these first four tunnels. Some folks might debate whether we will pass through all of the tunnels, but there is no question about this fifth tunnel. We all are going to die. The Bible says, "It is appointed unto man once to die."

And we are going to die sooner or later. Now, most of us expect it to be later, but it usually comes sooner.

Following the third bloody day at Gettysburg which was July 3, 1863, one of the survivors under General Picketts command approached his sergeant. After watching scores of his friends helplessly die in that futile assault, this foot soldier very poignantly said to his sergeant, "You know, Sarge, I have decided that actually there is not a lot of difference in dying today or tomorrow. The only difference is that most of us would like and expect to die tomorrow instead of today."

But for most, the visit of the dreaded pale horseman usually arrives before that expected tomorrow gets here.

Now, death is probably the shortest tunnel of all. In one Scriptural context it is spoken of as "in the twinkling of an eye."

But we need to understand death as simply a short tunnelway that leads from this life to the next. It is simply a passageway that leads us from this world into the presence of our God.

Richard Baxter, the Puritan Theologian of 17th Century England, said, "Through conversion, we enter into the kingdom of God; through death we enter into the glory of God."

I remember the second funeral service I conducted as a minister.

I was serving five little country churches that were spread over three counties. I was the pastor of that circuit for six years, and I learned to love those people so very much.

The strongest and most active church on the charge was the little Pleasant Hill Methodist Church. Every third week in July, the dear people in that church have their revival. When I was there, we always had it the third week in July. They had it the third week in July long before I came there, and they will always have their revival the third week in July. I believe there are some folks in that little church who do not believe there can be a visitation from God except during the third week in July.

One of my best pals in that church was a little 12 year old boy named Jimmy. Jimmy and I developed a very close friendship. The thing that impressed me about Jimmy was his spiritual maturity and a religious depth that was significant beyond his years. Jimmy loved to visit with me, and he especially enjoyed visiting elderly people and shut-ins. He could pray the prettiest prayers. When I went to visit, I took him with me. I did a lot of visiting when I was the minister on that charge. I especially enjoyed visiting around dinner time and supper time since I did not have a parsonage, and I did not have a wife.

I remember one day Jimmy shared with me these words, "When I grow up, I want to be a Methodist preacher." I honestly believe he had felt God's call upon his life at that very young age.

Jimmy was also a very smart little fellow. One day he said to me, "Brother George, you are the best preacher I've ever heard. As a matter of fact, you are the greatest preacher in the whole world." Like I said, Jimmy was a smart young man. He was brilliant, and he was wise beyond his years. Of course, I was probably the only preacher Jimmy had ever heard.

I remember that week when we were having our revival in July. Bobby Holiday was the guest evangelist for us. On Wednesday of that week, I was having lunch with Jimmy's grandmother, Mrs. Warren Harrison. She lived in a little frame house on the top of a hill, and she took every student pastor under her wing, and she made all of us feel like a million dollars. She cared for us, and she looked after us. When we finished our lunch on that Wednesday afternoon, I did what most folks in the country do. I took my place on the front porch in a rocking chair, and I began to rock.

A few moments later the silence of that hot and peaceful summer afternoon was broken with the screams of one of Jimmy's little friends who came running up the hill shouting at the top of his voice, "Brother George, Mrs. Harrison, come quickly and help me. Jimmy and I were swimming in the pond, and Jimmy went under the water, and he did not come up."

I remember I jumped off the porch and ran down the hill as fast as I could. When I got there, a neighbor had already arrived, and he had just pulled Jimmy's little lifeless body out of the pond. It was resting on the red clay shore that rimmed the body of water. Jimmy was gone.

Let me tell you something; in that little church and community, instead of having a revival, we had a funeral.

I remember the Friday of that funeral. The service was at noon, and it was so hot. There was no air-conditioning. The little church was filled to capacity, and the windows were raised.

I was the presiding minister at the funeral. As I look back, I honestly don't know if I was helpful to those dear people. I'm not sure that I provided any inspiration to them. I don't know that I conveyed to them any message of positive hope, but I want you to know that they certainly ministered to me.

I remember I shared with them those comforting words of Jesus when He said, "Let not your hearts be troubled; you believe in God, believe also in Me. In my Fathers house are many mansions; if it were not so I would have told you; I go to prepare a place for you, and if I go and prepare a place for you I will come again and receive you unto myself."

Then I thought of Jimmy as I shared these other words of Jesus when He said, "I am the Resurrection and the Life. Those who believe in me, though they die they shall live forever." And as I read those words I think for the first time I understood something about the true meaning and place of heaven.

As I lifted my eyes beyond that big, old King James Version of the Bible that rested upon the pulpit, and over the little casket, I looked into the faces of Jimmy's mother, Dot, his father, Allison, his uncle, Gene, his uncle, Bill, and his grandmother, Mrs. Harrison; and as I looked into their faces I saw a depth of faith I had rarely seen in other people. Through the tears as I looked into their eyes, I saw the light of faith.

Then a lady came and stood by an old upright piano and sang the most beautiful solo I think I've ever heard. It was beautiful because it had the anointing of God's blessed Spirit upon it. She sang:

> Beyond the sunset, Oh blissful morning,
> > When with our Savior heaven is begun.
> Earth's toiling ended, oh glorious dawning;
> > Beyond the sunset, when day is done.

I especially remember the third verse of that old hymn and how it touched and blessed me. She sang:

> Beyond the sunset, a hand will guide us
> > to God the Father, whom I adore.
> His glorious mercy, his words of welcome
> > will be my portion on that fair shore.

As she sang, I learned something about death.

Yes, during that funeral service those dear precious people ministered to me. They taught me something about heaven. They taught me something about faith. They taught me something about hope, and they especially taught me something about death; and what they taught me is a part of my theology that I have carried with me through the years. They taught me that death is a tunnel. Yes, it is a very dark tunnel, but in the midst of it there is a guiding hand that wants to take us and lead us through to the "glorious dawning" at the end of the way.

The tunnels of life! Have you passed through some of them? Are you in one of them today? The tunnels of despair, defeat, doubt, disappointment and death.

When you pass through one of these tunnels, always remember that a tunnel has light at both ends; and I especially challenge you to remember the words of our text, *"When you pass through the waters I will be with you. The rivers shall not overflow you. When you pass through the fire, the flame will not consume you,"* because our blessed Lord promises to be with us every step of the way, and He promises to bring us safely to the dry shore on the other side of the river. Yes, He promises to always bring us to the light at the end of the tunnel, and His promises never fail! Praise His Name!

SECTION IV

The Importance of A Good Finish
To finish well, we need:

Section IV

Chapter 25

<u>**The Importance Of A Good Finish**</u>

"I have fought the good fight, I have finished
the race, I have kept the faith."

(II Timothy 4:7)

A Commencement That Is Motivational

Part I

With this study we begin a four part series on the subject, <u>The Importance Of A Good Finish</u>.

Students have begun the fall term, and it is important that they finish well.

A Graduate student shared with me that she had started recently working on her dissertation. It is important that she finish well.

Perhaps you have just begun your faith journey, or maybe you are well into the trip; that does not matter, but what does count is that you finish well.

Our text is taken from the pen of one of God's servants who finished well. Listen as he writes from a cold prison cell, and hear him as he describes his finish in II Timothy 4:7, "I have fought the good fight, I have finished the race, I have kept the faith."

The importance of a good finish!

I remember reading some time ago the account of a newspaper reporter who was searching for a human-interest story. He went to one of the worst areas in a slum section of one of the largest cities in the East.

He found an old man who had been sleeping on cardboard and covering himself with newspapers. The old fellow had on a pair of worn out tennis shoes; a dirty, outdated, thread-bear suit; a soiled shirt, a stained tie, and he had not shaven, bathed or had a haircut in several weeks. There was the smell of cheap wine upon his breath.

The reporter engaged the man in conversation, and to his surprise, he discovered the man was very articulate and intelligent.

After further conversation, he learned that the man was the graduate of a prestigious school in the East.

And then after talking further, the old man reached in his pocket and produced an object that pointed to a better day. It was his pride and joy, as the old man held up a Phi Beta Kappa key. A good start; a bad finish!

Before my Dad went into the Methodist Ministry he worked for the Florida State Highway Department. In one of his sermons, I heard him share this moving story.

He told of how he deeply admired and looked up to his boss when he worked for the Highway Department. His young boss, who was in his early twenties at that time, was one of the sharpest young men he had ever met. His name was John. Everybody knew that John was destined to go to the very top. He was the very personification of quality, and I remember my Dad saying how much he greatly respected the young man's business acumen, his relational skills and his work ethic.

But then my Dad noticed his boss began to be late for work. He then observed that he started to miss several days. Along about that time my father resigned from the Florida State Highway Department to go back to school and prepare for the Methodist Ministry.

My Dad later heard that the tardiness and absenteeism of the young supervisor became blatantly obvious, and Dad discovered the reason for it was the man's excessive drinking. Word circulated that the fellow would drink all through the night, and in the mornings he just could not get up and make it to work on time. Many days he did not make it to work at all.

My father was deeply saddened when he heard that his former boss was terminated.

Some twenty years later, my Dad heard that his former boss was in the Veteran's hospital in Gainesville, Florida. At that time his former boss was in his early forties. Mother and Dad were in Gainesville, and they decided to go by the Veteran's hospital and visit with him.

When they got to the hospital, my Dad inquired at the information desk as to which room he was in. Mother and Dad went up to the third floor, and it was a big room, a ward, and there was only one bed in it. There was a bed in the corner, and my Dad noticed in the bed was an elderly looking man with white hair. The poor man was no more than skin and bones, and he was lying there curled up in an almost fetal position staring at the wall.

Dad walked over to where he was, and he peeped over his shoulder and then he said, "Excuse me sir, but I have the wrong room."

He then took Mother by the hand, and as they were walking through the door a trembling but stern voice came from the bed as the little man said, "Hello, Si. This is John!" A good start; a bad finish!

When I was in seminary at Emory in Atlanta, I became friends with a young man who was a theology student from another Annual Conference. He roomed with two theology students from our Conference.

He and I became friends because the two of us were taking Greek together. We were two of the few people in our class to take Greek, and I greatly admired his grasp of the Biblical languages. I was also impressed with the gifts and graces I felt he brought to ministry.

After we graduated, I lost contact with him. It was not until several years later that I heard his name. In the city where he served, there was a terrible murder. He was involved. He was brought to trial, convicted, and now he is in the Federal penitentiary. A good start; a bad finish!

I love to study American History, and one of the most intriguing characters to step upon the stage of American History was Benedict Arnold. One biographer tells of how Arnold started out as a respected public servant. He was also an able military man, and he distinguished himself with his gallantry at the Battle of Saratoga. Actually he was wounded at the Battle of Saratoga, and this author says that had he been killed at the battle he would have gone down in history as one of the great military leaders during the American Revolution. But Arnold was not killed, he was only wounded.

Later at West Point, he sold out to the British, and he became a traitor to his country.

In later years he became a dejected man as he was abhorred and loathed by the British, and he was hated and despised by the Americans. He was a man without a country, and he was a man without any friends. This author tells us that he died a broken man. A good start; a bad finish!

One of the most intriguing figures in the New Testament was a man by the name of Demas. The name of Demas is mentioned three times in the New Testament. The first time is in Philemon, verse 24, as Demas is mentioned along with Luke. In this verse you can sense the love, affection and confidence Paul has in Demas as he writes, "Demas and Luke my fellow workers." Notice, the name of Demas is first.

The second time is in Colossians 4:14. His name is mentioned secondary to Luke, and when you read it you sense a casualness, an almost coolness, about the place he held within the ministry of Paul.

And interestingly enough, the third time the name of Demas is mentioned is in the very chapter we are using for this study, II Timothy 4:10. It follows our text, and in these words you can sense the heartbreak and disappointment of Paul as he says, "For Demas has forsaken me, having loved this present world." A good start; a bad finish!

I think about Judas Iscariot. There has been much theological debate over Judas as to who he actually was, what he did, and why he did it.

In the midst of all of this theological discussion, for me, two distinctive facts about Judas stand out.

One, Jesus chose Judas to be one of the Disciples. Just think, out of all the people there in Palestine, Judas was one of the twelve chosen. There must have been something in the life of Judas that was attractive to the Galilean for He chose him to be a part of His inner circle. Scholars also tell us that Jesus must have trusted Judas in an extra special way because many of the times in Scripture that Judas' name is mentioned, it is associated with money, and there are those who feel that he was the treasurer of that group.

But *secondly*, Judas chose Jesus. Of his own volition, of his own will, of his own choice, he decided to follow the Christ.

I wonder what it was like when he became a part of the twelve. I wonder if it was during the bright sunshine of a beautiful morning when he became one of the twelve and joined the Nazarene as an honored Disciple.

I don't know, but I do know that one of the last times his name is mentioned is in

John 13:30, as it says, "So, after receiving the morsel, he immediately went out; and it was night." And Matthew 27:5 tells us he "hanged himself."

Oh, I know it was night because of the time and the hour, but I believe that little phrase has a deeper meaning as it refers to the dark shadow that rested upon the soul of Judas. It was night, and he went out and hanged himself. A good start; a bad finish!

Now, in our American culture, we like stories that end well. We like stories that finish well.

For example, we are fond of stories like Abraham Lincoln who was born in a log cabin house in Kentucky, and he went on to a white house in Washington, D.C.

We are fond of stories like Booker T. Washington who was born into slavery, and as the title of his autobiography says, he came Up From Slavery to become an innovative agriculturalist, a great scientist and a brilliant educator.

When I was in seminary at Emory, some of my friends in the medical school would talk about Dr. James Scarbrough, and when they would talk about him they would usually do it with full throats. They would tell of how he came to Emory from a little farm in Lowndes County. They would tell of how he walked on the Emory campus without any shoes on his feet and without any money in his pockets. He worked his way through old Emory College and then through the medical school. He established an exemplary record, and he became a leader in cancer research. He devoted his medical practice to the fight against cancer, and it is ironic that the very disease he sought to defeat is the disease that ultimately defeated him as he died with cancer.

And they would tell of how it was a moving experience to stand in front of the Emory Hospital and look across the way at the Dr. James Scarbrough Cancer Research Center, a perpetual memory and a lasting tribute to a great man and one of the outstanding physicians in the 20th Century.

Now we like stories that end well because ultimately it is only a good finish that really matters.

Now how can we finish well? Regardless of the endeavor; whether it is as a student, or whether it regards some particular project, or whether it pertains to your Christian walk, or whether it is just the journey of life, how can we finish well?

I believe we can finish well if seven needs are met within our lives. In this first study, I want us to look at the first need, and in the subsequent chapters we will discuss the other needs. We need:

I.   A Commencement that is **Motivational**
II.   A Goal that is **Measurable**
III. A Discipline that is **Masterful**
IV.   A Style that is **Malleable**
V.   A Spirit that is **Merciful**
VI.   An Attitude that is **Mindful**
VII. A Faith that is **Meaningful**

I.   A Commencement that is <u>Motivational</u>

First of all, we need a commencement that is motivational. We need to be motivated in our start. Now, it stands to reason that we are not going to finish well unless we get started and commence the journey, and the real tragedy is that many people never even get started.

One of my favorite baseball announcers was Joe Garigola. I remember when Tony Kubeck and he did the NBC Game of the Week on Saturday afternoons at 1:00 PM. That was before the expansion of television coverage and the proliferation of cable, and people everywhere looked forward to the Saturday game of the week with Joe and Tony.

Prior to his announcing career, Joe Garigola was a catcher for a National League Baseball team. Joe tells of a time when his team was playing the St. Louis Cardinals. They had a rookie pitcher on the mound, and he was catching. Stan "The Man" Musial came up to the plate. Musial was one of the most feared and dangerous hitters in the history of baseball.

Joe called for a fast ball, and the rookie pitcher shook it off. He then called for a curve ball, and the rookie pitcher again shook it off. He called for a slow ball, and the pitcher shook it off again. Joe then called for a change-up, and the young pitcher shook the sign off for a fourth time.

Joe then called for time-out and went out to the mound, and he said to the young rookie pitcher, "Son, I've called for the only four pitches we know, and you've shaken them all off. What do you want to do?"

The young rookie pitcher looked at Joe Garigola, and with a trembling voice said, "Mr. Garigola, do you realize that is Stan 'The Man' Musial at the plate. What do I want to do? I don't want to do anything. I just want to stand here and hold the ball!"

And many people are content to stand on the sidelines and just hold the ball. They never score a touchdown. They never cross home plate. They never even get to first base because they never really get into the game.

We teach our children to pray the prayer,
> *Now I lay me down to sleep,*
> *I pray the Lord my soul to keep.*
> *If I should die before I wake,*
> *I pray the Lord my soul to take.*

The problem is not that we are going to die before we wake, the problem is that we are going to die before we truly live. And there are so many people today who are not living. They are simply existing and getting by. They have not found the motivation to truly begin living.

After the death of her husband, Dylan Thomas, his widow Caitlin wrote a sad book with this unusual title, <u>Leftover Life to Kill</u>. In it, she says there is nothing to do but to get the time in. There is no purpose, no meaning, no direction and no motivation to live; just getting in the minutes and hours and days and weeks. There's no "end" in the sense of purpose for there is only the end that finishes everything.

I'm reminded of the poignant words of the mystic and sage of India, Rabindranath Tagore, when he wrote, "The music I came to sing remains unsung. I have spent my days stringing and unstringing my instrument."

How sad to have within us a song and never getting around to singing it.

How terrible to have within us a poem and never getting around to writing it.

How pitiful to have within us a sermon and never getting around to preaching it.

How sad to have within us a life with great potentiality and never find the motivation to truly start living it.

How pathetic to not finish because you never even begin.

And so, a starting point to finishing well is to find now the motivation to commence and truly begin the journey.

I'll challenge you this day to tap into the motivation that enables us to truly live. That motivation is found in our Great God. Won't you, this day, look to Him and make your prayer the words of the hymn,

> *Lead on O' King Eternal, the day of March has come;*
> *Henceforth in fields of conquest, thy tents shall be our home.*
> *Through days of preparation thy grace has made us strong;*
> *And now O' King Eternal, we lift our battle song.*

Looking to Him, following His leadership, finding strength in His grace, let us find in Him this very day the motivation to commence and begin the journey.

Chapter 26
The Importance Of A Good Finish
*"I have fought the good fight, I have finished
the race, I have kept the faith."*
(II Timothy 4:7)

A Goal That is Measurable
A Discipline That Is Masterful
Part II

I want us to look at the second study in our series on The Importance of a Good Finish.

Our text is taken from II Timothy 4:7. It is the account of a man who finished well. Paul wrote to his friend Timothy, and he said, "I have fought the good fight, I have finished the race, I have kept the faith."

The importance of a good finish.

It was the 1987 NCAA Regional Finals Basketball Tournament. LSU and Indiana were playing.

LSU got off to a good start, and they were playing well. They built up a sizable lead.

With only a few minutes left to play, LSU was leading by eight points.

Then they became aware of the time, and they started to watch the clock.

They completely changed their style of play.

Instead of playing aggressively, they started to play tentatively.

Instead of playing courageously, they started to play fearfully. As one announcer said, "Instead of playing to win, they were playing to keep from getting beat."

Indiana came back to win the game, and they went on to win the NCAA Championship game by beating Syracuse in the finals on a last second jump shot by Keith Smart.

In that tournament and in that game, for LSU, it was a good start, but it was a bad finish.

You see, it is important to begin well, but it is even more important to finish well. It is absolutely imperative that we finish well.

Now how can we finish well?

Whether it's as a student with your academic career, some particular project, or your life journey – how can we finish well?

I believe we can finish well if seven needs are met within our lives. In our last study we looked at Need One, "A Commencement that is Motivational." In this study and the other parts, we will discuss the other needs. They are:

I.   A Commencement that is Motivational

II.   A Goal that is <u>Measurable</u>
III. A Discipline that is <u>Masterful</u>
IV.   A Style that is <u>Malleable</u>
V.   A Spirit that is <u>Merciful</u>
VI.   An Attitude that is <u>Mindful</u>
VII. A Faith that is <u>Meaningful</u>

In our first study we spoke of a commencement that is motivational. In order to finish well, it is important for us to get started. We must have the motivation to commence the journey if we ever hope to complete the trip.

And so one is "A Commencement that is Motivational."

I want us to notice how each one of these needs builds one upon the other. And so, Need Two is:

II.   A Goal that is Measurable

If I were to ask you to write down on a piece of paper your ultimate goal in life, what would you write?

It is important to have a goal. Our church has a goal. Our Council on Ministries met, prayed and listened to input from several people, and we formulated a goal for our church. It is also our Mission Statement, and every act of ministry we do finds root in the fertile soil of this Mission Statement or this missional directive. And by the way, if you want to know what it is, it is on the back of your name tag. It says:

As Auburn United Methodist Church, we are called to share the Good News of Christ, to nurture people in spiritual growth and stewardship, to care for all people, and to equip people for ministry and outreach through Christ's Church.

But what is your measurable goal in life? It has been said that a goal is not really a goal until it is written down.

When I was writing my dissertation for my Doctorate, I had six Professors on my committee. It was a Joint program, and there were three Professors from Vanderbilt and three Professors from the University of the South, the Episcopal Seminary at Sewanee.

I remember when my Major Professor, my advisor and my reader shared with me that my dissertation was accepted. I was also excited when he shared with me that my grade was an "A".

He then told me that I needed to submit two bound copies of the dissertation as one was to go into the library at Vanderbilt, and the other was to go into the library at Sewanee.

He then told me that I was to enclose with the dissertation an abstract. I did not have any idea what an abstract was. My Professor then shared with me that an abstract was a cover letter with a paragraph summing up the content of the dissertation.

It was interesting for me to take one year of work and summarize and condense it into one paragraph.

If you were to write in one sentence or one paragraph the goal of the book of your life, what would it be?

Lou Holtz is the Head Football Coach at Notre Dame. When he graduated from college, he made a list of 107 goals. He showed them to his wife. She looked at them, and then she said, "Lou, Honey, those are 107 good goals. May I suggest goal #108?" He said, "Sure, Honey, what is that?" She said, "Get a job!" And that is not a bad goal.

But what is your measurable goal in life, with regard to your religion? Is it to nurture the deep spiritual recess of your soul and strengthen your faith?

As a student, is it to study hard and make good grades?

Just as it is important to be motivated to begin, it is also important to have a goal so we will know where we are going. As someone has said, "If you get to where you're going, where will you be?"

III. A Discipline that is Masterful

Again, I want you to notice how these first three needs build one upon the other.

One, we find the motivation to begin. *Secondly*, we have a goal so we'll know where the finish line is and where we are going, and three, we must discipline ourselves for the journey if we are going to make it, if we are going to finish well.

Discipline is so very important. Someone has well said, "Discipline is the price of success. Failure is the result of mediocrity."

Discipline is important on all fronts. Discipline is important in the life of a Professor as she must discipline herself to prepare stimulating lectures that can challenge her students. In addition to that, there must be discipline to do research in her respective field.

Discipline is important in the life of a student. It takes discipline for a student to go the library on Friday night instead of going to a movie so he can go the second mile in his studies and make good grades.

Discipline is important in the life of an athlete. It takes discipline to adhere to the right diet and to observe a proper exercise regimen.

Discipline is important in the life of a merchant in the business community as he must ever be mindful that the customer is the most important person.

Discipline is important in the life a minister as a minister must study and work hard if he is going to be effective. Phillips Brooks said, "The first task of the minister is to conquer the tyranny of his moods."

One of the things I enjoy about serving as the Senior Minister of the Auburn United Methodist Church is my association with the University.

This coming Tuesday, I am looking forward to speaking to the freshman honors group. I am real honored because they have invited me to speak for one hour. I've never been invited to speak for one hour at anything. As a minister, I am trained to speak for approximately 20-25 minutes. I am looking forward to speaking to those sharp young people, and I am especially looking forward to knowing that after 25 minutes they won't be looking at their watches.

Something else I enjoy doing is having the prayer for the Commissioning Service for the ROTC program at Auburn.

That is always an exciting time for me. This past August, following the summer quarter, they invited me to have the invocation and the benediction at the Commissioning Service. That can be a little dangerous if you invite a minister to have the invocation and the benediction. You vest a lot of power in him because you can't begin until he starts, and you can't finish until he gets through. But I look forward to attending that ceremony. It is always a moving experience for me.

For me, the moving part of the ceremony is when they actually commission those young men and women. It is a thrilling thing for me to see them as they are standing there at attention. And then in the background when the songs of the respective branches of the service are played, it makes cold chills run up and down my back. For the Air Forces there is "Off We Go Into the Wide Blue Yonder."

For the Army it is, "Over hill, over dale, we have hit the dusty trail as those caissons go rolling along."

For the Marines it is, "From the halls of Montezuma to the shores of Tripoly, we will fight our country's battles on the land, and on the sea."

But as I watch them stand there, with perfect military procession, it is a touching experience.

At the August Commissioning Service, our President, Dr. Muse, was the speaker. He gave one of the most stimulating and inspiring messages that I've ever heard. He talked about the ingredients that go into a plan for success. And I thought about how it applied not only to officers in the armed services, but to any field of endeavor. He said those ingredients are, "leadership, loyalty, character." And then he spoke of the importance of "discipline." And discipline is so very important in every area of life. It is vitally imperative if we are going to reach our goal and finish our work.

Discipline is so important, and as we inculcate disciplinary principles into our lives, discipline will become a way of life for us.

One of the great leaders in Church History was John van Ruysbrook. He was from Belgium, and he lived in the 14th Century. He wrote a book that is considered a spiritual classic entitled Spiritual Espousals. John van Ruysbrook was beautified by the

Roman Catholic Church in 1907 as the "Blessed John." Many of his books dealt with the important subject of discipline, especially as it relates to our spiritual lives, and the thrust of his writings is that as we master moral and spiritual values, they, in turn, will begin to master us.

Yes, when we are disciplined, it will not only enable us to finish our course, but it will be much more rewarding and a whole lot of fun in the process.

I close with this story. It was in the years following the Civil War. A man, his wife and little boy lived on a farm in the midwest.

Late one afternoon the little boy went to the barn to play. The darkness of night settled in while the lad was playing, and he could not see his way back to the house.

The back porch was in voice range of the barn, and the little boy began to cry and yell for his Dad.

His father was standing on the back porch. He cupped his hands to his mouth and said to his boy, "Son, there is a lantern and matches by the door of the barn. Strike a match, and light the lantern." The young boy did as his Dad instructed him, and then he lifted the lantern high for his father to see.

The father then yelled to the boy, "Son, as you hold the lantern high, what do you see immediately in front of you?" The little boy with a trembling voice responded, "Dad, I see the old oak tree." The father instructed the boy to walk to the oak tree by the light of the lantern. The lad made his way to the tree.

The father then instructed the boy to hold the lantern high again, and he said to him, "Son, what do you see now?" The young boy replied, "Dad, I can see the water pump just ahead." The father then instructed the young boy to walk by the light of the lantern to the water pump.

The father then instructed the lad again to hold the lantern in front of himself, and he said, "Now Son, what do you see?" The little fellow replied, "Daddy, I can see the white picket fence by the backyard." The father then told the boy to make his way to the white picket fence.

At the white picket fence, the father then shouted to his boy, "Lift your lantern, and tell me what you see now?" The little boy lifted the lantern, and with a smile upon his dirty little face he said, "Daddy, I can see you standing on the back porch with your arms outstretched waiting for me."

The father then made his way to the steps, and with his arms still outstretched, he said, "Son, I have been closely watching you every step of the way. I was not going to let anything happen to you. Now, my child, come on home" as the father then embraced his child.

Today, I ask you the question: Is that not a parabolic microcosm of life itself?

We find our motivation as God, through his Son Jesus Christ, lights the lantern of our faith.

With a marked and masterful discipline, we then move through life one step at the time. Yes, we make our journey and our trek even through the various stages of life.

Then, some glad day, like the Apostle Paul in our text, we will come to end of the journey. We will attain our ultimate objective and measurable goal as we become one with our Great Creator, God.

I believe the Apostle Paul caught a glimpse of this when he wrote in the words of our text, "I have fought the good fight, I have finished the race, I have kept the faith. Henceforth there is laid up for me the crown of righteousness, which the Lord, the righteous judge, will give to me on that day, and not only to me but also to all who have loved His appearing."

And it is my prayer that when the working tools of life have slipped from our tired and weary hands, and when we stand before our Lord having completed the journey, we will hear Him say to us, "Well done thou good and faithful servant. You have been faithful over that which I have entrusted unto you, now enter into that which I have prepared for you." As we make the trip, may that be our ultimate goal!

"I have fought the good fight, I have finished
the race, I have kept the faith."
(II Timothy 4:7)

A Style That Is Malleable
A Spirit That Is Merciful
Part III

Our text is the account of a man who finished well. He wrote to his friend Timothy and said in our text, "I have fought the good fight, I have finished the race, I have kept the faith."

Paul was a man who finished well. The question I want us to consider is, "How can we finish well?"

Maybe as a student you are thinking about your academic career.

Maybe you are reflecting upon some particular project in a field of endeavor.

Perhaps you are thinking about your spiritual walk.

Or maybe you are reflecting upon your life as a whole.

How can you finish well? I believe there are seven basic needs we all have, and when these needs are met in our lives, we will not only finish well, but we will also be productive as we make the journey in life.

In the way of review, allow me to say just a word about where we've been.

First, we need a commencement that is <u>motivational</u>. It is so important for us to get started. The reason many people do not finish well is because they do not even get started at all.

Secondly, we need a goal that is <u>measurable</u>. It is good to get started, but we also need to know where we are going. I believe Paul found his motivation in Acts (9:3-6) through his dramatic conversion experience on the Damascus Road. But I believe it was not until he wrote his letter to the Philippians (3:13) that he clearly articulated his measurable goal as he said, "Brethren, I do not consider that I have made it my own; but this one thing I do, forgetting what lies behind and straining forward to what lies ahead. I press on toward the goal (or the mark) for the prize of the high calling of God in Christ Jesus."

Again, it is important that we notice how each of these needs builds one upon the other.

Thirdly, we need a discipline that is <u>masterful</u>. We need to get started, and we need to know where we are going, but we need to discipline ourselves to get there.

And this leads us to the fourth need.

IV.   A Style that is Malleable

And *fourthly*, we need a style that is <u>malleable</u>.

Now Need IV, <u>A Style that is Malleable</u>, is in tension to and balanced with Need III, <u>A Discipline that is Masterful</u>.

For while we do need to discipline ourselves, it is so important for us to be flexible at times also. We need a style that is malleable. In other words, don't be so rigid about life, but learn to be flexible because there are times when you will need to "bend with the wind" and "go with the flow."

For example, if a tree is in the path of a hurricane, and that hurricane is packing strong winds, if that tree is rigid and stiff and will not bend, it might stand for a short while, but it will soon snap.

And the very same thing is true in your life. When the winds of adversity begin to blow, and when the rains of trouble start to fall and the storm comes, if you are not flexible, then like that tree, you will snap also. It happens everyday, and there are scores of people in mental institutions who could not cope with the storm and the stress, and they are testimony to this fact.

One of the ways that we have a style that is malleable is to develop a sense of humor. It is so important to learn to smile at people and laugh at life.

It is said that during the 1930's Will Rogers showed America how to laugh its way through the period of the Great Depression.

For you see, there are some situations in life, if you don't learn to smile at them and laugh with them then you will end up weeping over them.

Proverbs 17:22 says, "A merry heart does good like medicine." And I believe that if our hearts were merrier and we laughed more we would take far less medicine.

Solomon, the wise writer in Ecclesiastes said (3:1,4), "For everything there is a season, and a time for every purpose under heaven...a time to weep, <u>and a time to laugh</u>."

I agree whole-heartedly with the words of Charles Lamb, the English Essayist when he said, "We grow gray in our spirits long before we grow gray in our hairs."

William Makepeace Thackery said, "The world is a looking glass. Frown at it, and it in turn will frown back at you. Laugh with it, and it in turn will laugh with you, and it becomes a jolly good companion."

I read about some college kids who were partying a little too enthusiastically at Daytona Beach, Florida, during the spring holidays. They were arrested and taken to the police station. One young man, upon arriving at the station, immediately said to the Police Chief, "Sir, I know my Constitutional Rights, and I know I have the right to make a telephone call." The Chief was impressed with the young man's knowledge of the law, and he told him that he could certainly make his call.

The young man made the call, and fifteen minutes later a delivery car from Godfather's Pizza pulled up in front of the Police Station, and the delivery boy said, "I have one order here for a pizza supreme."

I don't agree with what the kid did, and I don't agree with were he was, but I do kind of like his sense of humor.

When I shared this with my congregation at Auburn United Methodist Church, a young college student came to me afterwards and said, "Dr. Mathison, it could have been that the kid did not have a sense of humor; it could have been that he was just hungry."

I said to him, "Well, I had never really thought about it. But for the sake of my sermon, I do hope that he had a sense of humor."

And I do know that you need to have a sense of humor if you are going to enjoy the journey and make a good finish; and this is what helps us have a style of living that is malleable.

V.   A Spirit that is Merciful

As you make your journey through life, you are going to meet some people who will disappoint you.

As they say, "It goes with the territory." As I say, "It goes with the roadway along the pathway of life."

And in addition to meeting people who will disappoint you, you will possibly, I would even say probably, meet somebody or some persons who will hurt you. Hopefully, it will not be on purpose, but it might well be intentional on the part of the person who hurts you.

It could well be that you are not the cause of the hurt that has been inflicted upon you by somebody else. It could be that hurt has stemmed from that particular person's insecurity, fear, envy or jealousy.

And one of the wisest things you can learn as you live life is to understand and accept the fact that you can't live other people's lives for them. You can't control what people say, what people think, what people do or how they act – even if it is directed toward you. The only thing you can control is how you respond and react to the hurt that has been inflicted upon you. It is a wise person who realizes that he is responsible only for his reaction to what has been said to him – or even about him.

Now, when somebody hurts us, how should we react? What should we do? Maybe you are thinking about some situation in your life right now. Keep in mind that I am addressing these remarks to those of us who are a part of the community of faith. I am directing this message to those of us who are followers of the Lamb. I believe we need to do three things.

One, we need to forgive that person.

Two, we need to love that person.

Three, we need to forget the experience, we need to put it behind us, and then we need to get on with our lives.

P.T. Barnum said, "When we forgive, that heals the wound. When we forget, that heals the scar."

Maybe you are saying to yourself, "But you don't know the hurt that has been inflicted upon me. You don't know what that person did to me when I was a little tyke. You don't know what he did to me when we went through that ugly divorce. You don't know how she mistreated me in that business transaction. I can't forgive, and I won't forgive!"

That is certainly your privilege if that is the route you choose to take, but if you don't forgive, an unmerciful spirit will do two things to you.

One, it will <u>hinder</u> you. You see, that unforgiving spirit will become like a ball and chain that you will drag through life with you, and if it does not prevent you from completing the journey and finishing your course, it will make life so miserable for you until it extracts all the joy from it. And if you are not careful, that unforgiving spirit will make you a bitter person. It has happened in the lives of many people, and perhaps you even know someone at this very moment who carries the root of bitterness.

You see, it is in your best interest to forgive. It is spiritually, emotionally and mentally therapeutic for you to forgive.

When you, with God's grace, forgive someone who has hurt you, then those shackle-like chains are struck away from you, the heavy load is lifted, and deep within you experience and feel and know the liberating freedom of God's grace that has enabled you to forgive someone else. But if you don't forgive, like that ball and chain, it will hinder your spiritual walk.

Secondly, it will <u>hurt</u> your relationship with your Lord. You see, one of the reasons we forgive is so we can experience God's forgiveness in our life. In the Beatitudes, Jesus says, (Matthew 5:7) "Blessed are the merciful, for they shall obtain mercy." Notice what Jesus says. He says those who are merciful are the ones who will receive mercy.

And when we pray the Lord's Prayer, we pray, "Forgive us our sins as we forgive those who sin against us." We are asking God to forgive us in direct relation to the way we forgive other people. You see, if we don't forgive others then we are burning the bridge over which we must pass.

In his book, <u>Love Is Eternal</u>, Irving R. Stone very graphically describes the scene after the assassination of President Lincoln.

A Mr. Parker was the man who was to have guarded the door through which John Wilkes Booth entered to shoot President Lincoln. Mr. Parker walked into the room with Mrs. Lincoln, and Stone describes him as "a heavy-faced man with half-closed lids." He trembled. Mrs. Lincoln, in a great outburst of emotion, said to him, "Why were you not at the door to keep the assassin out?"

Parker hung his head. "I have bitterly repented it. But I did not believe that anyone would try to kill so good a man in such a public place. The belief made me careless. I was attracted by the play, and did not see the assassin enter the box."

"You should have seen him. You had no business to be careless." she said. She fell back on the pillow, covered her face with her hands. "Go now. It's not you I can't forgive, it is the assassin."

And then her little boy, Tad, spoke. Doesn't the Bible say, "And a little child shall lead them?" Yes, little Tad spoke and he said, "If Pa had lived, he would have forgiven the man who shot him. Pa forgave everybody."

And in my opinion, President Lincoln, that one who said, "with malice towards none and charity for all," certainly embodied the Spirit of that blessed One who died upon the middle cross when He said, "Father, forgive them for they know not what they do."

And if we are going to have a spirit that is merciful, then we must have within us the spirit of our Saviour and Lord."

Yes, as we make our journey through life we need to have a spirit that is merciful because, quite frankly, the journey is too brief and life is too short not to.

The importance of a good finish. You've got to find the motivation to begin, and you've got to know where you're going. You've got to discipline yourself to get there, and that discipline must be balanced by a style that is malleable. And then right in the midst of it, there must be a spirit that is merciful permeating and touching every relationship, especially our relationship with God and those who have hurt us.

In his book, Restoring Your Spiritual Passion, Gordon MacDonald writes about a brilliant composer and famous musician. Late at night, or in the wee hours of the morning, this composer's son would come into the house. Many times he would be drunk, and he was loud and boisterous. He then would go to his father's piano, and he would begin to play a simple musical scale. He would play it slowly and loudly until he got to the final note. He then would stop and leave the scale uncompleted. The boy then would go to his room. The father would hear the scale of notes, and he would toss and turn in his bed, and it was not until he would get out of bed, make his way down the steps, go to the piano, and then play the final note that he was able to go back to bed, and as MacDonald says, then "surrender to his sleep once again."

The reason I am writing this series is very simple. The way we surrender to our sleep at night; the way we live productive lives during the day; the way we make the journey and the way we enjoy the trip; the way we complete the course, and the way we finish our lives well is to allow our great God to touch us with His grace and make us complete.

Then we allow our great God Jehovah to lead us "through this barren land" until we "tread the verge of Jordan and are finally at one with our Lord."

I'll challenge you today to allow Him to touch you and make you complete, and then allow Him to lead you forward.

Chapter 28
The Importance Of A Good Finish
"I have fought the good fight, I have finished the race,
I have kept the faith."
(II Timothy 4:7)

An Attitude That Is Mindful
A Faith That Is Meaningful
Part IV

(When I shared this study with the coaches on Monday morning, I then preached the message to my congregation at Auburn. It was in the month of November and during our stewardship program, and I shared the following story with them.)

During this time of year, many churches are involved with stewardship programs. I am especially appreciative of the fine response our church has made during this time.

I heard about a church that was in the midst of its stewardship program. A man called the Church, and he spoke with the Pastor's secretary. The man said, "May I speak to the Head Hog at the Trough?" The secretary said, "Sir, I beg your pardon. To whom do you wish to speak?"

The man replied again, "I wish to speak to the Head Hog at the Trough." The secretary said, "Sir, if you are referring to our minister, I demand that you treat him with more respect. He is a man of great dignity, and if you address him, you must refer to him as our fine pastor, the Right Reverend, or the good Doctor; but you must not refer to him as the Head Hog at the Trough."

The man then said, "Well, I have a check here for $10,000 that I want to give to the building fund." The secretary immediately replied, "Hold on, Sir, I believe the big pig just walked in!"

You can call Brother Andy and me anything you want to just as long as you get your commitment in.

With this fourth part, we bring our series on the theme The Importance of a Good Finish to a close. Our text is the same verse that we've used in the other parts, and it is taken from II Timothy 4:7 as Paul writes, "I have fought the good fight, I have finished the race (or the course), I have kept the faith."

The importance of a good finish.

I read recently about an insurance executive who shared these revealing and interesting statistics.

He pointed out that of 100 young men who are twenty-five years of age, in forty years, thirty-nine of them will be dead. He went on to point out that fifty-one of them will be dependent upon the government, charity or friends for their financial support.

Five will be financially secure and able to make it on their own. Four will be moderately wealthy, and one will be rich.

I thought as I read those statistics of how many people start, but they end up poorly.

Now, in our text we are reminded again that Paul finished well, but the question before the house is, "How can we finish well?"

Maybe you are a student and thinking about your academic career.

Maybe you are involved with some particular project.

Maybe you are thinking about your spiritual journey.

Or maybe you are thinking about your life as a whole. The question is, "How can you finish well?"

I believe we can finish well if seven needs are met within our lives. In our first three parts we spoke of Needs I - V, and in this chapter, I wish for us to study Needs VI and VII. It is important to notice how each need builds one upon the other. In the way of review, Needs I-V are:

I.   **A Commencement that is <u>Motivational</u>.** This is where it all begins as we must be motivated to commence the process. We must be motivated to begin.

II.   **A Goal that is <u>Measurable</u>.** Just as it is important to begin, it is even more important to know where we are going.

III.   **A Discipline that is <u>Masterful</u>.** We must discipline ourselves to attain our goal.

IV.   **A Style that is <u>Malleable</u>.** It is important that our discipline be balanced with a flexibility.

V.   **A Spirit that is <u>Merciful</u>.** With God's grace we need to have a merciful spirit that will touch every relationship within our lives.

Needs VI and VII are:

VI.   **An Attitude that is <u>Mindful</u>**
VII.   **A Faith that is <u>Meaningful</u>**

VI.   An Attitude that is Mindful

Perhaps it would be well to expand Need VI by referring to it as a positive attitude that is evermindful of God and others. There are several aspects of this attitude that I want us to consider. It should be:

One, an attitude of <u>thanking</u>. We are in the Thanksgiving Season, and this attitude of thanksgiving is upon the minds of many people. During this time, we instinctively have this attitude of gratitude. There are so many things for which we need to be thankful.

Ambrose of Milan, the saintly Bishop of the Fourth Century who led Augustine to faith in Christ said, "Our most urgent duty is to give thanks." Now, I am not real sure that I agree with Bishop Ambrose because I do not necessarily see thanksgiving as a duty. For me, giving thanks is a privilege. The hymn writer wrote, "What a privilege it is to carry everything to God in prayer." And thanksgiving is a part of prayer. For me, thanksgiving is not a duty nearly as much as it is a privilege that meets a need within my life.

Christina Rossetti wrote, "Imagine being in this glorious world with grateful hearts and no one to thank."

Yes, we need to thank God. There are so many things for which we need to thank Him. We need to thank Him for our faith, our family, our freedom and our friends. We need to thank Him for our health, our happiness and our homes. Yes, we need this positive attitude of thanks directed to God.

But we also need this positive attitude of thanks directed to other people as we express our gratitude to them.

Secondly, we should have a positive attitude of <u>serving</u>. As you make your journey through life, you will discover that some of your most enriching and fulfilling times will be while you are serving other people, and it is a wise person who realizes this.

Phillip Yancey, the writer, reminds us that Dr. Albert Einstein, towards the end of his life, went into his office and removed from the wall two portraits of the scientists Maxwell and Newton. He replaced them with the pictures of Ghandi and Schweitzer.

Somebody said to him, "Dr. Einstein, why did you do it?" He expressed to that person that the time for him had come to replace the image of success with the image of service.

Dr. Einstein said, "Only a life lived for others is a life worthwhile."

Thirdly, an attitude of <u>caring</u>. As we make our trek through life, we find many people by the roadside who feel as though they have not been loved, understood or cared for. People want to know that we care.

Keith Miller said, "The world is not waiting for advice on how to solve its problems. The world is waiting for somebody to listen to it and love it."

Bismark devoted all of his talents to uniting Germany. He said, "You may hang me as long as the rope with which you hang me ties Germany to the Prussian throne." As a church, as a community of faith, do we care so much about people, is our love so real that we genuinely and sincerely want to bind their hearts with the very throne of heaven.

Fourthly, an attitude of <u>encouraging</u>. Again, as we make our journey through life we find many people who have fallen out of the race of life, and they are discouraged. They feel as though life is not worth living, and they wonder if there is any point in pressing on. They no longer have any "fight" in them. They no longer adhere to the "faith," and they have no intention of finishing the course. They are discouraged with life.

Now, just as we need to be encouraged ourselves, so we need to encourage other people, and it is interesting to note here that when we encourage others it is then that we find encouragement building up within ourselves.

In his book, <u>Winning Life's Toughest Battles</u>, Dr. Segal shares this moving experience in the life of Vice Admiral Jim Stockdale.

One week ago Saturday was Veteran's Day. I have a great affection and appreciation for those brave souls who are a part of our Armed Forces. I especially identify with those who fought in Vietnam because they are my contemporaries.

Admiral Stockdale was a Prisoner Of War in Vietnam for 2,714 days.

His captors went into his cell room, they cuffed his hands behind his back, and they put irons upon his legs. They then very brutally and harshly dragged him out to a shaded courtyard. They made an example of him, and they told the other POWs that the same would happen to them if they failed to cooperate. They made Stockdale stand for three days without sleep, food or sunshine. He became very weak, and after repeated beatings, he was about to give up. He did not think he could go on anymore.

Then in the distant background he heard a beautiful sound. It was the sound of a towel snapping. Navy officials tell us that the Prisoners Of War in Vietnam developed an ingenious code system to communicate with one another. They would either snap a towel or tap upon a wall or some other object. A certain number of taps represented a letter in the alphabet.

After a terrible beating, Stockdale heard the towel snapping. In his mind, he deciphered the code, and it spelled out the letters G-B-Y-J-S. With tears in his eyes, a smile came over his pained face as he knew exactly what those letters represented. Those words of encouragement came as a soothing balm to his aching body and discouraged heart. He knew they meant, "God Bless You, Jim Stockdale. God Bless You, Jim Stockdale."

Stockdale said it was that expression of encouragement that enabled him to go on, fight the good fight, finish his course and keep the faith.

Yes, and all around us today there are those poor souls who are discouraged. They are about ready to give up. We need to have a positive attitude that is mindful of them, and when that attitude is expressed through action, it in turn enables us to press on towards our goal.

VII. A Faith that is Meaningful

A *meaningful* faith will do two things in your life.

One, it will give to you the courage to stand up for what you believe, and it is this courage that fortifies us and propels us onward.

It was a meaningful faith that gave Martin Luther the courage to stand before the Diet of Worms and speak those courageous words, "Here I stand! I cannot do otherwise. So help me God!" It was a meaningful faith that gave John Knox the courage to stand before Mary, Queen of Scots, and say, "Give me Scotland for God, or I die."

Yes, a meaningful faith will give to you the courage to stand up for what you believe.

Secondly, a meaningful faith will give to you the conviction to persevere to the end.

That is what this sermon is all about. That is what this series of messages is all about. That is what our text is all about. That is what Paul means when he says, "I have fought the good fight, I have finished the race, I have kept the faith."

I love to read the fascinating tales of Robert Lewis Stephenson. Stephenson told the story of a ship that was sailing through rough waters. The ship then encountered a terrible storm, and the passengers below became very frightened. They were deeply disturbed and distressed. The passengers were under orders to stay below deck.

One of the passengers disobeyed the order. He went to the top of the deck, and he made his way to the Captain. This seasoned seaman was faithfully discharging his duty as he was standing behind the wheel. As the passenger looked at him, he saw the Captain standing there with his shoulders erect, his chest out and his head held high. The Captain glanced over and saw the fear written upon the face of the passenger. The Captain then gave to the passenger a reassuring and convincing smile.

The passenger immediately turned, went below deck to the other passengers, and he spoke to them these words, "I have seen the face of the pilot, and he smiled. All is well!"

The reason Paul was able to persevere; the reason Paul was able to write, "I've fought the good fight, I've finished the race, I've kept the faith," was because Paul had been to the top. He had seen the face of his Pilot, and he knew that all was well.

Yes, a meaningful faith can give to you the courage to stand up for what you believe. It can give to you the conviction to persevere to the end, and it can enable you as you plow through the tempestuous sea of life to arrive safely in the harbor and finish your course well.

May our prayer be the words of the hymn:

> *Jesus, Savior, pilot me*
> *Over life's tempestuous sea;*
> *Unknown waves before me roll,*
> *Hiding rock and treacherous shoal.*
> *Chart and compass came from thee;*
> *Jesus, Savior, pilot me.*

Amen, and Amen!

Notes

Notes